I AM THE TRUTH

Cultural Memory

in

the

Present

Mieke Bal and Hent de Vries, Editors

I AM THE TRUTH

Toward a Philosophy of Christianity

Michel Henry

Translated by Susan Emanuel

STANFORD UNIVERSITY PRESS

STANFORD, CALIFORNIA

2003

Stanford University Press
Stanford, California

Assistance for the translation was provided by the French Ministry of
Culture, National Center for the Book.

I Am the Truth: Toward a Philosophy of Christianity, was originally
published in French in 1996 under the title *C'est moi la vérité:
Pour une philosophie du christianisme,* © 1996, Editions du Seuil.

© 2003 by the Board of Trustees of the
Leland Stanford Junior University

Printed in the United States of America

Library of Congress Cataloging-in-Publication Data

Henry, Michel.
   [C'est moi la vérité. English]
   I am the truth : toward a philosophy of Christianity / Michel Henry;
translated by Susan Emanuel.
      p.   cm.
   ISBN 0-8047-3775-4 (cloth : alk. paper) —
ISBN 0-8047-3780-0 (pbk.   )
   1. Christianity—Philosophy.   2. Man (Christian theology)
3. Truth (Christian theology)   4. Christian life.   I. Title.
BR100.H39813   2002
230'.01—dc21   2002007222

Original Printing 2003

Typeset by James P. Brommer in 11/13.5 Garamond

Contents

Note on Terminology   ix

Introduction: What Do We Mean by "Christianity"?   1

1 Truth of the World   12

2 The Truth According to Christianity   21

3 This Truth Called Life   33

4 The Self-Generation of Life as Generation of the
   First Living   53

5 The Phenomenology of Christ   69

6 Man as "Son of God"   94

7 Man as "Son Within the Son"   112

8 Forgetting the Condition of Son: "Me, I" / "Me, Ego"   133

9 The Second Birth   152

10 The Christian Ethic   171

11 The Paradoxes of Christianity   191

12 The Word of God, Scripture   215

13 Christianity and the World   234

   Conclusion: Christianity and the Modern World   259

Notes   279

Note on Terminology

Throughout the text, Michel Henry uses French *pathos* and *pathétique* in what amounts to the sense of these words' Greek roots. For *pathos*, that semantic domain extends from "anything that befalls one" through "what one has suffered, one's experience" (including its negative inflection in something like English "suffering"), to "any passive state or condition." The adjectival form—which we spell "pathētik" because in modern English "pathetic" has nearly reversed the meaning of its root, so that it applies to the object that arouses feeling rather than to the one who undergoes emotion—means "subject to feeling, capable of feeling something."

The author's capitalizations of nouns (e.g., "Life") have been retained throughout.

Thanks to Jeff Kosky for his work on this translation.

I AM THE TRUTH

Introduction

What Do We Mean by "Christianity"?

I do not intend to ask whether Christianity is "true" or "false," or to establish, for example, the former hypothesis. Rather, what will be in question here is *what Christianity considers as truth*—what kind of truth it offers to people, what it endeavors to communicate to them, not as a theoretical and indifferent truth but as the essential truth that by some mysterious affinity is suitable for them, to the point that it alone is capable of assuring them salvation. We are trying to understand the form of truth that circumscribes the domain of Christianity, the milieu in which it spreads, the air that it breathes, one might say—because there are many sorts of truths, many ways of being true or false. And we are also perhaps trying to get away from the concept of truth that dominates modern thought and that, as much in and of itself as in its multiple implications, determines the world in which we live. But before trying for a systematic elucidation of the concept of truth, so as to recognize the unexpected and buried truth specific to Christianity—a truth in total opposition to the one we naively take today as the prototype of all conceivable truth—a prior problem confronts us. How do we define, at least provisionally, the thing we are interrogating about the nature of the truth it professes: What do we mean by "Christianity"?

What we find expressed in a set of texts designated by the title *New Testament* is what we mean by Christianity—and rightly so, it would seem. Where else would we seek the "content" of Christianity, so as to reflect on what it considers truth to be, if not in the corpus constituted by the Gospels, the Acts of the Apostles, their Epistles (by Paul, James, Peter, John, and Jude), and last of all in the Revelation attributed to the same John? Were not the dogmas defining Christianity elaborated on the basis of this corpus? Does not the knowledge of Christianity—and thus all reflection on its possible "truth"—come by way of these texts? Only a meticulous analysis of them can lead, it would seem, to understanding of what Christianity is at its essential core.

This approach to Christianity, starting from the corpus of texts in which its contents are offered, presents two features. First, it implies an infinite amount of research concerning these texts and what one might generally call their authenticity. From when do they date, particularly those that are reputed to be canonical and on which dogma will later be founded? By whom were they written? By eyewitnesses to the strange events they relate, which gravitate around the life of Christ? Or much later, by people who would have at least heard the story from these witnesses? Or in a subsequent era were disparate elements borrowed from a vague oral tradition deriving from heterogeneous sources and then subjected to an effort at reconstruction, amalgamation, and invention, to the point where the very idea of an initial source becomes disputable? Does this mean that, in the presence of these reworked texts, whether arranged or quite simply fabricated—texts that are ultimately the product of a collective imaginary much more than a registering of events that supposedly really happened—we in fact find ourselves left not with a sacred memorial to the activities of Christ and his fundamental words, but rather with a simple mythology?

Indeed, many other questions can be raised about these texts. In what language were they written? Was it in Greek, according to the most frequent interpretation, or else in Hebrew, or else in a local language? A language is not simply a means of communication separate from whatever it aims to communicate. Rather, invested with multiple significations that cannot be reduced to those of language properly speaking, language is the vehicle of the practical and cognitive schemas that define a culture. With regard to Greek, all of Greek thought—a manner of thinking that is not only Greek but will reign over the whole Western world—hangs over early Christianity. All the Aristotelian and Platonic interpretations that will determine Christian theology, from the Church Fathers to the thinkers of the Middle Ages, are founded on this principle. If the first redactions were in Aramaic or in Hebrew (in which case they have totally disappeared), then the irrefutable references in the New Testament to the Old, which nobody denies, would be even more decisive. Paul's claim to introduce people directly to Christianity, by subtracting Judaism, or at least its practices and laws—in short, his presenting himself as the Apostle to the Gentiles, to the uncircumcised —lends itself to controversy. If the original writings were in Hebrew, reference to the Old Testament is not limited to a simple historical condition but inhabits the New Testament itself, to the point that the latter, instead of being detached from the Old (as it will be in the Marcion heresy), on the contrary risks appearing as one variant among others of Judaic writings. Such writings (arranged according to diverse strata) have given rise, as we know, to multiple commentaries, to commentaries upon commentaries, of which Christianity would be one among many, its heroes the simple reappearance of characters who have already played their role in the drama of the Old Testament. They might even be no more than the realization of metaphysical and religious entities whose evolution and avatars could be traced by erudite research.

The second feature of an approach to Christianity on the basis of the above-mentioned corpus of texts is not only that it leads to endless research. Accordingly if you wanted to question the Gospel about the salvation of your soul, then you would not merely, as in Kierkegaard's ironic remark, have to await the publication of the very last book on the question, you would still have to put everything else aside and throw yourself into study, which death would surely interrupt before you could obtain from so many realms of knowledge and exegesis even the first word in an answer to the single question that matters. This is because *what the answer depends upon, the truth of Christianity, has precisely no relation whatsoever to the truth that arises from the analysis of texts or their historical study.*

Let us begin with history. From the historical standpoint, criticism of the founding texts of Christianity splits into two parts. On the one hand, there is the critique of the events reported in these texts; on the other, the historical criticism of the texts themselves. For the first, history possesses a criterion—which is none other than its concept of truth. An event is historically true if it appeared in the world as a visible phenomenon of an objective sort. The visibility of the phenomenon—the fact that, being visible, it could be noticed by witnesses—is therefore the foundation of its objectivity. Or, if one prefers, "objectivity" in the realm of history as an objective science signifies two things in succession: first, that a phenomenon or event has shown itself and, second, that, having shown itself and thereby having been known (or having been able to be known) by some and by many, it has become "true"—in the sense of the truth recognized by science, which is called objectivity.

Let us set aside a circumstance that is particularly embarrassing for history and its concept of the truth. Let us suppose that an event has actually been produced in the form of a visible phenomenon in the world and that nonetheless nobody noticed or mentioned it, orally or in writing. Such an event would conform to the concept of the truth of history, or, more radically, to its ontological definition of reality, namely, the fact of becoming visible and thus of showing itself in the world under the heading of an objective phenomenon. Nevertheless, such an event would not escape the truth of history: it appeared but nobody saw it. Or else those who saw it have died without leaving any traces. Now *most events, those in any case that concern a particular individual or a limited group of individuals, are of this type: they all escape the truth of history.* What is at issue are not events or individuals: these individuals came into the world; they lived. What is at issue is the concept of the truth of history, its incapacity to grasp reality, the reality of those individuals and of everything connected with them.

Let us now suppose that the Whole of Reality is constituted by individuals, so that it is the Whole of Reality that escapes history, and escapes it by reason of its concept of truth—or, more radically, by reason of the ontological definition of reality that underpins that concept. It is precisely when one requires of a thing, specifically here an individual, that it show itself or be shown in the world such that its existence, attested to in this way, becomes an "objective" phenomenon, a historical fact, that this individual—and the quasi-totality of the individuals who have lived on the earth since its origin—slips beyond this kind of requirement, beyond the truth of history and its claim to establish objective facts that are thereby historically true.

This is why history itself, faced with the general disappearance of what it holds to be reality, namely, the history of men (since this is nothing other, and can be nothing other, than the history of an undetermined multitude of individuals), faced with the fact that this multitude escapes the concept of truth under which history intends to apprehend it, is obliged to do an about-face. Like any kind of knowledge that runs up against an insurmountable obstacle, it changes its object of study. Since individuals slip out of its grasp, it will stick to documents. And so from the history of men it turns into the history of texts. Thus, from the perspective of history and its concept of truth as appearance in the world, the corpus of writings composing the New Testament suddenly acquires a decisive importance, *becoming the sole mode of access to what these texts are about, to Christ and to God.*

The substitution of the analysis of texts for historical analysis, or rather the form henceforth taken by the latter forced to reduce itself to the former, places us in a quandary. The impossibility of reaching as far as the existence of specific living individuals, in that existence's furtive and now vanished appearance, led the historical approach to give itself over to a textual approach. But any analysis of texts in principle doubles back on itself. It does not consider merely a text in itself, its internal structure (which is, moreover, the object of many analyses and multiple theorizations). The reference of this text to reality, indeed, to a state of things foreign to the text itself is what constitutes its truth in the eyes of the historian. On the one hand, history holds the text itself to be a historical fact, placing it in the field of appearance that is the world taken as the universal milieu of the human events it studies. That "place" is its date, its dependence on a context that is social, economic, ideological, and religious. On the other hand, once situated in this field that overwhelms it on all sides, the text is worth nothing except in relation to that field. To establish the truth of a text—its date, the authenticity of its manuscripts, the original languages in which they were written—is, from the historical standpoint, to establish the truth of the events to which the text bears witness. The authenticity of primitive Christian texts, the knowledge and analysis of the first redactions—that is what would make their content more credible, this bundle of extraordinary events grouped around the person of Christ and his historical existence. Hence, for example, the effort of Christian analysis to situate the composition of the originals at a date as close as possible to the era in which the events they relate supposedly occurred, with the reliability of documents reflecting back on the reliability of facts. And hence the contrasting effort of skeptical criticism to contest this proximity, to discredit the texts and, through them, the story they recount, the story of Christ—even if Christianity itself is reduced to the historical truth of a certain number of objective facts, but specifically facts difficult or impossible to establish objectively.

Can the truth of Christianity be reduced to that of history? Is there even a way of considering Christianity from a historical point of view? Let us suppose that the exigencies, the criteria, and the methodologies by which historical truth is defined are fully satisfactory, to the extent that a truth of this sort ever could be. Let us suppose that the originators of the Gospels were accessible, that their authors were known, and that, as contemporaries of the facts that they relate, they were faithful witnesses whose testimony, gathered under the conditions most conducive to veracity, overlapped, and so on. Would the truth of Christianity be established thereby, even minimally?

By no means. The truth of Christianity is not that a certain Jesus wandered from village to village, trailing crowds after him, arousing admiration for his teaching as for his works, grouping around himself disciples in growing numbers—until his arrest by the priests and his crucifixion at Golgotha. Nor is the truth of Christianity that this Jesus claimed to be the Messiah, the Son of God and as such God himself—an affirmation, a blasphemy even, that was the cause of his arrest and his passion. Rather, the truth of Christianity is that the One who called himself the Messiah was truly that Messiah, the Christ, the Son of God, born before Abraham and before time, the bearer in himself of Eternal Life, which he communicated to whomever he wanted, making that which is be no longer, or else that which is dead come alive. The historical existence of Christ, just like the extraordinary declarations he unceasingly made about his own person, could indeed be established according to the rigorous criteria of history— and yet these declarations would still be no more than the maunderings of a lunatic or crazy person. The proof is that many of those who saw him and heard him did not believe him.

Let us suppose, on the contrary, that the composition of the canonical texts is pushed up to as late a period as skeptical criticism desires, so that the canonical Gospels date from the fourth century (which is quite implausible), and their content is suspect to the point that the historical existence of Christ becomes what it truly is: *as uncertain as that of each of the billions of human beings who have trod the earth since the human species first wandered its surface.* In this case the identity of Christ, his identification with Eternal Life, if it is true, would be no less true, despite the great emptiness of history, despite that fog in which everything that was supposed to have been shown there is lost to the world of the visible. The proof of this is that many of those who have neither seen nor heard Christ have believed and still believe in him.

The inability of historical truth to testify for or against the truth of Christianity, specifically the divinity of Christ, is more generally the incapacity of texts themselves. Whatever the respect with which they are surrounded, or, rather, whatever the sacred character conferred on them by believers, they are, despite everything, nothing more than texts. Their content in the Gospels is deployed in two distinct registers: first, there is a story relating a set of worldly events, Christ's movements, his meetings, his choice of disciples, his miraculous cures, and the like. Second, this story is punctuated with quotations that rend the simple fabric of facts and tear it apart. When Christ himself speaks, it is the very Word of God that we hear spoken, and this is so because Christ is defined as God's Word, his Spoken Word. Without being placed within quotation marks, other passages report in indirect style the words of Christ, notably those long and difficult passages in John's Gospel in which Christ offers an explanation of himself, returning endlessly to his own condition, to the dual and unique relation that he has with God on the one hand and with human beings on the other.

Despite their unexpected nature—or rather, their astonishing power—these words of Christ, like his most extraordinary acts, are spoken. In the Gospel texts, these are only fragments—signs or meanings borne by words, moments and parts of a language, of a speech, which can never do more than add one meaning to another, without ever getting beyond the abyss that separates any signifying truth from the reality it signifies. That is precisely the status of any text, including the Gospels: it is dual. Composed of words and meaning on the one hand, it is as such susceptible to many philosophical approaches; on the other hand, it is referential, meaning *that it relates to a reality other than that of the text itself, in such a way that the reality targeted in this text is never posited through it.* The one who says "I have a ten-franc coin in my pocket" does not thereby possess it. Similarly, one who says "I am the Messiah" is not the Son of God merely through the effect of his words—inasmuch as we are dealing with human speech composed of words and meanings, as is the text of Scripture.

It is not just under the gaze of history that the text admits its inability to posit through itself the reality that it utters, offering itself up to the blade of criticism, requiring infinite verifications. Within history, the powerlessness of the written document to posit the reality of the event to which it wants to testify in fact reiterates the powerlessness of the event itself to posit itself within being. This double powerlessness describes a circle within which any historical or textual truth self-destructs. The disappearance of singular existences into the darkness of time, where they vanish, can only be overcome in the annals of history. But these annals are true only if these existences really existed. The extraordinary facts and actions of Christ, his companions, those mysterious women who served him, are known to us only through the texts of Scripture. But Scripture is true only if these deeds and actions, despite their extraordinary character, really happened.

It is remarkable that this criticism of language is formulated in the New Testament itself. It endlessly discredits the universe of words and speech, and not simply by force of circumstance, according to the vicissitudes of the story, but for reasons of principle: because language, or text, leaves true reality outside itself, thus finding itself totally impotent with respect to that reality, whether to construct it, modify it, or destroy it. This inherent powerlessness of language is opposed in a radical way by what in the eyes of Christianity alone matters and counts as what is Essential, specifically, power: "For the kingdom of God is not a matter of talk but of power" (1 Corinthians 4:20). How far this power surpasses our idea of it, which we are able to experience in our own body, and, by virtue of this surpassing, how this power belongs only to God, is something the Apostle Paul unfailingly repeats: "So that you may know . . . his incomparably great power." This power gives proof of its extraordinary grandeur in the inconceivable Act around which the New Testament is organized, the act by which God raises the dead Christ: "The power is like the working of his mighty strength, which he exerted in Christ when he raised him from the dead" (Ephesians 1:17–20).

The powerlessness of language to posit a reality other than its own does not leave it totally bereft. One power remains to it: to speak this reality when it does not exist, to affirm something, whatever it may be, when there is nothing, to lie. Lying is not one possibility of language alongside another with which it might be contrasted—speaking the truth, for example. This possibility is rooted in language and is as inherent in it as its very essence. Language, as long as there is nothing else but language, can only be lying. Hence the fury of Christ against language professionals, those whose job consists in the criticism and analysis of texts, ad infinitum—the scribes and Pharisees: "Woe to you, teachers of the law and Pharisees, you hypocrites! . . . Snakes! You brood of vipers!" (Matthew 23:1–36). To the powerlessness of language is added all the vices belonging to powerlessness in general: lying, hypocrisy, the shrouding of truth, bad faith, the over-throwing of values, the falsification of reality in all its forms—including the most extreme form, that is, the reduction of this reality to language and ultimately, in this supreme confusion, their identification with each other.

Language has become the universal evil. And we can certainly see why. What characterizes any word is its difference from the thing—the fact that, taken in itself, in its own reality, language contains nothing of the reality of the thing, none of its properties. This difference from the thing explains its indifference to the thing. Since a word has nothing in itself that is identical or similar to what is in the thing, it could as well be united with any other thing whatever. One could use the same name for two different things or else attribute several names to the same thing. But because, in and of itself, the word contains nothing that is real and ignores everything about that reality, it could just as well bring reality back to it-self, identify with it, define it, in such a way that everything the word says becomes reality, and pretends to stand for it. Emerging from its own pow-erlessness, the power of language suddenly becomes frightening, shaking up reality, twisting it up in its frenzy. This frenzy burns everything, as the hallucinatory text of James's Epistle (3:3) expresses in its grandiose concise-ness: "When we put bits into the mouths of horses to make them obey us, we can turn the whole animal. Or take ships as an example. Although they are so large and are driven by strong winds, they are steered by a very small rudder wherever the pilot wants to go. . . . Consider what a great forest is set on fire by a small spark. *The tongue is also a fire, a world of evil among the parts of the body.* . . . With the tongue we praise our Lord and Father, and with it we curse men, who have been made in God's likeness."[1]

If language praises and curses in turn what is the Same (the Lord and his image, God and his sons), if, for want of penetrating the interior of what it pretends to say, it can only mis-speak, whether in praise and in blame, and therefore if it is by itself incapable of giving access to reality in general, to that which is at issue here, namely, the truth of Christianity—then should not the relation of language to this truth be inverted? *It is not the corpus of New Testament texts that can offer us access to the Truth, to that absolute Truth of which the corpus speaks. On the contrary, it is Truth and Truth alone that can offer us access to itself and by the same token to that cor-pus, allowing us to understand the text in which Truth is deposited and to recognize it there.*

This is one of the most essential affirmations of Christianity: that the truth that is its own can testify only to itself. Only Truth can attest to it-self—reveal itself in and through itself. This Truth that alone has the power to reveal itself is God's truth. It is God himself who is revealed, or Christ as God. More radically, divine essence consists in Revelation as self-revelation, as revelation of itself on the basis of itself. Only one to whom that revelation is made can enter into it, into its absolute truth. Only one who has entered into that absolute truth can, illuminated by it, hear what is said in the Gospel, which is nothing other than that absolute Truth that, revealing itself to itself, reveals itself to that person. That the absolute Truth revealing itself to itself also reveals itself to someone to whom it is given to hear it—that is what makes the person who hears it the son of that truth, the son of God, according to the thesis that, as I will demonstrate, constitutes the essential content of Christianity. But in no text is the truth of this ultimate thesis given to be promulgated or heard.

Therefore language cannot blaze a trail to either reality or truth—which for the time being we are still treating separately. Language passes as the means of communication par excellence, that is, as the means of communicating or transmitting the truth. But that is its greatest illusion, since the single truth that it can transmit is a truth that already exists, has already been revealed, revealed to itself by itself, independently of and prior to language. This poverty of language, which comes along to contradict and annihilate the purpose with which one usually defines language's essence, does not pertain only to the decisive fact that it does not constitute in itself and through itself our access to reality, that it is not itself a producer of truth. A more radical reflection, to be developed below, will show that language is the negation of this reality, of any conceivable reality—unless one exempts that pallid reality that pertains to language as a system of significations and that finds itself in principle to be an unreality. This fundamental unreality is precisely the truth of language.

History is no less impoverished. Its poverty bursts into the light of day as soon as we stop defining the discipline on the basis of a restrictive concept, as specialists do, and instead speculate on its condition of possibility, on the horizon where all events—and especially human events, the historical facts that history takes as its subject of research—become visible. This horizon is none other than the world. It is also, as we shall see, the horizon of Time. This horizon of the world's visibility as the horizon of

Time: this is the truth of history, a truth such that everything that appears in history just as quickly disappears. In it, as we have said, each of the billions of human beings who have inhabited the earth since prehistoric times is forever lost, dissipated, vanished in the haze.

But the truth designated here as that of history in its very condition of possibility is also that of language, since, as I will try to show, language is possible only if it lets what it speaks of and what it says about it be seen. But the making-seen in which any language, especially that of the Gospels, reveals what it says and what it is talking about is not possible, in turn, except on that horizon of visibility that is the world, that is Time and the truth of history.

The truth of history and the truth of language are identical. By restoring vanished human events to the documents in which they are supposedly preserved, history appeals only to its own truth, and likewise to language's truth. The documents are as fugitive and uncertain as the facts they report. It is important to grasp why these two truths, not content with letting what ought to be their object escape, also allow the truth of the Gospels to escape, to the point where these texts are not able to say a word on this subject. Truth of history, truth of language, the truth of Christianity—these are three forms of truth. But why does the third have the power to reduce the two others to insignificance? At this point, we are hearing the anguished question that Pilate, faced with the tumult aroused by the priests, addressed to Christ: "What is truth?" (John 18:38).

1

Truth of the World

There are many kinds of truths. "The sky is getting dark and it's going to rain" is one of them. "In a circle all the radii are equal" is another. These two truths differ in that the first is contingent (the sky could be blue), whereas the second is necessary: it is impossible that the radii of a circle not be equal. Philosophers say of contingent truths that they are a posteriori: it is experience that teaches me that the sky is darkening, since it could equally well clear up. And they say that necessary truths are a priori, since it is by the very law of a circle's construction, and thus before the actual construction of any particular circle, that the equality of its radii is implied. Of both contingent truths and rational truths we nevertheless say, despite the difference separating them, that they are "truths." What is it within them that is equally "truth"?

What is true is what shows itself. It is because the sky shows itself with a threatening aspect that we can say: "The sky is threatening." The truth of the proposition refers back to the prior truth of a state of things, to the appearance of a darkly colored sky. It is this appearance as such, it is the fact of the sky showing itself, that constitutes the "truth." Suppose that, in the manner of logicians, we wanted to isolate the proposition from the state of things to which it naturally relates—to consider in itself the proposition "the sky is threatening" without going to the window to verify whether this is correct. Then this proposition, reduced to itself, put into quotation marks, would still show itself to us, and this appearance—in this case, of the proposition and not the sky—would confer on itself its own truth, making it, too, a phenomenon, something that appears and that, in this way, is true. What we have just said about "contingent truths," about the state of the sky or the proposition that expresses it, we can just as well assert about "necessary truths," about a geometric state of things and the statements that formulate it.

From these brief preliminary indications it follows that the concept of truth is twofold, designating both what shows itself and the fact of self-showing. What shows itself is the gray sky or the equality of radii. But the fact of something showing itself has nothing to do with what shows itself, with the gray of the sky or with geometric properties, and is even totally indifferent to what shows itself. The proof of this is that a blue sky can show itself to us as well, just as geometric properties, other forms, or even the fury of people killing each other, the beauty of a painting, the smile of a child. The fact of self-showing is as indifferent to what shows itself as is the light to what it illuminates—shining, according to Scripture, on the just as well as the unjust. But the fact of self-showing is indifferent to all that shows itself only because by its nature it differs from all that, whatever it may be: clouds, geometric properties, fury, a smile. The fact of self-showing, considered in itself and as such—that is the essence of truth. Inasmuch as it consists of the pure fact of showing itself, or else of appearing, of manifesting itself, of revealing itself, we can just as well call the truth "monstration," "apparition," "manifestation," "revelation." Moreover, it is under these three equivalent terms—apparition, manifestation, revelation—that the truth is designated in the New Testament, as well and as often as under its proper name of Truth.

If it is in the very essence of truth—in the sense of a pure manifestation, of a pure revelation—that the fact of self-showing consists, then everything that shows itself is true only in a secondary sense. It is only because the pure act of appearing takes place, and that, in it, the truth deploys its essence beforehand, that everything that appears is susceptible of doing so —that the sky shows itself and, likewise, geometric forms, the fury of people, the painting, the child's smile. Thus any truth concerning things—beings [*étants*, that is, beings], as the Greeks said—any ontic truth, refers back to a pure phenomenological truth that it presupposes, refers back to the pure act of self-showing, considered in itself and as such.

If any truth concerning things—again, for example, the manuscripts of the New Testament or the events they relate—refers back to a preexisting truth, to the absolute phenomenological truth that consists in the pure act of self-showing that is implied in everything that shows itself, then it is of the greatest importance to know what this act of self-showing consists of, and what the nature of the original truth presupposed in any particular truth might be. Modern philosophy—and more precisely, Husserl's phenomenology—first posed this fundamental question explicitly. But because phenomenological truth precedes and determines everything that is true, whatever the particular nature of what is true each time (images, circles, manuscripts, historical events), the question of truth in this radical sense has had to be posed and truly resolved at least implicitly by philosophy ever since its inception, and perhaps even before the birth of philosophy properly speaking, through common sense and its most proximate language.

In Greece, things are called "phenomena." "Phenomenon," *phainomenon*, comes from the verb *phainesthai*, which carries within it the root *pha-*, *phōs*, which means light. *Phainesthai* therefore means "what shows itself by coming into the light, by coming into daylight."[1] The light into which things come in order to show themselves in their quality as phenomena is the light of the world. The World is not the set of things, of beings, but the horizon of light where things show themselves in their quality as phenomena. The world thus does not designate what is true but rather Truth itself. The phenomena of the world are things inasmuch as they show themselves in the world, which is their proper "monstration," their appearance, their manifestation, their revelation. Already implied in the Greek interpretation of things—beings—as "phenomena" is an intuition that will be taken up by contemporary phenomenology and will serve as its fundamental principle, to wit, the idea that what is (cloud, circle, etc.) "is" only inasmuch as it shows itself, precisely as a phenomenon. Consequently, what is is that which is true, in such a way, ultimately, that the being of everything that is, Being as such, is the truth as such, the pure fact of self-showing considered in itself, as appearance and as pure manifestation.

The interpretation of what is as what shows itself, and thus the interpretation of Being as Truth, dominates the development of Western thought. If you consider, for example, the philosophy of consciousness that appeared in the seventeenth century, you soon realize that consciousness is nothing other than the act of self-showing grasped in itself, pure manifestation, the Truth. On their side, things are reduced by this philosophy to what shows itself to consciousness, to their status as phenomena. The shift from the ancient and medieval philosophy of Being to the modern philosophy of consciousness is generally interpreted as one of the great breakthroughs in Western thought. However, such a shift changes nothing in the definition of the thing as phenomenon but on the contrary carries it to the absolute level. The phenomena of consciousness are its representations, its objects. The relation of consciousness to its objects allows us to discern with greater precision the nature of that pure manifestation that is consciousness, the nature of truth. To re-present anything to oneself, for consciousness is to place it before oneself. In German "to represent" is *vor-stellen* = to place (*stellen*) before (*vor*). "Ob-ject" designates that which is placed before, in such a way that it is the fact of being placed "before" that renders the object manifest. Consciousness itself is nothing other than this manifestation that consists in the fact of being placed before. What is placed before is the ob-ject, that which is true, that which shows itself, the phenomenon. The fact of being placed before is the truth, manifestation, pure consciousness. The fact of being placed before is equally well the fact of being placed outside: it is the "outside" as such. The "outside" as such is the world. We say "the truth of the world," but the expression "the truth of the world" is tautological. It is the world, it is the "outside," that is manifestation, consciousness, truth.

As we now see, consciousness in no way refers to a truth of another order than the truth of the world. Quite the contrary, the emergence of the modern philosophy of consciousness marks the moment when the world ceases being understood in a naive fashion as the sum of things, of beings— and this because things cease themselves to be understood just as naively as what is quite simply present before us, as what we supposedly have access to, without the possibility of acceding to these things posing a problem. However, it is precisely this "being-there-before-us" that makes things phenomena. But this "being-before" is nothing other than the "outsideness" that is the world as such, its truth.

To this original truth of the world is subjected everything that is true, every phenomenon, whatever its nature, whether a sensory reality, like the blue of the sky, or an intelligible one, like the equality of the radii of a circle—everything we can perceive, conceive, imagine, or name through language. A thing exists for us only if it shows itself to us as a phenomenon. And it shows itself to us only in that primordial "outsideness" that is the world. It matters little in the end whether the truth of the world is understood through consciousness or through the world itself, if in either case what constitutes the capacity of self-showing, truth, manifestation, is "outsideness" as such.

The capacity of self-showing that finds its possibility in the "outsideness" of the world implies that everything that is susceptible of being shown in it is in principle different from it. We recognize here an essential trait perceived from the start of our analysis: the division of the concept of truth between what is true and truth itself. This division is made manifest, as we have seen, in the indifference of the light of the truth to what it illuminates, to what is true. It is precisely when the truth is understood as that of the world that this indifference is borne into evidence: in the world everything and anything shows itself—children's faces, clouds, circles—in such a way that what shows itself is never explained by the mode of revealing specific to the world. What shows itself in the world's truth is shown in that truth as other than itself, as forsaken by it, uncovered as this or that, but a "that" which might be different from what is shown, a content that is contingent, abandoned to itself, lost. What is true in the world's truth in no way depends on this truth: it is not supported by it, guarded by it, loved by it, saved by it. The world's truth—that is to say, the world itself—never contains the justification for or the reason behind what it allows to show itself in that truth and thus allows "to be"—inasmuch as to be is to be shown.

The world's truth is not merely indifferent to everything it shows. Much more seriously, it undermines that which draws its truth from it, which is not "true" except by showing itself in it. And this is because the world is not some inert and ready-made milieu that preexists things, into which they have only to penetrate in order to find themselves illuminated by it, by the light of that "outsideness." In the philosophies that place consciousness at the foundation of truth, consciousness is defined as an active transcendence that projects beyond beings the horizon on which they become visible. The placing of the being in the condition of "ob-ject" and "opposite us" [*en-face*], and thus of a phenomenon, is only possible through the production of that transcendent horizon of visibility that is the world itself. Consequently the world "is" not, but unceasingly intervenes as a horizon that unceasingly takes shape, but only on the condition of a power that unceasingly projects the horizon. In Kant this power is called the transcendental imagination; it is the imaging of a world that is itself nothing other than this imaging. And it is in this imaging, in this imaginary site, that every being in turn shows itself to us as an image, a representation, an ob-ject, something opposite us, a phenomenon.

It is not necessary to connect this production of a horizon of visibility as an imaging of a world with a consciousness and with a particular power of this consciousness called imagination. It rather suffices to think of this pro-duction of the outsideness of the world for itself as a primary and absolute fact. It is the "outside" itself that is externalized, of itself and through itself. The "world's truth" is nothing other than this: a self-production of "outsideness" as the horizon of visibility in and through which every thing can become visible and thus become a "phenomenon" for us. Nature as conceived by the Greeks was undoubtedly no different from this self-production of "outsideness" as the original truth of the world. As for modern consciousness, it was merely an inexact way of formulating this same truth. Consciousness is foremost understood as a subject that relates itself to an object. But this subject risks being confused with something else, some conscious or spiritual substance that would have the property of relating itself to objects. This is why it is important to understand that consciousness is nothing other than this relation to the object. It is "consciousness of something," pure intentionality moving beyond itself toward the object and foremost toward that "outside" where everything is shown as an "ob-ject," as "opposite us," as "phenomenon."

The self-externalization of the externality of the "outside," which we call the world, is not a metaphysical or speculative affirmation of a kind to leave the reader uncertain or in doubt. To say that the world is truth is to say that it makes manifest. What we now need to understand is how the world makes manifest, how this pure manifestation is achieved. It so happens that this self-externalization of the externality where the horizon of visibility of the world is formed, its "outside," has another name that we know still better: it is called time. Time and the world are identical; they designate that single process in which the "outside" is constantly self-externalized. Such a process should be examined on two levels: in itself, where it is literally just the formation of a "world," the coming outside of that horizon on whose screen every thing shows itself to us. According to the unconsidered but constant experience we have of it, this horizon is discovered to be that of Time. Ceaselessly being hollowed out in front of us is a "future," where things and events take place toward which we are projecting ourselves—I will go to work, to the station, etc.; and a "present," where our immediate environment is held—the room, the table on which I am writing; and finally a "past," into which everything that has just been present for us slides away—those thoughts I have just had while writing. The horizon of the world is thus deployed before us in the form of three temporal dimensions and is constituted by them. The expanses of externality, which Heidegger called the three temporal "ek-stases," are not fixed but slide into each other, from the future to the present and to the past, thus constituting a continuous flux that is the flow of time. It is this three-dimensional horizon of time that fashions the visibility of the world, its truth. It is against the background of this horizon that everything that shows itself to us becomes, as temporal, visible.

Here we may perceive the seriousness of the way in which the world's truth undermines everything it makes seen, everything that it makes true. To the extent, then, that the truth is a placing outside, seizing everything to render it manifest, it actually casts the thing outside itself at every instant. This putting-outside-itself by no means signifies a simple transfer of the thing from one place to another—as if, in such a displacement, it remained similar to itself, at most receiving this new property of showing itself. Rather, this coming-into-appearance in the "outside-itself" of the world signifies that it is the thing itself that finds itself cast outside itself. It is fractured, broken, cleaved in two, stripped of its own reality—in such a way that, now deprived of that reality that was its own, emptied of its flesh, it is no longer outside itself, in the world's Image, but just its own skin, a simple image, in effect, a transparent film, a surface without thickness, a piece of naked externality offered to a gaze that slides over it without being able to penetrate into it or reach anything but empty appearance.

This coming-into-appearance as coming-into-the-world—which, according to phenomenology, should confer Being on everything that shows itself—now withdraws Being from it, making of this Being its contrary, a sort of naught of itself, depriving each thing of its substance in order to deliver it to us, but in the form of an appearance foreign to reality, and foremost to the reality that ought to be its own, which this coming-into-appearance can make seen only by destroying that reality. This making-seen that destroys, which consists in the annihilation of everything it exhibits, not letting it subsist except under the aspect of an empty apparition, is time. Time is passage, a slipping away in the form of a slipping into nothingness.

But time is not the incessant annihilation through the effect of a property to which we would be subject without understanding it, in the manner of a mysterious fatality. It is because the coming-into-appearance is here the coming-outside that, casting every thing outside itself and tearing it away from itself, it precipitates it into nothingness. It is the way of making a thing appear as drawing its essence from the "outside itself" that is the annihilation. How time passes! It's already autumn! Already my lamp is out! But time is not truly a slipping from the present into the past, according to the celebrated analyses that approach common sense. *In time there is no present, there never has been one, and there never will be one.* In time, things come into appearance, but since this coming-into-appearance consists in coming-outside, things do not rise into the light of this "outside" except as torn from themselves, emptied of their being, already dead. It is because its power to make manifest resides in the "outside-itself" that time annihilates everything it exhibits. But time's way of making manifest is the world's. It is the world's way of making seen, the truth of the world, that destroys.

Thus the "world's truth" does not refer to some judgment delivered from on high upon the world and everything that shows itself in it, upon the course of things. Because the truth of the world lies in its manner of making each thing appear, it inhabits this thing as its way of appearing precisely and of standing out in our experience, of giving itself to us and touching us. The truth of the world is the law of the appearance of things. According to this law, things being given outside themselves, being deprived of themselves, being emptied of themselves in their very appearing, never give their own reality but only the image of that reality that annihilates itself in the moment they are given. They are given in such a way that their appearance is also their disappearance, the incessant annihilation of their reality in the image of it. This is why there is no present within time: because this coming-into-appearance that defines the very present as a phenomenological present, as a presentation of the thing, destroys the reality of that thing in the process of its very presentation, making of it a present-image homogeneous with the image of the future as well as with the image of the past. The coming-into-the-present as a coming-into-a-future that slips into the past is thus nothing other than the modalization of an Imaginary—that modalization of the image of the world that is time itself as the world's time, as this deployment of the "outside-itself" that is the world's truth.

I said that the world's truth is indifferent to what it illuminates:

clouds, forms, smiles, manuscripts, events in a history. Starting from the appearance of the world, one can, in fact, never deduce what appears in it each time. But appearing in the world confers on everything that appears in that way a state of being cast outside itself, emptied of its reality, reduced to an image—since it is the manner of being cast outside itself that constitutes appearance as such. Everything that appears in the world is subject to a process of principled derealization, which does not mark the passage from a primitive state of reality to the abolition of that state but rather a priori puts everything that appears in that way into a state of original unreality. It is not that a thing would first be present and then later would pass away. From the beginning this thing was passing away. When it was still only future, it was already traversing the successive phases of this future existence; through them, without halting in the present, it was propelled toward its nothingness in the past. At no moment did it cease being this nothingness. If everything appeared to us in this way—if there existed no other truth than that of the world—there would be no reality at all anywhere but only, on all sides, death. Destruction and death are not the work of time being exercised after the fact on some reality preexisting time's reach; rather, they strike a priori everything that appears in time, as the very law of its appearance—everything that is shown in the truth of the world, as the very law of this truth. It is this essential connection that links destruction and death to the very appearance of the world, to what he calls its form, that the Apostle was thinking of in this striking phrase: "For, indeed, the form of this world is passing away" (I Corinthians 7:31).

Any form of truth, except the truth of Christianity. This is what we must now elucidate and understand, in its radical foreignness with respect to everything that common sense, philosophy, and science call (and continue to call) "truth."

2

The Truth According to Christianity

The truth of Christianity must be understood according to the pure phenomenological meaning that we have granted this concept. It is not a matter of a truth of the type: "The French took the Bastille on July 14, 1789." Nor of another kind of truth, formally similar to the preceding one: "Christ came into the world in order to save humankind." In these two examples, our attention is drawn to a certain content, specifically a historical fact or—since a fact of this type is never present in isolation—to a certain state of things that is itself historical. It is this state of things that constitutes the theme of thought and that alone matters as far as that state of things is concerned, to wit, that the French took the Bastille on July 14 or that Christ came into the world. What makes the two states of things true is situated, according to ordinary thought, at the very level of the state of things and depends upon that state. That the French did in fact take the Bastille on that day, brandishing the head of the governor at the end of a pike, is what makes the truth of this state of things, and accordingly of the proposition that expresses it. Because the verity of the state of things seems of the same order as the state of things, and ultimately is one with it, its affirmation appears as a sort of tautology in relation to the state of things, a quite useless way of expressing it a second time. After the spontaneous realization of the state of things—the taking of the Bastille—what interest is offered by the variation: "It is true that the French took the Bastille on July 14"? What does the "It is true that" add?

Nothing less than the truth of the world. If a state of things seems to count in itself and to be proof of its own truth, it is only to the extent that it shows itself: it is on condition of a manifestation that owes nothing to the head of the governor, any more than to the howling crowd escorting it—a manifestation without which, however, nothing of that kind would exist. And this pure manifestation, totally different from what it makes manifest, is the "outside-itself," the "outside," that cavity of light sketched by the horizon of the world, where there becomes visible for us everything that is susceptible of being known by us. The philosophical question of truth as such is thus not superfluous, except in the view of a naive kind of thought that, hypnotized by the content of what it perceives or studies on each occasion, ignores the content's coming into the light of day in its quality as a phenomenon, which, along with Kant, we must call the transcendental condition of the possibility of experience.

Thus, the philosophical question of Truth cannot be eluded. We see this clearly when, on the empirical plane itself, the truth of the state of things presents a problem—for example, when it concerns the coming of Christ into the world. Did this coming really happen? Is it true? And the texts announcing it, the Scriptures—are they also true? What "being true" means is now no longer the superfluous duplication of a prior and self-sufficient state of things. Quite the contrary, the state of things is true only if it manifests itself or was once manifest—more radically, if this manifestation manifested itself, in itself and as such. *The coming of Christ into the world is subordinate to the coming of the world itself, to its appearance as the world.* Because if the world had not first opened its space of light—if it had not been shown to us as that horizon of visibility cast beyond things, as that screen against which they are detached—then Christ would never have been able to come into the world or show himself to us, or at least to those who were given the privilege of seeing him.

Now, did Christ really come into the world? Were people favored with being witnesses to his extraordinary acts; did they hear his staggering words? Were the writings into which these words and these acts were consigned written by witnesses, or at least by contemporaries? Or are they instead collections of bits and pieces of diverse provenance belonging to a much later redaction? These questions, with which any approach to Christianity begins, it would seem, lose their preliminary character, becoming no more than secondary, if they are subordinated to the prior question of the appearance of the world, and thus to a much more original Truth than that of Christianity itself—if the latter means we are concerned only with knowing whether Christ actually came into the world, whether his historical existence is an established fact or not.

Moreover, when during our earlier approach to Christianity these questions of the historical truth of the events related in Scripture (or, these events having themselves disappeared, of the authenticity of the texts that relate them) were mentioned in passing, did it not appear that the truth of both the events and the texts immediately referred back to that more original essence of the truth of the world and the nature of this truth? It is because in the time of the world any particular reality is effaced and disappears, it is because language in turn leaves this reality outside itself and, like time, enlightens only through the negation of that reality, that the truth of Christianity appears so precarious, as if fading. At the end of the day, it is not facts or things that are precarious, fugitive as the years, but rather their mode of apparition. It is pure phenomenological truth that, as the world's truth, determines any particular form of truth for us—that of history, for example, or that of language—as a sort of evanescent apparition, eroded by nothingness.

It is then decisive to note that *the Truth of Christianity differs in essence from the truth of the world.* Like the latter, it is true—and as we shall see, even more true: it is a pure phenomenological truth, in an absolute sense. Consequently, it concerns not what shows itself but the fact of self-showing, not what appears but the way of its appearing, not what is manifest but the pure manifestation, in itself and as such—or, to put it another way, not the phenomenon but phenomenality. The fact of self-showing, appearing, manifestation are pure phenomenological concepts precisely because they designate phenomenality itself and nothing else. Other equivalent terms, already mentioned because they are those of Christianity, are "apparition," "truth," and "revelation." As soon as concepts of truth, manifestation, or revelation are understood in their pure phenomenological signification, a crucial question arises: What does this truth, this manifestation, this revelation, consist in? What within them makes true, makes manifest, reveals? It is not a power situated behind manifestation, behind revelation, behind truth—that of making manifest, making true, revealing —because such a background power does not exist. It is truth itself in its very deployment that makes something true; it is manifestation as it itself manifests itself that makes manifest; it is revelation in revealing itself that reveals. But how? What does the phenomenological effectivity of this revelation consist in, each and every time?

Here appears the radical difference separating the truth of Christianity from that of the world, as well as from all forms of truth that draw upon the world for their own possibility—the truths of science, of knowledge, of perception. How the truth of the world makes manifest is something that has long been a subject of analysis. Let us recall from this analysis some essential conclusions so as to understand how the truth of the world and the truth of Christianity contrast with each other on all points. The truth of the world makes each thing seen by placing that thing outside itself, in such a way that it is the externality of the "outside-itself" that makes seen, which is phenomenality. It is because the truth of the world consists in the externality of this "outside-itself" that it differs from everything that is given within this externality, from all the things that are shown within it as "objects" or beings. From this follows a decisive consequence: the division of the concept of truth between the truth and what is true does not belong to the concept of truth in general. *It is only when the truth is understood as that of the world, when it makes everything seen by placing it outside itself, that the division in the concept of Truth, the difference between the truth itself and what it shows—what it makes true—is produced.*

It is the first decisive characteristic of the Truth of Christianity that it in no way differs from what it makes true. Within it there is no separation between the seeing and what is seen, between the light and what it illuminates. And this is because there is in that Truth neither Seeing nor seen, no Light like that of the world. From the start, the Christian concept of truth is given as irreducible to the concept of truth that dominates the history of Western thought, from Greece to contemporary phenomenology. This traditional concept of truth determines not only most of the philosophical currents that have succeeded one another until the present day but even more so the ideas currently held about truth within the domain of scientific knowledge and within common sense, which is more or less impregnated with the scientific ideal. It is precisely when the Christian concept of Truth ceases to determine the collective consciousness of society, as it did in the Middle Ages, that its divorce from the Greek idea of a true knowledge and a true science appears in full force. And the consequence is, if not the suppression of the Christian concept, then at least its repression into the realm of private life, or even superstition.

What, then, is a truth that differs in no way from what is true? If truth is manifestation grasped in its phenomenological purity—phenomenality and not the phenomenon—then what is phenomenalized is phenomenality itself. The phenomenalization of phenomenality itself is a pure phenomenological matter, a substance whose whole essence is to appear—phenomenality in its actualization and in its pure phenomenological effectivity. What manifests itself is manifestation itself. What reveals itself is revelation itself; it is a revelation of revelation, a self-revelation in its original and immediate effulgence. With this idea of a pure Revelation—of a revelation whose phenomenality is the phenomenalization of phenomenality itself, of an absolute self-revelation that dispenses with whatever is other than its own phenomenological substance—we are in the presence of the essence that Christianity posits as the principle of everything. *God is that pure Revelation that reveals nothing other than itself. God reveals Himself.* The Revelation of God is his self-revelation. If by chance "the Revelation of God" were addressed to people, this would not consist in the unveiling of a content foreign to its own essence and somehow transmitted to a few initiates. To reveal Himself to people could only signify for God that He gives to them a share of his eternal self-revelation. Christianity is nothing other, truly, than the awe-inspiring and meticulous theory of this givenness of God's self-revelation shared with man.

Where can we see something like the phenomenalization of pure phenomenality as its immediate and original self-phenomenalization, as the self-revelation of what we are presumptively calling "God"? Nowhere. But it is also clear that such "seeing" is out of the question here. Seeing is only possible in a "world." Seeing presupposes the distancing of what must be seen and thus its coming-outside—more precisely, the prior coming-outside of "Outside" itself, the formation of the world's horizon. It is the coming-outside of "Outside," the "outside-itself" as such, that constitutes the visibility of everything that, situated in this "Outside" before our gaze, will be susceptible of being seen by us, as a being-seen as such. And this concerns not only sensory seeing but equally so intelligible seeing, any form of experience in which one accedes to what is experienced as an *en-face* or as an "ob-ject."

That God's revelation as his self-revelation owes nothing to the phenomenality of the world but rather rejects it as fundamentally foreign to its own phenomenality is something that powerfully emerges in Christ's final prayer on the Mount of Olives: "I am not praying for the world" (John

17:9). Now, it is not the circumstances, tragic as they may be, that explain this terrifying declaration; instead, it finds its striking justification in a proposition whose theoretical character cannot easily be challenged: "My kingdom is not of this world" (John 18:36). Here again one would be sorely mistaken if one imagined this to be primarily a matter of moral judgment. Everywhere in Christianity, the ethical is subordinated to the order of things. "Kingdom" does not mean a sort of domain across which divine power extends, a terrain reserved for its action. It is the very essence of Christ as identified with "the Revelation of God," with His absolute self-revelation, that is designated foreign to the world: "even as I am not of [the world]" (John 17:14).

However, if the Revelation of God owes nothing to the world's truth —if its pure phenomenological matter is not identified with the horizon of light that is the world, in such a way that this Revelation cannot show itself within the world and will never show itself there—how then can we have access to Revelation? And how can we even think it? Thought is only one mode of our relation to the world. To think is always to think something that thinking brings into sensory or intellectual seeing, and thus brings under the condition of the world. Any form of knowledge—and especially the scientific method of research, including the phenomenological method—proceeds according to a play of intentional implications constantly deployed so as to result in evidence and thus in a seeing. It is in this seeing, and thanks to it, that any advance in knowledge is constituted. How could the work undertaken here concerning the Truth of Christianity, that is to say, concerning God's self-revelation, produce results if that self-revelation in principle slipped away as a target of thought, inasmuch as thought always presupposes the prior opening of a world?

The irreducibility of the truth of Christianity to thought, or to any form of knowledge or science, is one of the major themes of Christianity itself. Such a situation does not merely confirm the opposition of Christianity to a tradition of Western thought oriented toward the world and toward obtaining knowledge that is objective and, as such, scientific. Precisely because this opposition refers back to a final irreducibility (of the truth of Christianity to any worldly form of knowledge and science), it, too, finds itself formulated in an extremely forceful manner by Christ himself: "I praise you, Father, . . . because you have hidden these things from the wise and learned, and revealed them to little children" (Matthew 11:25).

What is meant by "little children" and their mysterious appropriation of divine Revelation is something we will try to catch sight of. But an initial difficulty must first be overcome, that which a priori deprives thought of any possibility of access to divine revelation, because the phenomenality of everything that shows itself to thought is itself incapable of making manifest this divine revelation—because the phenomenality of this Revelation is never phenomenalized as "outside" the world. Still, the question of access to divine Revelation does not concern us either first or principally, we people who think, even if it would inevitably be a matter of knowing, at some moment or other, how we could arrive at this revelation or how it came to us. Although it is not thought or some other form of knowledge, although it is not the truth of the world, that gives access to the Revelation of God, at least a single possibility persists, already mentioned as a simple matter of fact and now rendered unimpeachable. *Access to God, understood as his self-revelation according to a phenomenality proper to Him, is not susceptible of being produced except where this self-revelation is produced and in the way self-revelation does so.* There where God originally arrives in himself, in the phenomenalization of phenomenality that is his own and is thus like the self-phenomenalization of this phenomenality proper—there alone is access to God. It is not that thought is lacking and so we cannot accede to the Revelation of God. Quite the contrary, it is only when thought defaults, because the truth of the world is absent, that what is at stake be achieved: the self-revelation of God—the self-phenomenalization of pure phenomenality against the background of a phenomenality that is not that of the world.

Where is a self-revelation of this sort achieved? *In Life, as its essence, since Life is nothing other than that which reveals itself*—not something that might have an added property of self-revealing, but *the very fact of self-revealing, self-revelation as such.* Everywhere that something like a self-revelation is produced there is Life. Everywhere there is Life, this self-revelation is produced. If, then, the Revelation of God is a self-revelation that owes nothing to the truth of the world, and if we ask where such a self-revelation is achieved, the answer is unequivocal: in Life and in Life alone. Therefore we are in the presence of the first fundamental equation of Christianity: God is Life—he is the essence of Life, or if one prefers, the essence of Life is God. Saying this we already know what God is, but we do not know it through the effect of some knowledge or learning—we do not know it through thought, against the background of the truth of the world. Rather we know it, and can know it, only in and through Life itself. We can know the essence of God only in God. But this observation is premature.[1]

The assertion that Life constitutes the essence of God and is identical with him is constantly made in the New Testament. Here we shall be content with brief indications—"I am the First and the Last; I am the living one" (Revelation 1:17), "the living God" (1 Timothy 3:15), "by him who is declared to be living" (Hebrews 7:8), "He who is living" (Luke 24:5)— not to mention the decisive declarations that occur during a more developed elaboration of the divine essence, and to which we shall return: "For as the Father has life in himself, so he has granted the Son to have life in himself" (John 5:26). Of the Word that is at the Beginning, John's celebrated prologue declares: "In him was Life."

To the definitions of God as finding his essence in Life, as well as the many propositions in which he appears as the Living, people will not fail to contrast those definitions that make reference to Being. Thus Yahweh, the God of Abraham, Isaac, and Jacob, who names himself in a way that can be approximately translated "I am who I am," by all accounts refers to this concept of Being. Revelation also says of God: "I am the Alpha and the Omega . . . He who is, who was, and who will come, the Almighty" (Revelation 1:8). We observe, too, that the concept of being even intrudes into statements that identify the divine essence with life, such as the following: "He who is living." In order to clear away from the start the massive misconception that equates the essence of the Christian God with Being, and thus with a concept proper to Greek thought—opening the path to the great Western theologies that reduce the God of Abraham to that of the philosophers and scholars (to that of Aristotle, for example)— we must remember that, restored to its ultimate phenomenological foundation, the concept of Being is related to the truth of the world, designating nothing other than its apparition, its clearing, which suffices to deprive it of any pertinence to the Truth of Christianity, that is, to God himself.

More precisely, the word "Being" belongs to human language, which is that of the world. This is because, as we have previously suggested and will have occasion to establish at length, any language makes seen the thing of which it is speaking as well as what it is saying about this thing. Such making seen arises from the world and its own Truth. To the extent that the language of Scripture is the one spoken by people, the word "Being" is found there at every step, even when it involves God identifying himself to people *in the language that is their own*. When, on the contrary, this language is explicitly referenced to God to the point of becoming his own Word, this Word is then given unfailingly as the Word of Life and as Living Word —but by no means as "the word of Being," which from a Christian viewpoint does not mean anything at all. "The words I have spoken to you are spirit and they are life" (John 6:63); "'Go, stand in the temple courts,' he said, 'and tell the people these words of life'" (Acts 5:20). We will have occasion to cite many other passages in which the divine essence is explicitly stated to be that of Life, "the bread of life" (John 6:48). As for the many metaphors used in New Testament texts, which will give rise to an entirely new iconography and generate a specifically Christian art that will change the course of Western art, they all converge toward another truth, in the phenomenological sense, than that of the world. Things do not appear merely as bearers of "mystical" significations. Rather, their worldly being actually dissolves in symbols of fire or water—"the water of life." In a passage to which we will return, deer drink from the source of life, flowing "down the middle of the great street of the city. On each side of the river stood the tree of life" (Revelation 22:2).

What is specific to life as self-revelation is therefore the fact that it reveals itself. This apparent tautology implies two distinct meanings that we must now separate for the first time. Self-revelation, when it concerns the essence of Life, means, on the one hand, that it is Life that achieves the revelation, that reveals—but, on the other hand, that *what Life reveals is itself.* And it is here that the mode of revelation specific to Life differs fundamentally from that of the world. The world, too, reveals and makes manifest, but within the "outside," casting a thing outside itself, as we have seen, in such a way that it never shows itself as other, different, external, in its setting of radical exteriority that is the "outside-itself" of the world. Hence it is doubly exterior: external to the power that makes it manifest—and this is where the contrast between Truth and what it makes true intervenes— and also exterior to itself. It manifests itself only in its own exteriority to itself, emptied of its own substance, unreal—emptied of this unreality that comes to it from its own mode of apparition, from the truth of the world. If, then, Life reveals itself not only in the sense that it achieves revelation but also because it is itself that it reveals in such a revelation, then Life is possible only because its own mode of revelation ignores the world and its "outside." *Living is not possible in the world.* Living is possible only outside the world, where another Truth reigns, another way of revealing. This way of revealing is that of Life. Life does not cast outside itself what it reveals but holds it inside itself, retains it in so close an embrace that what it holds and reveals is itself. It is only because it holds what it reveals in this embrace, which nothing can pull apart, that it is and can be life. Life embraces, experiences without distance or difference. Solely on this condition can it experience itself, *be itself what it experiences*—and, consequently, be itself that which experiences and which is experienced.

In the self-revelation of Life reality is given birth, any possible reality. And we can understand why. It is clear from the start that reality of whatever sort can be established only if the conditions that make it a priori impossible are excluded and are thus incapable of performing their destructive work. Where the "outside" that casts everything out of itself and strips it of its reality has neither place nor power—there alone, in the essence of Life, can something like reality be possible. This is why, from now on (and even if we will have to return to the point at greater length), we must reject an idea found in Hegel's philosophy—and in its by-products such as its most tenacious expression, Marxism—before determining in turn many of the commonplaces of modern thought. This is the idea that Christianity is a flight from reality, inasmuch as it is a flight from the world. But if reality resides in Life and only in Life, this reproach disintegrates to the point of ultimately appearing as non-sense.

Thus, reality resides in Life not merely because what Life experiences, being experienced without distance or any kind of difference, is not emptied of itself within the "outside-itself" of a world, in the noematic unreality of what can only be seen—because what Life experiences is still itself. The content of Life—what it experiences—is Life itself, refers back to a more fundamental condition, to the very essence of "Living," to a mode of revelation whose specific phenomenality is the flesh of a pathos, pure affective material, in which any cleavage, any separation, finds itself radically excluded. It is uniquely because such is the phenomenological matter of which this revelation is made that we can say that in this revelation what reveals and what is revealed are one and the same. It is this *pathētik* phenomenological substance of living that defines and contains any conceivable "reality."

When we say that in the Living where any reality takes place—in the self-revelation that constitutes the essence of life and thus of God himself—what reveals is the same as what is revealed, is there not a distinction to be apprehended (at least in rough outline) between the first of these terms and the second, even though we are declaring them the same? Is this distinction not overcome by, or supposedly overcome by, an identification that in fact presupposes it? Similarly, with regard to an "experiencing" that expresses nothing except Living, when we affirm that what experiences is the same as what is experienced, have we not already broken up what we had taken as the primordial unity of Living? But these potential differentiations, as well as the copula that overcomes them, belong to the morphology of language and are ultimately rooted in the world in which this language is the only language. Experiencing oneself as Life does is to enjoy oneself [*jouir de soi*]. Enjoyment does not presuppose any differences similar to those in which the world is born: it is homogeneous phenomenological material, a monolithic affective body whose phenomenality is affectivity as such. The self-revelation of Life is not a formal structure that can be conceived on the basis of "outside oneself" and in terms of its own structures, since these are bypassed, overcome while being maintained in this very bypassing. The self-revelation of life is its enjoyment, the primordial self-enjoyment that defines the essence of Living and thus of God himself. According to Christianity, God is Love. Love is nothing other than the self-revelation of God understood in its *pathētik* phenomenological essence, specifically, the self-enjoyment of absolute Life. This is why the Love of God is the infinite love in which he eternally loves himself, and the revelation of God is none other than this Love.

Urgent questions arise here. If the truth of Christianity finds its essence in Life, and if this essence of Life is that of God himself, then what relation can such a Life have with what we usually call by this name, and which seems to be the privilege not only of God but of all the living? More precisely, what relation does Life have with what science means by this term—with the subject of biology? Doesn't biology, which concentrates within itself the spectacular progress made by contemporary research and which possesses extraordinarily sophisticated and complex methodologies, shed an entirely new light on life? Does the archaic discourse of Christianity, encumbered by theological considerations as well as by an obsolete kind of learning, still hold some interest for people today? How can we think man himself in the light of the Christian conception of Truth, as meaning the single idea of life? Doesn't the Greek elaboration of what constitutes the humanity of man in terms of his specific difference from animals—as an animal possessing *logos*, reason, and language, as capable of thinking, reflecting, and reasoning—lead us much nearer to who we really are? And leads us, moreover, in such a way that it is impossible, even dangerous, to see in man nothing more than a living.

3

This Truth Called Life

The elaboration of the Christian concept of Truth has made truth appear to find its essence in Life. Inasmuch as it is identical with Truth, Life is understood from the start as phenomenological. That Life is Truth signifies that it is manifestation and revelation, in the original meaning we have granted these terms. Life is not "true," which would mean nothing more than that it manifests itself, shows itself. In that case, nothing would distinguish it from any other phenomenon, from everything that shows itself in general. Such a proposition would not only remain indeterminate but would also leave unexamined the problem of Truth, notably the truth proper to Life. That which shows itself is not the only thing that presupposes a "monstration," a prior manifestation without which nothing would ever be manifest to us, no phenomenon of any sort. But the central question of phenomenology, which is directly implicated in the understanding of Christianity, is knowing *how* manifestation makes manifest everything it manifests, or more essentially how it manifests itself. Before making manifest whatever it may be, and in order to be able to do so, manifestation must manifest itself in its purity, as such that it is. Before illuminating something, light shines in its own luster. It is when the central question of phenomenology is posed that we discover the extraordinary originality of Christianity, the decisive cleavage on which it altogether rests. To the Greek concept of phenomenon that will determine the course of Western thought—the interpretation of the manifestation of things, or, more rigorously, the interpretation of the manifestation of this manifestation as truth of the world, a truth whose phenomenality is that of "outside"—Christianity solidly opposes its conception of Truth as Life. Life thus receives in Christianity a phenomenological meaning that is as original as it is radical. Life designates a pure manifestation, always irreducible to that of the world, an original revelation that is not the revelation of an other thing and does not depend on anything other, but is rather a revelation of self, that absolute self-revelation that is Life itself.

Through its phenomenological essence—because it is thereby Truth, pure manifestation, revelation—the Life of which Christianity speaks differs totally from what biology studies. What characterizes biology—whether it has to do with neurons, electric currents, chains of amino acids, cells, or chemical properties, or else their ultimate constituents, which are physical particles—is something wholly foreign to phenomenality. Certainly these diverse elements—physical, chemical, or specifically biological—are all phenomena or refer back to phenomena, without which no science, however elaborate or sophisticated its methodologies, would be able to know anything. But these diverse phenomena do not in fact retain their own phenomenality, their capacity to show themselves to us. Rather, they owe this capacity to be shown, and thus to become the object of possible knowledge, to a power of manifestation foreign to them—whereas in themselves they are "blind." And this power of manifestation foreign to elements that are themselves blind, those that biology studies, is the truth of the world.

The radical opposition—between, on the one hand, the phenomenological matter of which Life is made as self-revelation, as original truth, and, on the other hand, the nonphenomenological matter of the elements constitutive of chemical or specifically biological properties—raises an embarrassing but unavoidable question, that of the relation between the approach of Christianity and that of contemporary science, a relation that can only appear, it would seems, conflictual. Christ did not know about all the marvelous discoveries of twentieth-century biology, and, such being the case, the discourse he professed about life takes no account of them. When he declares, in a sentence to which we will return, that "I am . . . the Life" (John 14:6), he does not mean that he is a composite of molecules. And even those among his contemporaries who see him as only a man, or at most a prophet, do not therefore consider him a "neuronal man."

One might point out that, at the time Christ lived, science had not yet been born. What was known about a man could be reduced to the immediate expression of the data of sensory perception—a naive understanding upon which was erected the whole set of anthropological and religious conceptions that constitute common belief. What Christ taught concerning what is most essential in man, and his supposed relation with the absolute derived from ignorance.

This is a strange ignorance, since in its negative definition—as ignorance pure and simple—ignorance would be unable to produce anything at all, not even the collective representations of an era, which are also assigned a particular origin (despite their pejorative denotations) in immediate and ordinary perception. It is this sensory perception of things, as well as the sensory networks habitually established among them and serving as the foundation of various ways of judging, reasoning, and evaluating, that together constitute the ideology of a given society at any moment in its history. This common way of thinking determines the behavior, customs, and ultimately the ethics of that society. But the teaching of Christ unfortunately has nothing to do with this sensory, immediate, empirical, and practical knowledge that constitutes the bedrock of a society. One could say that he pursues the very opposite. In the universe of ordinary perception, one sees the bodies of the dead decompose in the earth rather than returning to life in "Heaven." In the universe of perception, wealth decays and clothing is devoured by worms, metals are eaten by rust. In the universe of perception, dwellings are built by people's hands. But Christ speaks of a wealth that does not rot away, and James and Paul of a metal that does not rust, of dwellings that are not built by people's hands.

And it is not only things but people and their actions that suddenly obey other laws than those of ordinary perception. In the blinding illumination of Life, in its unapproachable light, along come the livings, staggering as if drunk, their customary behavior turned upside down. The one who would be first finds himself seated in the last row, the one who hoards money is deprived of his wealth, the one who has nothing now possesses everything, the one who is thirsty is no longer thirsty, the one who is hated by all should be glad because he suffers, and the one who suffers is happy. The one who knows nothing knows everything, the one who knows everything knows nothing. It is difficult, in truth, to attribute such propositions to the knowledge of ordinary perception, to the naive ideology of an era.

Could the chemistry of molecules tell us more about these paradoxes, which after all concern the life of everybody every day? Should we think that, if Christ had had the opportunity to take classes in biology at any institute of biology, he would have been led to modify in any appreciable way his conception of life—a conception according to which, for example, "whoever wants to save his life will lose it, but whoever loses his life for me will save it" (Luke 9:24)? Might we rather say, either to avoid polemics or to remove a real difficulty, that Christianity and biology are not speaking about the same thing, that their discourses do not interfere with each other, that any comparison between them makes no sense? Or, to the contrary, that *there is only one Life, that of Christ, which is also that of God and men,* and that, to this single and unique life that is self-revelation—and, moreover, the self-revelation of God himself—only the word of Christ can testify?

We have been supposing that in Christ's era people knew nothing (or nothing much) about life. Now let us propose the reverse hypothesis. Let us suppose that today, at a time when biology has achieved its most incisive progress, a mounting ignorance is developing on the subject of what life really is—and that, far from involving only biology, this ignorance extends to the whole realm of scientific expertise, which, thanks especially to the cult made of it, ends up infecting the whole public mind. In this case, it would indeed be that the latter—the spirit of our times, the modern spirit, and thus each person determined by it—would know less than ever what life is, what a person is. And since it cannot be a matter here of a simple hypothesis, let us bring this line of reasoning as much to bear on the scientific knowledge of our era as on its collective (and to a certain extent popular) ideology.

As for what science is, we cannot forget the initial decision from which it proceeds and which will altogether determine it, as well as the world that is its own—which is our own. The conclusions reached by Galileo at the start of the seventeenth century assign to the new science the task of knowing the real universe, which is constituted of an array of material objects measurable in space. Henceforth, the knowledge that should make accessible to us the reality of the universe cannot be sensory knowledge, as had been the case in the past—the variable knowledge of one individual or another, which is incapable of resulting in universal propositions and is especially ill-suited to the reality to be known. That reality is not, in fact, sensible, and the sensible properties of things do not inhere in the essential nature of things themselves: they are content to express the empirical and contingent structures of the animal nature within us—our factitious biological organization. To know the universe in an adequate way therefore implies that, these sensible properties having been set aside as illusory, we will grasp the measurements of real bodies—a study relating to geometry, a rational and rigorous science. The mathematical determination of the geometric properties of real bodies, as proposed by Descartes in the wake of the new Galilean science, conferred on that science its modern physiognomy: a physical and mathematical approach to the material particles that constitute the reality of our universe.

Even a moment's reflection on the genesis of this science that will upset the world, thus opening the way to what we conveniently call modernity, is enough for us to catch sight of the initial reduction that it implies—namely, the exclusion of the sensible qualities of the universe. To take the measure of such a reduction—to grasp its importance for the future of humanity not just in a historical but in a properly metaphysical sense, one that affects the destiny of man himself—is to understand that the exclusion of sensible qualities implies the exclusion of the sensibility without which these sensible qualities would not exist. But to exclude sensibility is to exclude the phenomenological Life that defines the Truth of Christianity, and of which sensibility is only one modality. This is so because feeling is possible only in this place where "experiencing oneself" reigns, in the original self-revelation of which Life is the essence. Considered from the viewpoint of scientific development, the exclusion of sensible qualities might appear a methodological postulate whose legitimacy relates to its extraordinary practical fecundity. In addition, sensible qualities belong to the object, at least under the guise of apparent qualities: like the object itself, they appear in the world. Science believes that it continues to operate in its own proper domain when it reduces these properties to their material physical substrate. What escapes science is that sensible qualities never exist as the simple properties of an object. Before being projected onto that object, they are pure subjective impressions that in fact presuppose sensibility, that invisible essence of Life that is Christian Truth.

The exclusion of life by the Galilean decision that inaugurates modern science concerns biology above all. In this field that decision manifests its most remarkable effect, orienting research toward the chemical and then the physical substrata of biological phenomena and their specific functioning. The absolutely necessary consequence is that at the culmination of such research, one finds only physical and chemical processes, and nothing that resembles the internal ordeal that every living undergoes of its life—nothing that resembles the very fact of "Living," meaning the original self-revelation that characterizes Life as a pure phenomenological essence and the truth in the sense given it by Christianity. This consequence does not follow from the research itself, from its progress or its own vicissitudes, but rather from its initial methodological postulate. In its inaugural decision, having placed sensible life, phenomenological life in general, outside its field of study, Galilean science would assuredly not be able to discover it again through research, even though it calls itself biology. And in fact biology never encounters life, knows nothing of it, has not the slightest idea of it. When by some extraordinary circumstance it is biology itself that speaks—biology and not a biologist who is imbued with the ideals or prejudices of his time—it pronounces a sentence on itself, declares truthfully and lucidly what it is: "*Biologists no longer study life today.*"[1] We must take it at its word: *in biology there is no life; there are only algorithms.*

Thus it is not the case that in the time of Abraham or of Melchizedek and in the time of Christ people knew nothing about life, whereas at the end of the twentieth century, before our amazed and vaguely uneasy eyes, the veil has begun to lift from secrets hidden since the world's origin. Rather, the contrary is true: today, despite the marvelous progress of science, or rather because of it, we know less and less about life. Or, more exactly, *we no longer know anything about it, not even that it exists.* And this is what biology tells us, saying that under its gaze, in its field of investigation, which is scientifically circumscribed and defined, nothing whatsoever of the "Living" of life is ever shown. In truth, biology does not say even that, because to say it you have to at least know what this "Living" is, have a vague idea of it. But biology does not know this, hasn't the faintest idea of it.

Biologists themselves know what life is. They do not know it in their capacity as biologists, since biology knows nothing about it. They know it like everyone else, since they, too, live and love life, wine, and the opposite sex; they get jobs, have careers, and themselves experience the joy of new departures, chance encounters, the boredom of administrative tasks, the anguish of death. But these sensations and emotions, these desires, this happiness or resentment—all those experiences and ordeals that are just so many of life's epiphanies—are in their eyes only "pure appearance."

"Appearance" implies in the first place that there is no need to study it. "Appearance," "pure appearance," or "mere appearance" in effect designate an apparition that has no intrinsic value, which does not contain its own raison d'être, that is not explained by itself. "Appearance" means the appearance of another thing; it refers back to that other thing and finds its sole explanation there. Therefore biologists do not concern themselves with the appearances that are the modalities of life; their phenomenological status does not interest them. They never perceive them in themselves as impressions, sentiments, desires, joys. In these appearances, or rather through them, they seize upon electric currents or chains of neurons. The reduction of absolute phenomenological Life to the content of biology—this reduction that biology never completes and of which it in fact has no idea—is practiced by biologists as a matter of course. Instead, for the self-revelation of absolute phenomenological Life, of which they have knowledge only from inside this self-revelation and through it (inasmuch as they are of the living, living from this phenomenological Life and it alone), they substitute at one fell swoop, without even being aware of it, the material content of biology.

This is an absurd reduction if it means asserting that what is experienced in the infrangible *pathētik* embrace of suffering or joy is in reality something that experiences nothing and is in principle incapable of doing so: material particles. This is an untenable reduction, since the phenomenological laws of life—those, for example, exhibited by Christianity in its ageless truth—have no relation to biological, chemical, or physical laws, which have never pretended to be the laws of absolute phenomenological Life. Never has nonphenomenological matter presented itself as the phenomenological matter of life, as its self-revelation—which it certainly is not. Science has never practiced any reductionism unless of a purely methodological sort. It is scientists, forcing science to say what it does not say, who profess this reductionism. Those who murder life are those who, depriving life of the self-revelation that constitutes its essence at the same time as that of all livings, and thus denying the very fact of Living and holding it to be nothing, reduce everything that lives, and experiences itself as living, to a set of blind processes and to death.

Reductionist illusions set aside, we must stick to the effective content of science. The true question will henceforth be the following: Why does the living of life never appear in the field of phenomena taken up by biology? As important as its role in the definition and development of modern

science has been, does the Galilean reduction suffice to explain why, paradoxically, *life absents itself from the field of biology, as it does, moreover, from
any field of scientific investigation*? Is it really this act of ruling out the sensible qualities of things that has caused to vanish, at the same time as these
qualities themselves, the sensibility to which they necessarily refer back—
and thus phenomenological life itself, even though it is present in sensibility as that which originally makes life sensible, as the "feeling of oneself"
without which no sentient thing would ever feel anything?

However, let us consider the world before the Galilean reduction—
the sensible world in which people live, where there are colors, odors, and
sounds, tactile qualities such as hard and soft, gentle and rough, where
things are never given to us except as clothed in axiomatic qualities such as
harmful or advantageous, favorable or dangerous, friendly or hostile. We
are then forced to recognize that, despite these sensible or affective determinations that return everything to life—to such an extent that contemporary phenomenology has called this world of concrete experience, this
world before science, the lifeworld (*Lebenswelt*)—*life never shows itself in
it*. And it is for this reason alone that life is not shown in any field of theoretical investigation (especially that of biology) either: whatever the importance of the processes of abstract purification in preparation for a specifically scientific treatment, this field of investigation has already assumed
the form of a world, having had at the outset to offer itself to view and
thus to the truth of the world. Thus we are sent back to the decisive thesis
of Christianity, to wit, that the Truth of Life is irreducible to the truth of
the world, so that it never shows itself in the world. It is this reciprocal
exclusion between the Truth of Life and that of the world that we must
examine more closely.

In the world, do we not see, apart from inanimate things, living beings, and even our own life, as more or less similar to that of animals? It is
true: *we see living beings but never their life*. If we reflect a bit more on the
perception that we have of such beings, we realize that a signification is inherent in that perception—the signification "living being"—and it is that
signification, coupled with an intuitive grasp of their objective bodies, that
make of these bodies living bodies and make of these beings what they are
for us: living beings. But grasping this signification is by no means equivalent to the perception of life itself. To signify means to aim "into the void"
in such a way that no intuition of reality yet corresponds with this target.

When I form the signification "dog," for example by using the word "dog," I do not perceive a real dog. Similarly, when I perceive livings, I confer on them the signification of "livings" without perceiving their own life in itself, as they experience it. It is precisely because we do not perceive Life in itself that we arrive at it only in the form of an empty signification or, to use Husserl's term, of a noematic, unreal signification. This signification is invested in the living being and determines its perception to the point that the living being is not conceivable without it. To take another example from Husserl: "these eyes are perceived as 'eyes that see,' these hands as 'hands that touch'" [trans. modified].[2] Such significations nevertheless remain empty, incapable of containing reality. Whatever the philosophical analysis one offers of them, they merely signify life without being able to give it in person.

Here we should introduce a radical difference between significations relating to life, and thus to the whole set of the living, and those referring to things. When we say, "The tree is green," we have formed the meaning "tree" and the meaning "green" without any tree or any green color being present before us as the "real" tree or "real" color. Like any signification in general, these take aim at their object with empty intentions without really furnishing an effective intuition of that object. But these empty intentions can be filled in at any moment. This is what happens in my experience when, after having thought of a green tree or having spoken of it, I suddenly apprehend one. Then the empty signification is converted into a full intuition, which we call a perception. *Any empty signification concerning things—whether sensible or intelligible—is susceptible of changing into a filled-in intuition, into a perception. But this never happens in the case of a signification intending life.* Such a signification—for example, "living"—is incapable of being transformed into a real perception of life or of a particular life. And this is not because this life "would not exist," but precisely because it is incapable of giving itself to a perception, of becoming visible in the truth of the world.

The incapacity of modern biology to give access to life itself is not specific to biology. It is not specific to science in general and thus does not result from the Galilean reduction from which this science proceeds. There is a similar impotence in any knowledge that opens onto a world or, more profoundly, in any form of experience that demands and borrows its phenomenality from that of the world, from the world's truth. But the presupposition that every form of experience borrows its phenomenality from that of the world will come to dominate Western thought. This whole manner of thinking misses Life in the sense we are giving it—in the sense Christianity gives it: that of the phenomenological Life whose essence is that one experiences oneself in one's "Living." This phenomenological Life that experiences itself, this actual life that is ours, that inhabits each of our joys and sufferings, desires and fears, and above all the most humble of our sensations, therefore constitutes the great absence in the philosophical and cultural tradition to which we belong. But how could such an absence go undetected? Why does it not present itself as the greatest paradox, unbearable to all those who live this life, who borrow from it at every instant, without ever being able to pay off the debt—their own condition as living?

The dissimulation of the absolute phenomenological Life that is the sole real life, which does not cease in its "Living" to experience itself—this will be a principal theme in our reflections. And because this dissimulation of life is also, in each living, that of its veritable condition, that condition will by the same token constitute a privileged subject in our study. These questions are those of Christianity, too. For the time being, let us be content with a more limited line of questioning: When a tradition has traversed the centuries to result in European culture, how has such a culture been able to function in relation to the essential reality that is our life without placing it at the forefront of its preoccupations, without making it the keystone of its various systems of conceptualization? The answer is powerfully simple: it was by substituting, for this essence dissimulated in life, the consideration of each and all that lives. But for this substitution to work, for it to result in the occultation by Western thought of the original essence of life and its "Living," it was necessary that this substitution be reproduced on the very plane of the living that came to replace life before the gaze of that thought. It was necessary, with regard to each and every living, that *its external appearance in the truth of the world be substituted for its self-giving in the Living of life, for the self-revelation of that life.*

And this is what has happened since classical antiquity, and no doubt took place even before that. The living is a being that shows itself in the world among all the other beings and in the same way as they do—among all the other beings, living or not, and subsequently sustaining with them multiple relations that are themselves worldly, that are disclosed in the world and draw their character from it. The living's belonging to the world is so forceful that it determines it from the moment of its birth—which consists of nothing other than its coming into the world and is exhausted in so doing. It remains to be known what distinguishes this living being from all others, inasmuch as their mode of apparition is the same—this same and unique world, with its identical modes of appearance for all, those spatial and temporal intuitions and the reciprocal correlations to which they are subject. When Life in its Living is absent, in the truth of the world, what would make a being that claimed the title of "living" worth more than some other thing that is not living? Its properties and characteristics, of which the other thing is deprived. But these properties and characteristics are objective, they appear in the world: properties and functions like mobility, nutrition, excretion, reproduction. And it is these functions unfolding in the form of objective processes, and taken as such, that allow us to characterize the beings possessing these functions as living beings and to define them as such.

We are left with the enigma of understanding why such functions are considered to be characteristics of life. It is not their role as distinctive criteria that is the problem, since one could just as well choose any criteria—decide that the phenomena bearing one group of properties are to be placed in the class "A" and those without them in the class "not-A." But why are the phenomena in the first class designated as "living?" Why are functions like nutrition, mobility, and so on, considered specific to life and hence capable of differentiating specifically vital qualities? After all, they are only objective phenomena, none of which reveals within itself life in its "Living," such as life is revealed to itself. On the level of sense perception, it is true that these phenomena spontaneously receive the signification "living being." They are perceived as such, or, as Husserl said, as hands that touch, eyes that see. That which touches within them is life. That which sees within them is life. But within the objective process to which the act of touching is reduced, since it is shown in the truth of the world, we do not see and cannot see life—we cannot see it touch, if it is life that touches. In the objective movement of the eye or the glance, since it is shown in the truth of the world, we do not see and cannot see life—we cannot see its Seeing, if it is life that sees. Why then do we attribute to them this meaning of being the movements of life itself, if life itself never reveals itself in their worldly appearance?

We have said that significations concerning life, unlike those relating to things, are incapable of receiving an intuitive fulfillment, of being transformed into a perception. Now we can say a little more. It is not only the impossibility that the signification "living" or "living being" can give us life that is at issue, but the origin of this signification itself. Where does it come from, if life is never shown in the world, if the very idea of life—its meaning—cannot proceed from the truth of this world? It is not only the possibility of having access to life in the world that is barred. The issue is the very possibility of perceiving in the world a being endowed at least with the signification of being a living being, an "organism," if the origin of this signification remains unknown.

That it is impossible for life to be revealed in the truth of the world becomes evident in Galilean science. As in the case of naive sense perception, it is the living being, not life, that science studies. What it retains from this being, as does immediate perception, are the characteristics by which that being is given as living: functions, biological and physiological phenomena, considered in their specificity. With sensibility having been subtracted, it is these objective biological phenomena reduced to material processes—themselves reduced to the parameters that express them—that constitute its object. There is no longer anything of life's Living, anything of the living. Thus the idea that even the most minor of these phenomena relates to living beings and belongs to them concerns biology no more than does life itself. And with good reason, since the signification of "living" or "living being" fundamentally makes no sense once it has been stripped of any relation to the Living of life. Biology studies phenomena of the class "A." The concepts of life and of living are archaic metaphysical entities, no longer current. "In biology there is no life; there are only algorithms." The final survival of these obscure entities—"life," the "vital force," the "living"—in a biology that has achieved a full understanding of itself, of its object and tasks, lies basically in what it is called—the name of this discipline, this *bios* that no longer corresponds with anything and has no value except as an external and conventional designation of phenomena of the class "A."

If we consider the sum of the failings of Western thought with regard to the question of life, we can find a significant example at the endpoint of this thought's history in the philosophy of Heidegger. And this is not by chance, if it is true that, despite his repeated criticism of the history of Western metaphysics and his own efforts to put an end to it, Heidegger's phenomenology recognized (thought through and took to the limit) only the phenomenological presuppositions that had guided, or rather misguided, this thought from the start. By inexorably and ingeniously unveiling the implications of the Greek concept of phenomenon, these presuppositions led to the truth of the world being laid bare. This phenomenology was not about things but rather about nothingness, not about what is shown but rather the "unapparent." Far from turning us away from the world and its "insight," this phenomenology concerns itself with nothing other than the original event in which this insight is produced.

With respect to the question of life, the immediate consequences of these presuppositions are overwhelming. The first is the fact that we know nothing about a mode of revelation other than that in which the illumination of the world occurs. Life has no phenomenological existence if we understand it as a specific mode of the phenomenalization of pure phenomenality. The phenomenological nonexistence of life in this radical sense leads back to the substitution exposed above, which has been recognized as one of the most enduring traits of Western thought: the substitution for life of what is called the living being. Certainly this being presents characteristics different from those of any random being; it has a particular type of Being. Like any being, though, it derives its Being solely from its quality as phenomenon. How the living being shows itself to us—how we have access to it, and, accordingly, how we have access to a life that reveals itself to us only in the form of this being—is the question posed and answered in *Being and Time*: "Life, in its own right, is a kind of Being, but essentially it is only accessible in *Dasein*."[3]

Given that the *Dasein* that pretends to define the essence of a person is essentially an opening into the world, a Being-in-the-world, *In-der-Welt-sein*, it follows that life is accessible only in the truth of the world. Life is not truth. It is not, in itself and through itself, a power or mode of phenomenalization. Life is not what gives access, what clears a path to—nor is it what shows, makes manifest, reveals. Life is not the path to follow if you want to arrive at what makes the essential-Being of man, his veritable reality. Nor is life the path to follow if you want to arrive at life. *It is not life that gives access to itself.* It is because life is not a power of revelation that it is also not what gives access to itself, what reveals itself—that it is not self-revelation. If the living arrives at life and enters into the condition of living, this is not thanks to life. It is only because he is open to the world, in relation with the truth of the world and defined by this relation, that man is related to himself. But it is for the same reason that he is related to life. If it is not as living that a person has access to life, then neither is it as living that he knows what life is. It is only to the extent that a person is open to the world that he is related, and can be related, to living beings—to life. This set of aporias is not specific to Heidegger's thought; it results from the phenomenological presupposition according to which "to show oneself" means "to show oneself in a world," in the ek-static truth of its "outside."

It is because the truth is reduced to that of the world, to a horizon of visibility, that life, stripped of truth, of the power of revealing, finds itself reduced to something that shows itself in the truth of the world, in the illumination of its "outside"—finds itself reduced to an entity. The calamitous confusion of Life with a living being, or to use another kind of language, with a living organism, results directly from the phenomenological failing of Western thought, from its permanent powerlessness to conceive of Life as truth—and, moreover, as the original essence of truth. What is true of living organisms as objective empirical beings appearing in the world according to the mode of appearing specific to that world, is attributed without question to life itself. Once its self-revelation inside Life is eliminated, the manifestation of the living is no longer anything other, in fact, than its external appearance in the form of a being or a living organism endowed with the particular "kind of Being" that life, reduced to and defined by the empirical properties of this entity, has become.

Such a reduction, similar in appearance to the Galilean kind and like it concerned only with worldly phenomena, is in fact totally different. The Galilean reduction has, in principle, only a methodological significance: it leaves outside its field of interest the decisive phenomenological question of knowing whether there exists a mode of revelation other than that in which the phenomena of the world give themselves to us. It is from the radical negation of such a mode of revelation that Heideggerian thought proceeds. If such a mode of revelation, as a self-revelation foreign to the "outside" of the world, constitutes the essence of life, then its negation signifies nothing less than the impossibility of any form of life, and thus amounts to the murder of life—not accidentally but rather in principle.

It is thus the affirmation that life at least is "a particular kind of Being" that causes a problem. It is indicative of Heidegger's embarrassment that his approach to life is obliged to pursue different paths. To the extent that our access to life reveals *Dasein* and takes place in the world, the philosophical problematic of life resembles the scientific approach more than it might wish. Once and for all, it is living organisms considered from the outside, and the objective processes of which they are the site, that furnish the material for analysis and impose a method. Like the biologist, the philosopher then chooses the simplest of organisms, protoplasmic, single-celled creatures, to sketch by means of example a theory of the organ, a theory whose aim is not so different from that of science. Moreover, it is from science, from the biology of his day, that Heidegger borrows the knowledge he uses to construct his interpretation of life. Although, regarding certain problems, such an interpretation may have at its command more elaborate concepts borrowed from the *Dasein* analytic, it does not escape the aporia into which science itself tumbles. *Is it not paradoxical for someone who wants to know what life is to go and ask protozoa, or, at best, honeybees? It is as if we had a relation with life that was every bit as totally external and fragile as the one we have with beings about which we know nothing—or very little. As if we were not ourselves living.*

The application of this totally extravagant methodology leads us, then, to some disheartening conclusions: from now on, man must know nothing about his own life, and the life in him must know nothing of itself, in order that single-celled organisms can become the new masters of our understanding of life. Life is repressed into a closed domain, that of animal nature, so that it now presents itself as a set of enigmas. That this life is part of man, whether he is understood as a rational animal or as *Dasein*, which could only be a living *Dasein*, with hands to connect him to the "present-at-hand" (*Vor-handen*) or to the "ready-to-hand" (*Zu-handen*)—does not prevent life from remaining in him and for him an unknown, whose mystery can be only partially resolved by recourse to protozoa and bees. And the reason for all these aporia and paradoxes and absurdities is that only this external relation to objective organisms, that is to say, in the end only the world's truth, is recognized as the bearer of truth—whereas *that which makes each of the living a living, its internal relation to life as a relation with life itself, as its original and essential self-revelation, finds itself totally conjured away.*

How far such legerdemain goes we see when Heidegger turns to consider living Being no longer as some being subject to a power of revelation that is foreign to it—specifically, as *Dasein*—but as bearing within itself, despite everything, a power that alone is capable of differentiating that be-ing from some sort of thing or tool—of some dead being. An animal be-haves; it has the capacity to move and to react to specific stimuli. This capacity is foremost that of being affected by those stimuli, of being in relation with an environment, and relating to an environment is possible only in the form of Being-in-the-world. The bee returning to its hive, guided by the sun, is open to that sun, in such a way that the sun can act on it, excite it, and determine its behavior. It is Being-in-the-world, a Be-ing-in-the world now internal to the animal, that accounts for animal na-ture and all the properties by which one defines it, in ignorance of the mode of revelation specific to life. Thus the failing of the Heideggerian interpretation is exposed. First of all, it does not consider life as phenom-enological in its essence, as having the power to reveal. It is up to Being-in-the-world to give us access to the living. Second, when this power is con-ceded to it, life is not understood either in its originality or in its origination, but as a fallen mode of the only known power of manifesta-tion, that of Being-in-the-world. If, all the same, man is an animal and *Dasein* a living thing, it is the relation, *in them*, of Being-in-the world, open to the world despite the somnambulistic forms taken by this relation, that remains enigmatic. And still more enigmatic is the capacity of the drive, as much in man as in animals—to be in possession of oneself and thus to be able to act.[4] Only the insights offered by the Christian concept of man will permit us to penetrate this ultimate mystery.

Is it correct to assert that life remained the poor relative of Western thought, the object of its disdain? Without mentioning exceptional thinkers or mystics who viewed it as the loftiest authority, how can we forget its irruption into the foreground of European thought when Schopenhauer published his major work, *The World as Will and Representation*, in 1818? By "representation" Schopenhauer meant nothing less than the manner of ap-pearing of the world as it had recently been redefined by Kant in the great renewal of critical thought. It is this truth of the world that Schopenhauer questioned in such an inspired way, not by ignoring it, but by radically sub-ordinating it to what he calls the will, which is just another name for life. Instead of leading to arbitrary or debatable assertions, the determination of the entire world of representation by the irrepressible power of the will-to-live is destined to result, through the intermediaries of Nietzsche and Freud in particular, in a reestablishment of European culture on entirely new foundations. These foundations are supplied by this way of thinking about life and are so powerful that in effect they reduce the faculties that traditionally defined *humanitas* to a secondary role and the intellect itself to the rank of a mere "valet" of the will-to-live. Moreover, this revolution is not limited to the sphere of philosophy or thinking, properly speaking: all realms of culture will find themselves turned upside down—literature, theater, morality, painting, art in general, cinema. In each of these realms, the work of the greatest creators appears as the expression or evidence of this tide of the will-to-live, to the point of remaining unintelligible without initial reference to that idea.[5]

The most remarkable characteristic of the advent of life in the foreground of modern cultural preoccupations, as the Schopenhauerian tide submerged Europe in the final decade of the nineteenth century and the first two or three decades of the twentieth, was however the denaturation and falsification of life itself, a denaturation so serious that it resulted in life's very destruction. This singular overthrow of life in death is strikingly illuminated by radical phenomenology. It is precisely when life appears in the foreground of the European cultural scene that its power of revelation finds itself not only obscured but explicitly denied. This negation of the specific power of revelation of life has a phenomenological dimension as well. Because, for Schopenhauer as after him for Freud, the power of making manifest, what they call "consciousness," resides in representation—in the fact of being placed before, in the "outside" of the world—life, which is alien to this "outside," inevitably finds itself deprived of the power of accomplishing in and through itself the work of revelation—it becomes blind and unconscious. A blind and unconscious life, a life that desires without knowing what it desires and without even knowing that it desires, is an absurd life. An absurd, blind, unconscious power, life can then be charged with every crime. In its murderous frenzy, entering millions of times into a struggle against itself, it becomes the source of all that ravages the universe—to the point that the concept, now eminently suspect, can be associated in scandalous fashion with the atrocities, monstrosities, and genocides of which our century has been the theater.

Polemics aside, how could we not notice the very disturbing link between these diverse ways of slandering life? The first, improperly attributed to biology by many of those who think they speak in its name, consists of reducing life to material processes. The second, which pretends to be philosophical, oscillates between the confusion of the living with a being made manifest through being-in-the-world and the definition of the phenomenality proper to the living by attributing to it a fallen and almost hallucinatory form of this same being-in-the-world. The third makes life the metaphysical principle of the universe, but by stripping it of the capacity to reveal itself, to experience and to live, by stripping it of its essence. Life is only a blind entity, like the processes to which Galilean science reduces it. Underneath these diverse ways of despising life, it is easy to recognize the common root: the incapacity to construct a phenomenology of life.

By way of an awesome and timeless antithesis, Christianity opposes to these disparaging views on life its own decisive intuition of Life as Truth. It is like a trumpet call prefiguring the angels of the Apocalypse who echo Christ's words: "I am the Way and the Truth and the Life" (John 14:6). We begin to understand the two final terms of this proposition, though we seldom read them in that order. Not only does Christ say—against the scientism and positivism of all ages, against Greek phenomenology, against Schopenhauer and against Freud—that, far from being absurd, blind, or unconscious, alien to phenomenality, Life is Truth. He affirms, more fundamentally, the contrary, that Truth is Life. The primordial Revelation that tears everything from nothingness by enabling it to appear and thus to be is for the first time revealed to itself in an embrace that precedes all things, that precedes the world and owes nothing to it— in a state of absolute self-enjoyment that has no other name than Life.

This radical phenomenology according to which Life is constitutive of the primordial Revelation, that is to say, of the essence of God, is joined with an entirely new conception of man, his definition on the basis of Life and also as constituted by it—of man as living. What we must perceive clearly is the extent to which such a conception is novel, alien in any case to Western thought. In the classic conception originating in Greece, *a man is more than a living*, a man is a living endowed with *Logos*, that is to say, with reason and language, as we have seen. It follows, reciprocally, that life is less than man, or in any event less than what makes his humanity. Hence Heidegger's assertion that life can only be understood in a negative or privative way, on the basis of what is specific to man: "The ontology of life is accomplished by way of a privative Interpretation; it determines what must be the case if there is to be something that is more than just life" [trans. modified].[6] According to Christianity, on the contrary, Life is more than man, by which we understand more than what makes his humanity in the eyes of classical thought, more than *Logos*, more than reason and language. Life that speaks not a word knows everything, or in any case much more than reason. And this is as true of man as it is of God.

But—and here is another absolutely decisive thesis of Christianity— Life is equally more than man adequately understood as living. Life is more than the living. And this thesis also applies to God.

It is these two decisive theses of Christianity that we must first explore, if we still wish to understand a word about this kind of thought, or rather, this religion that is Christianity.

To the extent that Life is more than man understood as living, it is from Life, not from man, that we must begin. From Life means from God, since according to Christianity, the essence of Life and that of God are one and the same.

To the extent that, in God himself, Life precedes the living, it is in Him, too, through Life, through the eternal and immutable process whereby Life is made, that we must make a start.

The relation of Life to the living is the central thesis of Christianity. Such a relation is called, from life's viewpoint, generation, and from the living's viewpoint, birth. It is Life that generates any conceivable living thing. But this generation of the living can be accomplished by Life only insofar as it is capable of engendering itself. A Life that is capable of engendering itself, what Christianity calls God, we are calling absolute Life—or, for reasons that will emerge later, absolute phenomenological Life. Insofar as the relation of Life to the living occurs inside God himself, it is produced as the generation of the First Living at the core of Life's self-generation. Insofar as such a relation concerns not just God's relationship with himself but also his relationship with man, it is produced as the generation of transcendental man at the core of God's self-generation. We will see how this generation of transcendental man within the self-generation of God implies the generation, within this self-generation, of the First Living.

What is generated in Life as the First Living Christianity calls the firstborn Son, or the only Son, or, in Hebraic tradition, the Christ or Messiah. What is generated in Life as man, that is to say, as man himself, it calls "Son of God." Absolute Life, as it engenders itself and, in doing so, engenders the First Living, is what Christianity calls Father.

Our analysis must therefore follow this path:

1. The self-generation of absolute Life as the generation of the First Living, of the "firstborn and only Son"—which we will call, for reasons to be explained later, the transcendental Arch-Son.
2. The self-generation of absolute Life as the generation of transcendental man, of his transcendental "me," of his transcendental ego—or the generation of man as the "Son of God."

In both cases, we are dealing, in Christianity, with a transcendental phenomenology whose central concepts are those of Father and Son. The Christian concept of the transcendental birth subverts our customary idea of birth, in the same way that Christian concepts of Father and Son will overturn the current representations of "father" and "son." This is the reason why we are introducing the philosophical concept "transcendental," which does not refer to things such as we see them—a birth, a father, a son—but refers back to their most interior possibility, to their essence. But the possibility of birth, of something like a father or a son, is not seen, because this possibility resides precisely in Life, which is not seen either. This is why we also call this Life a transcendental life. "Transcendental" life is not a fiction invented by philosophy but refers to the only life that exists. As for the natural life that we think we see around us in the world, it does not exist, any more than does the supposed "biological" life. This is why there are neither natural fathers nor sons in the sense of a father or son belonging to "nature" and open to explanation on that basis. "Do not call anyone on earth 'father,' for you have one Father, and he is in heaven" (Matthew 23:9). But these are already the radical and disconcerting propositions of Christianity that we must seek to understand.

4

The Self-Generation of Life as Generation of the First Living

   Christianity concentrates on the relation of life with the living, in God as well as in man. This is why the elucidation of what Christianity means by life, more precisely, its interpretation of life as phenomenological in essence, as self-revelation and as Truth, furnishes the indispensable preliminary to understanding its teaching. Without rigorous knowledge of what Christianity takes as life, such a teaching is reduced to a tissue of enigmatic propositions barely heard, and only by "believers," those who make such assertions without understanding them. On the other hand, for someone who penetrates the interior essence of Life, the enigmatic content of Christianity is suddenly illuminated in a light of such intensity that anyone perceiving it in this light finds himself profoundly unsettled. Everything that appeared until then to be self-evident—this so solid and certain world in which it is hardly possible not to believe, the things that populate it, the affairs of men that form the subject of their everyday cares and preoccupations, the kinds of knowledge concerning objects as well as activities, the network of sciences developing today with impressive rigor and rapidity, the technical prowess that results—all that suddenly tumbles into insignificance. How can the mysterious Life of God, set forth in a series of "dogmas," be capable of producing in us such an effect? How can we penetrate it in order to share in its Revelation and find ourselves transformed by it? These are precisely the questions of Christianity, to which we are already able to give partial answers.

According to Christianity there exists only one Life, the unique essence of all that lives. This does not mean an unchanging essence or an ideal archetype, like that of a Circle that is present in all circles, but rather an active essence, deploying itself with an invincible force, a source of power, the power of engendering that is immanent in anything that lives and unceasingly gives it life. Inasmuch as this Life is that of God and is identified with Him, the Apostle could write: "One God and Father of us all, who is over all and through all and in all" (Ephesians 4:6). To the extent that God alone is this unique Life that generates all living things, Christianity appears as a monotheism. What separates it from other monotheisms (except Judaism), as well as from the rational or natural theologies in which these monotheisms have sought a form of expression liable to rally all reasonable people, is that this unique God is not thought by the mind. It is not a Being endowed with all the conceivable attributes conferred on an absolute power, or an infinite Being, "a being than which nothing greater can be conceived"[1] and who for this reason necessarily exists. If the Christian God has nothing in common with the infinitely great Being of Saint Anselm, which will be taken up in all the classical proofs of the existence of God and will serve as their pillar, any more than it does with Aristotle's prime mover, or else with the author of the best of all possible worlds, or with the simple concept of a unique God with whom no other will later be able to compete—this is for the decisive reason that God is not something to which our thought can provide access. Thus any rational representation, even more so any proof of God's existence, is absurd in principle—because to prove is to "make seen," to make seen in the light of ineluctable evidence, in that horizon of visibility that is the world and in which life is never revealed. We will have occasion to return to this point.[2]

If God is Life, then the first results of the phenomenological analysis of life make it possible to understand the fundamental arguments of Christianity. Life never being shown in the world, as we have just recalled, it is therefore impossible to perceive it there, unless in the form of illusory significations coupled to objective processes, significations whose origin remains unexplained as long as one sticks to the appearance of the world and seeks this origin there. Absent from the world, life is thus also absent from the field of biology, which is a worldly one. Hence the question arises: Is it still possible to have access to Life, that is to say, to the essence of God himself? And if so, where and how?

The answer, according to the phenomenology of life we have sketched here, is as follows: we do have access to Life itself. Where? In Life. How? Through Life. That it is only in Life and through it that we can accede to Life implies a decisive presupposition: it is Life itself that comes forth in itself. This was precisely our first phenomenological approach to life, its definition as truth, or rather the definition of Truth as Life: life is self-revelation. Within life, it is life itsel that achieves revelation; and itself that is revealed. This is because it is life itself that originally comes forth by itself, inasmuch as it is self-revelation and it comes first. Nothing and no one could ever come forth if its coming forth in Life did not depend on the very coming forth of Life in itself—and, beyond that, if its coming forth in life were not identified with the original coming forth of Life in itself.

What comes forth in Life is the living. How the living emerges in Life is what we have just glimpsed for the first time: the living comes forth in Life by depending on the very coming forth of Life in itself, by identify-ing itself with it—with the self-revelation of life itself that is identical with the revelation of God.

Two urgent issues now arise, concerning the interior essence of God, on the one hand, and the possibility of entering into relationship with that essence, on the other. How does life come forth? How does the living thing come forth in it? Since the living thing cannot come forth in life except on the basis of the original coming forth whereby life comes forth in itself, the first question subsumes the second.

What we must steadfastly rule out of the analysis of life—at least if we want to grasp life as coming forth in itself and, moreover, to understand the manner in which it does so—is the concept of being. As we have already observed, we are not using the verb "to be" on the subject of life—saying, for example, "life is," and then taking this fallacious proposition as a piece of evidence, even though we are speaking of life in human language, which is that of the world—which is precisely that of Being. Life "is" not. Rather, it occurs and does not cease occurring. This incessant coming of life is its eter-nal coming forth in itself, a process without end, a constant movement. In the eternal fulfillment of this process, life plunges into itself, crushes against itself, experiences itself, enjoys itself, constantly producing its own essence, inasmuch as that essence consists in this enjoyment of itself and is exhausted in it. Thus life continuously engenders itself. In this self-generation without end the active phenomenological effectuation of the coming-into-itself of life takes place as the coming into the experiencing-of-oneself within which any conceivable living resides. Sustained by the coming-into-itself of life and completing it, the "experiencing-oneself" is itself a process in which what is experienced occurs as always newly experienced, whereas Living resides in this process as what it always experiences anew. Life is a self-movement that is self-experiencing and never ceases to be self-experiencing in its very movement—in such a way that from this self-experiencing movement nothing is ever detached: nothing slips away from it, away from this self-moving self-experience. The movement by which life does not cease to come into itself and thus to enjoyment of itself—the movement of its own living, which itself does not cease, is never detached from itself but remains eternally within itself—such is therefore the process in which the essence of life consists, its self-generation.

Since the coming-into-itself of life is its coming into the "experience-of-itself" in which, when experiencing itself, it enjoys itself, it follows that this enjoyment of self, this "feeling of oneself," is the first form of any conceivable phenomenality. But the coming-into-itself of life is not merely the originating birth of phenomenality, that is to say, of revelation. In it is unquestionably revealed the manner in which this phenomenality is phenomenalized, in which this revelation is revealed: as pathos and in the affective flesh of pathos. Hence nothing else is revealed in it, if not itself. This is what "to experience oneself" means: to experience what is, in its flesh, nothing other than that which experiences it. This identity between experiencing and what is experienced is the original essence of Ipseity. And now this, too, can no longer escape us: In the process of self-generation of life, that is, the process whereby life comes into its own, is crushed against itself, experiences itself and enjoys itself, an essential Ipseity is implicated as the condition without which and outside of which no process of this sort could ever be produced. Ipseity is not simply a condition of the process of life's self-generation: it resides within it as the very way this process is achieved. Thus is created, conjointly with the coming-into-itself of life in the experiencing-of-itself and the enjoyment-of-itself, the original and essential Ipseity from which the experiencing-itself derives its possibility, the Ipseity in which and as which every experiencing-itself comes about.

This process whereby life generates itself is, as we know, a phenomenological process. Life generates itself inasmuch as it propels itself into phenomenality in the form of a self-revelation. But it is only because this self-revelation is produced, and insofar as it is, that the process of self-generation is one with it, that the living of life is actualized.

How can the process of self-generation of life be its self-revelation? In the sense that life's coming-into-itself, in the experiencing-itself in its *pathētik* embrace, is its enjoyment of itself. The pathos of this enjoyment defines the phenomenality of this coming-into-itself, the concrete phenomenological mode according to which, and thanks to which, the process of life's self-generation becomes that of its self-revelation. Because an original and essential Ipseity is required by the process of life's self-generation, it also belongs to that self-revelation. Moreover, the Ipseity in which life's *pathētik* embrace takes place, generating itself by experiencing itself, is the concrete phenomenological mode by which this process of self-generation is produced as its own self-revelatory process. Thus Ipseity belongs to life's self-generation as that in which this self-generation is achieved as self-revelation. This original and essential Ipseity belongs to life's self-revelation as that which makes it possible.

Inasmuch as the process of life's self-generation, being achieved as its process of self-revelation, is actually the same process—inasmuch as life being cast into the self enjoys itself—the Ipseity that it engenders is also an active process, and a singular one. It is a singular Self that embraces itself, affects itself, experiences itself and enjoys itself, in such a way that this embrace of itself in which this Self embraces itself is no different from the embrace in which life grasps itself, possesses itself, being simply the mode in which it does so. Life can embrace itself, and thus reveal itself to itself in the enjoyment of itself, only by generating in itself this Self that embraces itself as the phenomenological effectuation of its own self-embrace. This singular Self within which life embraces itself, this Self that is the sole possible mode in which this embrace occurs, is the First Living. Thus, in its absolute self-generation, Life generates within itself He whose birth is the self-accomplishment of this Life—its self-accomplishment in the form of its self-revelation. The Father—if by this we understand the movement, which nothing precedes and of which nobody knows the name, by which Life is cast into itself in order to experience itself, this Father eternally engenders the Son within himself, if by the latter we understand the First Living in whose original and essential Ipseity the Father experiences himself.

Given that the process of Life's self-generation cannot come about without generating within itself this Son as the very mode in which this process takes place, the Son is as old as the Father, being, like him, present from the beginning. This is the reason we call the Son the Arch-Son, not just the originating Son, not merely the one who, as in a human family, came along first, before his brothers and sisters, but the One who inhabits the Origin, the very Beginning—the One who is engendered in the very process whereby the Father engenders himself. Given that the process of Life's self-generation is also that of its self-revelation, then the mode in which its essential Ipseity is phenomenalized—meaning the Son—is the very revelation of God Himself, his Logos—not the Greek *logos*, whose phenomenality is that of the world, but the Logos of Life, whose phenomenality is the phenomenological substance of this life itself, its emotional embrace, its enjoyment. Given that there is only one Life, and thus that the process in which it eternally engenders itself is unique, then what is engendered within it as the mode of this self-engendering is also unique, the Unique Son as the Word with which he is identical, inasmuch as the self-engendering of Life is its self-revelation.

That the process of Life's self-revelation engenders in it the First Living as the Arch-Son is what places us in the presence of the concept of an Arch-birth—meaning a birth that does not take place in a preexisting life but that belongs as a constituent element to the upsurge of this life itself, to the process, we might say, of life itself—implicated in it, one with it. We characterize this Arch-Son, his Arch-birth, and also the process of absolute Life's self-generation, as "transcendental," so as to dissociate them completely from any natural or worldly process, although the practical reason for this characterization will only emerge later on. The concept of the transcendental Arch-birth belongs only to the Arch-Son and, to be precise, applies only to him. Its explanatory capacity is felt, though, well beyond its initial sphere of pertinence. From the concepts of the Arch-Son and his Arch-birth, the concept of birth receives an unexpected and yet singularly truthful meaning, one that manages to subvert the ordinary concept of birth to the extent of rendering it meaningless.

To be born, according to the ordinary use of the term, means to come into Being, to enter into existence. In the same way, to die means to depart from existence, to enter into nothingness. But in the same way that Being always refers back to an appearing that grounds it in reality (since only what shows itself to us exists for us)—in the same way, to put it in philosophical terms, that ontology always refers back to a prior phenomenology, conscious or not—so the statement "to come into Being" should be rewritten phenomenologically. Thus "to come into Being" would be rewritten as "to come into appearing," meaning, according to Western thought, to show itself in the world's truth: *to come into the world.* To come into the world: Isn't that what being born signifies to each of us, philosopher or not?

And it is here that Christianity wholly breaks with all the ordinary representations and conceptions of birth: in the world, according to Christianity, no birth is possible. Many things come into the world, that is to say, they appear in it, in this horizon of light that is the world itself, in its truth. They appear and disappear without this appearing in any way constituting a birth or this disappearing a death, unless metaphorically. Stones were there on the road, and then they are removed. A house was built, and now it is just a ruin. A star that had never been seen before appeared in the firmament, and others disappeared. Of none of these things, even while it is making its appearance in the world, do we say that it is born. Therefore coming into the world as such cannot imply a birth. We are saying not only that many of the things that come into the world are not thereby born, but, more radically, that *the prior coming into the world precludes any conceivable birth, if it is true that in the "outside-itself" of the world, the self-embrace of life would be sundered before being produced—if Life's Truth is irreducible to the world's.* We cannot say that everything that comes into the world will die there, but rather that everything that is manifest in that way is foreign to life's Living. For any living, to come for good into the world, and to no longer be anything other than what is exhibited in the world as such, amounts to being offered as a cadaver. A cadaver is just that: a body reduced to its pure externality. When we are no longer anything but something of the world, something in the world, that is indeed what we will be before being buried or cremated there.

To be born is not to come into the world. To be born is to come into life. We have to understand this statement clearly, because it carries at least two meanings, of which the more obvious is not the more essential. To come into life means, of course, to come to life, to enter into it, to accede to this extraordinary and mysterious condition of being alive now. This mysterious character relates to the phenomenological status of life which we have as yet only touched upon, so that a more radical elucidation of this status will be one of the tasks of a phenomenology of birth, which is possible only within a phenomenology of life. But it is the second meaning of the statement "to come into life" that should preoccupy us for a moment. To come into life here means that it is in life and from out of it alone that this coming is capable of being produced. To come into life means to come from life, starting from it, in such a way that life is not birth's point of arrival, as it were, but its point of departure. By placing oneself from the outset within life as within the original presupposition out of which something like a birth is alone possible, we are in a position to understand how this birth occurs: in other words, how life engenders the living in, and on the basis of, itself. This decisive question has just been answered by the theory of the generation of the First Living within the self-generation of absolute phenomenological life. What was clearly established was this: absolute Life experiences itself in an actualized Ipseity, a Self that is itself actualized and, as such, singular. It is in this way that the self-engendering of the Father implies within it the engendering of the Son and is one with it. Or rather: the engendering of the Son consists in the Father's self-engendering and is one with it. No Life without a Living. Not a Living without Life. We should not say that Life's engendering itself engenders Living, because why would this living being be this one here and not that one there? And why would there be only one such thing, rather than several or a multitude? And why would this one, rather than that one, be the first? We should instead say: *Life engenders itself like the Living that Life itself is within its self-engendering.* And this is why that Living is the Unique and the First—"That man," as John says (1:33).

Let us return to the "content" of Christianity. We can better perceive now why it certainly cannot be reduced to the worldly existence of Christ and to his story, as astonishing as the latter is. Reduced to that story, Christ's existence presents two more or less contradictory characteristics. On the one hand, it truly is an extraordinary story, to the point that many whose imaginations cannot get past the ground level have cast doubt upon it, taking it as the product of a fabulating imagination of which they themselves are so cruelly bereft. On the other hand, it is a story that takes place in the world, and it dissipates itself in the fog of the world's truth—where any individual existence is effaced, and likewise even thousands and millions and billions of them. It is hard to find a mention of Christ's existence in the historians of the period—an obscure riot in Jerusalem, perhaps. This is the contradiction: between the astonishing character of this story and the traces it left or did not leave in history—which, despite its scientific pretensions, more resembles a colander than an approach, however weak, to reality.

Foreign to history and more generally to the world's truth, the "content" of Christianity consists in the network of transcendental (therefore acosmic and invisible) relationships that we can formulate as follows: the relationship between absolute Life and the First Living—between the Father and the Son, between God and Christ; the relationship of absolute Life to all living things—of the Father to his sons, of God to "men"; the relationship between the Son and sons, between Christ and living people; the relationships among sons, living people, and mankind—what is called in philosophy intersubjectivity. One decisive criterion for the rigorous examination of such relationships is whether the possibility of reversing them exists. The one between the Father and Arch-Son is reversible, but that between the Father or the Arch-Son and sons is not. On the level of intersubjectivity, the question of relationships among sons is meaningless. All these relationships, though, offer a common and overwhelming characteristic that lifts them out of the realm of customary representations and determines them from top to bottom: they are nonintentional relationships. Or, stated more positively, they put Life into play. Not only do the terms of these relationships imply Life, inasmuch as they concern life's relation to the living or the relations among living people, but it is the relation itself that is constituted as a relation with Life, that draws its essence from within it.

What is a relation that draws its essence from within Life, and how does it differ from a relation in the ordinary sense? A relation is the link that unites two or more terms. But the ultimate possibility of such a relation is phenomenological, it is the "outside-itself" that places the terms one outside the other, while externality assures their phenomenality and thus their unity, and thus the relationship itself. It is in the externality of space that any conceivable spatial relationship is deployed, and in the externality of time that any temporal relationship is, and in an ideal externality that any mathematical relationship is—in short, in the truth of a world, whatever it may be, and ultimately in the world's truth. But when rapture is experienced and thus enjoys itself, the link that unites it to itself is not outside itself, and thus does not appear in any world. The link that unites it with itself is the phenomenological substance of life. It is within life and within it alone that joy or anguish can "experience themselves," inasmuch as "Living" inhabits them. But life is not a phenomenological milieu where, as in a river's flow, everything that is living bathes, a sort of "interior world" that would not decide what is revealed within it any more than the world of "outsideness" decides what appears in its light. Life, as I have said, is a process, and this process generates within it all living things, making of each of them precisely what it is. Life is the relation that itself generates its own "terms." The content of Christianity is the systematic, and moreover unprecedented, elucidation of this relation between Life and all the living, a relation that is generation or birth as such.

What is now at issue is the generation of the First Living within Life's self-generation, specifically the relation between Father and Son, which constitutes the first and most important of the relations considered by Christianity. The radical phenomenology of life developed here has supplied us with the key to understanding this essential relation. If we consider more closely Christianity's content, we see that the Father/Son relation not only constitutes its most essential kernel, but that it is also the subject of an explicit discourse, namely, *the constant discourse Christ holds about himself, and that he offers as the only thing that matters.* The only thing that matters is the salvation of all mankind as defined not by means of thought but by Life. And this salvation consists exactly of "believing" what Christ says about himself, that is to say—and as the problematic of Faith will show—not of accepting it as "true" as thought defines truth and thus as the world defines it, but rather of rendering it consubstantial with the Truth of Life, in its phenomenological embodiment and in its enjoyment.

So as accurately to explain the initially incredible discourse that Christ holds about himself, which constitutes the heart of the New Testament, it is necessary to have a clear answer to a prior question: Who holds this discourse, and by what right? This is precisely the question the Jews asked Christ. (Let us note in passing that, notably in the Johannine texts, "Jews" designates not Jews in general but those among them who did not recognize Jesus as the Messiah, it being elsewhere understood that those who did recognize him or would recognize him as such are also, in the majority, Jews, at least in the early days.) Here is the "question of the Jews": "And while Jesus was walking in the temple courts, the chief priests, the teachers of the law, and the elders came to him. 'By what authority are you doing these things? And who gave you the authority to do them?'" (Mark 11:27–30). We know by what detour Christ avoids answering them on this occasion, sending them back to a question that embarrasses them ("John's baptism—was it from heaven, or from men?") to the point where they prefer to be quiet ("We don't know"): "Then neither will I tell you by what authority I am doing these things" (11:33). In this confrontation, which will be repeated in an increasingly tense and ultimately tragic way, two characteristics are particularly remarkable: on the one hand, the pertinence of the question, which unfailingly refers the authority to do what Christ does back to the nature of the one who has or does not have this authority, and, on the other, Christ's dodging of this essential questioning: Who are you, then, to assume such a right? Or else: "Who do you think you are?" (John 8:53). And eventually, in its final formulation, this time by Pilate: "Where do you come from?" (John 19:9).

That the answer is at first eluded and then endlessly deferred—enveloped in parables, delivered in a way that is fragmentary, indirect, and enigmatic, before being suddenly quashed in an act of extreme brutality—is something one would be tempted to explain by referring to motivations that belong to the world and to human affairs. Formulated baldly, finally made as transparent as possible and freed of equivocations, what Christ says about himself will mean his condemnation to death. We understand, then, that what he had to say about himself had been held back for as long as Christ thought it necessary to accomplish his mission. But now explained in this way in the light of the world, and illuminated by it, Christ's words about himself become largely unintelligible—because the Truth of which Christ speaks, and which he moreover presents as his very essence, is precisely not that of the world, but a Truth that has nothing to do with the world's truth.

From the world's point of view, Christ's condemnation is perfectly comprehensible, and even legitimate. From the world's point of view, Christ is a man and, as his discourse gradually emerges from its initial dissimulation to appear in the light of day, what he affirms about himself appears crazy or scandalous. Here is a man who declares he was born before another one, specifically Abraham, who actually preceded him in history by several centuries; who pretends to be able to make what is in fact not be, and make what in fact is not be—to pardon sins, to resuscitate the dead; who claims never to die and, to cap it all, who quite candidly identifies himself with God. These statements are crazy, not because they contradict common sense or the beliefs of a given society, but because they defy the phenomenological structures of the world itself, the way the world comes to exist by appearing as such—the temporality of this world, for example, or its irreversibility, with Christ saying he is not concerned by either.

Who, then, is the one whose words about himself, breaking with everything we know about the world, remain inconceivable in its light? There is only one answer: it is on the condition of escaping, in effect, from the phenomenological structures of the world that Christ can say everything he does about himself. Only his condition as transcendental Arch-Son co-generated in absolute Life's self-generation is capable of legitimating assertions that strictly speaking belong only to God. And this is what is placed before us, especially in John. Christ's designating of himself as the Son of God merely comments on his condition as Arch-Son, in the way that a radical phenomenology of life could establish it—whereas applied to a man of this world and coming from him, such a statement would appear quite simply as absurd, demented—as it did in the eyes of the priests of his time and as it would even more so to people today, if by chance it occurred to them to pay attention to it. The extent to which Christ's designating of himself as the Arch-Son is merely the immediate transcription of his condition is something we can establish, point by point. What emerges is a series of fundamental tautologies, the founding tautologies of life, which we will also call the decisive implications of Christianity. Arranged in an order that will make them comprehensible, these are as follows:

"As for me, I was born" (John 18:37). If, as the phenomenology of birth has established, birth is possible only in life and nowhere else, then Christ, in this final declaration to Pilate, has already identified the type of truth in which his original Apparition occurred. This truth is that of life. However, to come into life, again as the phenomenology of birth has shown, does not mean to come to life already within the condition of living, but to come to life from life, and in this way alone, meaning to come to life out of that self-engendering of absolute Life that is the Father. In all that Christ says about himself, this is the weightiest and most categorical affirmation, one that will be constantly reiterated, with great tenacity. "It is from God that I have come and to Him I go" (John 8:42).

In the sort of "story" the Gospels tell, at the point when this affirmation occurs, the text suddenly becomes strained, as in the argument between the Pharisees and the one born blind whom Jesus has cured: "'We are disciples of Moses! We know that God spoke to Moses, but as for this fellow, we don't even know where he comes from.' The man answered, 'Now that is remarkable! You don't know where he comes from, yet he opened my eyes. . . . If this man were not from God, he could do nothing'" (John 9:29–33). And in what is presented as the final, or one of the final, of Christ's prayers, his declaration that he was sent by the Father returns like an obsessive leitmotiv: "That the world may believe that you have sent me. . . . To let the world know that you sent me. . . . [These men] know that you have sent me. . . . They knew with certainty that I came from you, and they believed that you sent me" (John 17:21, 23, 25, and 8, respectively).

But how could Christ believe what he claims for himself, that he came from God and as such from a divine condition? Who will bear him witness? Here arises one of the central questions of the Johannine text, that of testimony, remarkable in that it occurs in direct connection with Christ's affirmation of his condition as the Son of God, making him equal to God. Immediately after the prologue in which Christ is identified as the Word and the Word as God, John's Gospel invokes the testimony of John the Baptist: "I saw the Spirit come down from heaven as a dove and remain on him. . . . I have seen and I testify that this is the Son of God" (John 1:32, 34). On the one hand, we have to believe what John the Baptist says and, on the other, to forget that Christ later declares that he has not received testimony of his divine provenance from any man: "Not that I accept human testimony" (John 5:34). So in fact he renders testimony to himself, and this is precisely the accusation made against him by the "Jews."

Christ's answer is twofold. At a loss at first, he seems to recognize the weight of the objection: "If I testify about myself, my testimony is not valid" (John 5:31). Then who could do so? An other, his Father, God! "And the Father who sent me has himself testified concerning me" (John 5:37). But if it is God who renders testimony that Christ is his Son, who would be able to recognize this testimony, or rather, understand it? To this end, would it not be necessary to know God himself in order to hear his own testimony—the testimony that declares: "This is my Son, whom I love; with him I am well pleased" (2 Peter 1:17)? That they do not know God and cannot therefore recognize the testimony of God regarding his Son—this is what Christ throws in the faces of those who contradict him: "You have never heard his voice nor seen his form, nor does his word dwell in you" (John 5:37–38).

If only one who has heard the very voice of God and what he has said, one who has seen his Face, one in whom God dwells, could bring testimony about the Son of God and say, "That is the Son," then only Christ is capable of doing so: only he can testify to what he is. "If I testify about myself, my testimony does not count as true. There is another who testifies in my favor, and I *know* that his testimony about me counts as true" (John 5:31; my emphasis). If it is an other—God—who testifies to Christ, then one must know God and in this way know that the testimony is valid, that it has value for one who knows God and hears his testimony. "Even if I testify on my own behalf, my testimony does indeed count as true, for *I know where I came from*, and where I am going. But you—you have no idea where I come from or where I am going" (John 8:14; my emphasis).

If ultimately, then, only Christ can testify about himself, he could not do so as a man, *but only as one who knows where he comes from*—his transcendental Arch-birth. It is the transcendental Arch-Son who testifies about himself, about his condition as Arch-Son, and he alone can do so as a function of this condition of his—which is that of God finding a home in him. Thus the structure of the testimony that Christ offers about himself is threefold: testimony that comes from the Arch-Son, that bears on the Arch-Son, and whose possibility resides in the condition of Arch-Son.

"Testimony" in the Johannine context means the same thing as "truth." To give testimony to the truth means that it is Truth that gives testimony to itself. And it does so since it is Life and since Life is self-revelation, that which originally reveals itself to itself—or, in Johannine language, that which testifies to itself. In what Christ says about himself, it is not really the self-revelation of absolute Life that is at issue, it would seem, but rather Christ's testimony about himself—the testimony of the Arch-Son, as we have said, about his condition as Arch-Son, and made possible by that. This condition is that of being generated in the self-generation of absolute Life as the First Living, in the essential Ipseity of which life eternally engenders itself—such that this generation of the First Living is no different from the self-generation of eternal Life, from its self-revelation as the revelation of God himself, as his Truth, as his testimony. "In fact, for this reason I was born, and for this I came into the world, to testify to the truth" (John 18:37).

To the extent that the generation of the First Living is no different from the self-generation of absolute phenomenological Life itself, so the self-generation of Life is no different from the generation of the First Living, taking place in the form of the latter—to the extent, consequently, that the revelation of the Son is no different from the self-revelation of God himself. Therefore, the first relationship constitutive of Christianity's content, the relationship between the Father and the Son, can be defined with absolute rigor as a relationship of reciprocal interiority, since the Son is revealed only in the Father's self-revelation, while the Father's self-revelation takes place only in, and as, the revelation of the Son. The primordial Father/Son relationship is not merely this relation whose essence is constituted by Life, nor is it merely this relation whose essence generates the terms. Rather, it also generates them as internal one to the other, such that they belong together, one and the other, in a co-belonging that is more powerful than any conceivable unity, in the inconceivable unity of Life whose self-engendering is one with the engendering of the Engendered. Monotheism is a naive religion, or rather it is a religion of understanding, of abstract thought that thinks of an abstract unity. The God of monotheism is this abstract unity, accompanied if possible by a consciousness capable of conceiving of it, and by a prophet capable ad hoc of enunciating it. As soon as God no longer "is," no longer is the subject of reason—the absolute unity conceived by our intellect, for example—then nothing that one could see or understand, starting with the divine essence and including any phenomenological mediation alien to its own phenomenality, imposes itself as the phenomenological actualization of absolute Life and thus as its self-actualization in the Self of its essential Ipseity. Abstract concepts give way to the fundamental phenomenological characteristics of life and to the network of relations that link them.

Since the reciprocal interiority of Father and Son—that is, Life's self-generation as the generation of the First Living—is essentially phenomenological, it could be framed in terms of "knowledge," such that knowledge of the second is not possible without knowledge of the first. "'You do not know me or my Father,' Jesus replied. 'If you knew me, you would know my Father also'" (John 8:19). It is precisely because they do not know the Father that they do not know the Son. "Though you do not know him, I know him. If I said I did not, I would be a liar like you, but I do know him" (John 8:55); and again: "just as the Father knows me and I know the Father" (John 10:15). So strong is the reciprocal phenomenological interiority of Father and Son, to the extent that the revelation of the Son is the self-revelation of the Father—that the first is not possible without the second, nor the second without the first—each appears in turn as the condition of the other. Granted, revelation is most often given as the means of gaining knowledge of God, knowledge of such a sort that there, present in the very speech of the Son, is his mission: to make God known, to reveal Him to men—"No one comes to the Father except through me" (John 14:6). Yet we cannot forget the many strange passages in which it turns out that one can reach the Son only by way of the Father and to the extent that the Father wishes it: "No one can come to me unless the Father has enabled him" (John 6:65); "All that the Father gives me will come to me" (John 6:37); "No one can come to me unless the Father who sent me draws him there" (John 6:44).

These are not random assertions, or even copyists' mistakes. It is the apodictic order that prescribes a priori that *the path that leads to Christ can only be the repetition of his transcendental Arch-birth within the Father,* namely, the process of Life's self-generation that generated Christ in his condition as First Living. If life were not cast into itself to experience itself in its enjoyment of itself, then neither would the essential Ipseity that life generates in its self-generation, any more so than the singular Self that belongs to it in principle, ever themselves have come into life.

But, in the end, did not Christ actually come into this world to save it, by making the world know God? Only a phenomenology of Christ can answer this question.

5

The Phenomenology of Christ

The phenomenology of Christ concerns the apparition of Christ, which has assumed many guises, and so the question itself has had many formulations. It cannot be limited to one of his apparitions—the first, for example—but must take into account all the others as well. The phenomenology of Christ therefore encounters questions of this kind: Where was Christ born? Who were his parents? Where did they come from? Did Christ have brothers? And so forth. In the Gospels we find diverse information on this subject—more, in fact, than brief indications. The genealogy of Jesus occupies the long prologue to the Gospel of Matthew: "A record of the genealogy of Jesus Christ, the son of David, the son of Abraham. Abraham was the father of Isaac, Isaac the father of Jacob, Jacob the father of Judah and his brothers . . . Eleazar the father of Matthan, Matthan the father of Jacob, Jacob the father of Joseph, the husband of Mary, of whom was born Jesus, who is called Christ" (1:1–16). This genealogy of Jesus is also taken up in Luke: "Now Jesus himself was about thirty years old when he began his ministry. He was the son, so it was thought, of Joseph, the son of Heli, the son of Matthat . . . the son of Enosh, the son of Seth, the son of Adam, the son of God" (3:23–38).

However, this genealogy of Jesus, as set forth at the outset of these two Gospels, is immediately subject to correction. It is not Joseph, according to Matthew and to Luke, who is the father of Christ. What a strange genealogy, to be laid out only to be straightaway refuted! Moreover, the status of the Virgin has embarrassed theologians to the point that they have seen no other solution but to make it an article of faith—which, however, in no way amounts to indirectly supporting and reaffirming the human genealogy of Jesus, if it is indeed true that the Virgin bears the Child only upon the intervention of the Holy Spirit, meaning God. Whether a subject of embarrassment on the part of believers or of irony on the part of nonbelievers, the affirmation of Mary's virginity scarcely conceals, behind its apparently absurd content, the essential argument of Christianity, namely, that *no man is the son of a man, or of any woman either, but only of God.*

The singular character of Christ's human genealogy is no less apparent in its reprise by Luke, which is found in two passages. The first consists of a relatively minor modification: "the son, so it was thought, of Joseph." But the second offers an incredible list that, after having designated Cainan the son of Enosh, Enosh the son of Seth, and Seth the son of Adam, suddenly declares the last to be the son of God, as if one could put the two filiations on the same footing, as if it were the same thing, in effect, to be the son of a man or the son of a god—or, more precisely, as if god only intervened in some speculative fashion when, no other person having presented himself as a man's father, this role could now be conferred only on one presumed to be God.

But if Adam cannot be said to be the son of God in the same way as Seth is said to be his own son—the son of Adam—then one seriously has to ask what the difference is between these two conditions: that of being the son of a man, like Seth is of Adam, and that of being a son of God, as is the case with Adam. We will formulate the answer in the following terms: the essential difference between the condition of being the son of a man and that of being the son of God resides in the Truth, or, to be specific, the kind of Truth at issue in each case. *In the truth of the world any man is the son of a man, and hence also of a woman. In the Truth of Life any man is the son of Life, that is to say, of God himself.* But if both these truths speak of birth, meaning the possibility of a living person coming into life, one of them is undoubtedly de trop. Seth cannot be the son of Adam if Adam can only be the Son of God. Inversely, Adam does not need to be the Son of God if Seth can be his own son. Therefore one has to choose, to state unequivocally of whom a man can be the son: of another man or only of God.

What the birth of man, and thus his condition as son *in the truth of the world*, consists of is something we all know today, aided by the amazing progress in biology and by the dissemination of theories believed to derive from it. I will make only the briefest allusion to these theories, inasmuch as the phenomenology of birth has already demonstrated the absurdity of any worldly interpretation of birth, whether as a coming-into-the-world or as the result of a process rooted in this world, for example, an objective process. The absurdity relates, as we have seen, to the fact that *in the world and in the externality of its "outside," no "Living" is possible—and consequently no livings either.*

What the condition of Son, and thus of birth, consists of *within the Truth of Life* is something we will ask of Christ himself. On the one hand, according to an essential phrase that has already been cited, Christ names himself "the Truth and the Life." He is himself that original Truth that is Life. On the other hand, it is in the light of this Truth that he analyzes his own condition as Son. But can one examine this condition in the light of any other Truth than that of Life? Can we speak of it otherwise than Christ does himself, if there is no Son and no birth except in Life, if coming into life is conceivable only on the basis of life?

From the outset of this volume we have been considering the discourse that Christ offers about himself to be the essential content of Christianity. It appears that this discourse not only holds good for Christ but concerns all human beings as well to the extent that they, too, are Sons. In fact, they exist only in Life, engendered by it. All Sons are Sons of Life and, inasmuch as there is only one Life and this Life is God, they are all the Sons of God. If Christ is not merely the transcendental Arch-Son immersed in an eternal symbiosis with the Father, if in people's eyes he stands as an emblematic and radiant figure who causes them to tremble within, it is because this figure is that of their own true condition as Sons. Thus Christ's discourse about himself, consisting in the radical elucidation of the state of Son, suddenly outstrips its initial and "proper" domain—the autarchic enjoyment of divinity, the self-sufficient system of Life and of the First Living—in order to rebound upon the entire human condition and to place it in a light that no kind of thought, no philosophy, no culture or science had dared project onto it before.

For this reason Christ's discourse about himself, when it turns to people, can well arouse their emotions yet remain incomprehensible—because people do not understand their own condition except in the light of the world's truth. To be a son for them means to be the son of one's father and mother. To be born means to come into the world, to appear at such a point in space, at such a moment in time—to come out of the mother's belly in this place and at this moment, in such a way that before this birth the baby or fetus was already in the world, ultimately in the form of seeds in the bodies of the father and mother. This is the modern interpretation of birth and thus of the condition of son, which perceives and understands everything within the framework of the world's truth. Among people of antiquity, alongside this objectlike vision of humanity's origin was mysteriously juxtaposed the idea of a divine provenance. Far from being reduced to a simple presumption, such an idea spontaneously expressed the true life of man, his transcendental and invisible life as he immediately experiences it. Despite constantly experiencing life themselves, these people did not manage to arrive at a correct understanding of life, or even an image of it, owing to its invisibility. Their metaphysical and religious beliefs were linked to crudely realistic representations. This state of affairs came to an end with the advent of modern thought. By deliberately removing transcendental life from the scope of human knowledge, which was subsequently restricted to objective knowledge of the material universe, Galileo's reduction and the science that evolved from it carried the worldly interpretation of birth and thus of sonhood to an absolute limit. If the modern discourse on man resulted in his thoroughgoing denigration, his abasement, and ultimately the elimination of his individuality in favor of anonymous and unconscious processes, thus amounting to his negation pure and simple, it did so by pushing the worldly interpretation of man's birth and of his condition as son to its outermost limit—where birth, son, and man become nothing but metaphors.

It is this worldly interpretation of birth that Christ's discourse about himself shatters into pieces. It is remarkable that in speaking of himself, and in locating his Arch-birth within Life as the principle of any conceivable birth, the First Born, the transcendental Arch-Son, proves capable of conferring upon birth its true meaning. Now every birth finds itself understood as transcendental, generated within and by means of absolute Life. Simultaneously with the concept of birth, the concept of Son is also subverted, torn from any natural interpretation. But this condition of Son, thought of as transcendental, as issuing from a transcendental birth, is that of man: it is man who is torn from nature and returned to Life. To place the concepts of birth and the Son within the safekeeping of the transcendental Arch-Son is necessarily to refer to absolute Life, of which the Arch-Son is merely the self-realization in the form of his self-revelation. It calls inevitably on another Truth than the world's, on this Truth of Life outside of which there is neither birth nor Son, no livings of any sort.

What we are saying, then, is that each time Christ speaks of himself, he violently rejects the idea of a human genealogy, that is, a worldly one, with respect to himself. This genealogy can be called worldly because it is in the world that people interpret their own genealogy, which in that world appears "human," each person offering himself as the son of the one who preceded him, and as the father of the one who will follow. Thus, each individual understands his condition as son on the basis of his own father's condition, which will later be his own. Let me quickly explain why this human and worldly genealogy is absurd. In effect, to be a father means—at least if we wish to give the term its proper meaning—to give life. But each of these human fathers, who calls himself or believes himself a father, is first one of the living; he is within life and thus is far from having the power to give life to others or to himself. Living, whether he appears as son or as father, he depends on life. Only life itself can give life: none of the living is in a position to do so, since that living, far from giving life, constantly presupposes it within himself. If we say that God is living, designating him, for example, as "the Living God," it is in an entirely different sense, one in which God is capable of giving Life to others only because he is first capable of giving life to himself. Before being living, he is himself Life, the eternal coming-into-itself in which Life eternally engenders itself. It is to this self-engendering of Life, which he calls eternal Life—a Life that precedes and will eternally precede all the living—that Christ gives the name of Father, and this is why he says, in the luminous language of absolute truth: "Do not call anyone on earth 'father'; for *you have one Father, he in Heaven*" (Matthew 23:9; my emphasis).

The addition "he in Heaven" is not without interest. No doubt this expression suffices to discredit Christianity in the eyes of people today who are believers in the world. In the world's truth, heaven designates merely a part of this world, the one explored by astronauts. Apart from a "heaven" that has become the domain of science, nothing corresponds with this term. The "Heaven" of Christianity is only a void, or at most an imaginary place for the phantasmagoric satisfaction of desires that cannot realized here below. In contrast, the connection that Christ's discourse constantly establishes between the father and Heaven gives the latter the value of a rigorous concept: *that of a Life that does not appear in any world and is revealed only in itself.* In its absolute self-engendering, Life is the Father of whom Christ is the Son. Because in his discourse about himself Christ thinks of himself as this Arch-Son co-engendered in the self-engendering of absolute Life, he can only vehemently reject the idea of his human or worldly genealogy, which he does in different ways, according to the slyness or foolishness of his interlocutors.

The questioners prove their cleverness when, knowing that the Messiah could only come from God, they forbid Jesus, with whose modest origins they are familiar, to claim this title: "But we know where this man is from; when the Christ comes, no one will know where he is from" (John 7:27). It is the same argument, but in a more naive form, that was previously formulated by the "Jews": "At this the Jews began to grumble about him because he said, 'I am the bread that came down from heaven.' They said, 'Is this not Jesus, the son of Joseph; whose father and mother we know? How can he now say, 'I came down from heaven'?" (John 6:41–42). Christ's response, as is sometimes the case, begins with a concession: "Yes, you know me, and you know where I came from" (John 7:28). We do not need to reiterate that everything they know or think they know concerns his human genealogy, his apparition within the world's truth. This is why Christ's concession is only a feint—a contradictory viewpoint, or appearance, or illusion, against the dark horizon of which he is going to make manifest his true condition as the Messiah or Christ. This condition—that of being the Arch-Son co-engendered in the process of Life's coming-into-itself as the essential Ipseity in which Life reveals itself—is co-engendered as the True (for what is more true than that which reveals itself completely in and of itself?), in such a way that Life knows itself in that essential Ipseity that in turn knows it, being merely the site of Life's self-revelation, which remains unknown to the world and alien to its truth. Immediately after having declared, "Yes, you know me, and you know where I came from," the text continues: "I am not here on my own, but he who sent me is true. You do not know him, but I know him because I came from him and he sent me" (John 7:28–29).

Christ's human genealogy is neither so modest nor so insignificant that it can be dismissed with a wave of the hand. Do we not find alongside Joseph—a humble carpenter who is in fact *not* the father of Jesus—some prestigious ancestors, prophets and more than prophets, the founders of the religion in which Jesus was raised—David and Abraham, to mention only two? What is staggering, and could not fail to appear so to the priests of his day, is to see Christ deliberately undertake to compare himself with these pillars, so to speak, of Judaism. And to make this comparison so as to demonstrate unequivocally the infinite superiority of his own essence over theirs: his state as Arch-Son precisely in the sense that we have discussed, as meaning his equality with God.

The extreme cleverness of the argument, if not the mockery it conveys regarding his Medusan adversaries, cannot mask the decisive character of the reference to David. If David considered the Messiah sent by God as the equal of God and as God himself, designating him as such, how could the Messiah issue from David within the lineage of a human genealogy? "What do you think about the Christ? Whose son is he?" David's? "If then David calls him 'Lord' . . . how can he be his son?" (Matthew 22:42–45; see also Mark 12:35–37 and Luke 20:44).

The clash over Abraham, which will lead to Christ's being condemned to death, is even more titanic. Calling themselves the sons of Abraham because they are faithful to him and adore no idol but God, the Jews consider themselves by the same token to be Sons of God: "'We are not illegitimate children,' they protested, 'the only father we have is God himself'" (John 8:41). To be the son of Abraham here means to behave as a faithful disciple of the father of the faith, to refuse to adore anything that is not god, and thus to consider him, the God of Abraham, as the sole God. But their spiritual attitude remains that of human beings trapped in the human and worldly genealogy of which Matthew speaks and which leads back to Adam. It is because Christ calls himself the Son of God in quite another sense, in the sense of the Arch-Son consubstantial with the Father, that the conflict erupts. On the one hand, Christ declares his work superior to Abraham's, the founder of the faith, inasmuch as Christ's work is inseparable from his state as God's self-revelation: "me, a man who has told you the truth that I heard from God. Abraham did not do such things" (John 8:40). Moreover, this Truth of God, learned from him, Christ has revealed to Abraham himself, who was overwhelmed by it: "Your father Abraham rejoiced at the thought of seeing my day: he saw it and was glad" (John 8:56). And it is at this point that everything explodes and stones start flying, when the radical difference is discovered between the worldly state of son—the son of Abraham, certainly, and the son of God but only within the world's truth, as a property and quality of men issued of human lineage—and the state of Arch-Son generated in Life's self-revelation and identical with it: "They picked up stones to stone him" (John 8:59).

The abyss that separates the Arch-Son in this life from other sons according to the world's truth, apprehended within human genealogy— whether or not these sons think of themselves as sons of Abraham or God —is expressed in the overturning of this genealogy and of its temporal orientation. Lord of David, Christ places himself before David, rather than after him as a son. Still more explicit is the astonishing declaration with which he ends his polemic against the "Jews": "Before Abraham was, I am!" (John 8:58). This affirmation that so insults common sense is not to be taken in isolation, not a simple, rather paranoid assertion, one that can only be blindly "believed" or not "believed" by trusting Reason. The reason behind it is given quite precisely, in the form of an absolute justification: *the nonworldly condition of Christ*—the fact that, co-engendered in the self-engendering of absolute phenomenological Life that is alien to the world, the Arch-Son is himself alien to this world and its temporality. So it is really not a matter of a simple reversal of human genealogy and its temporal order, as if, placed at first "after"—Christ, son of David, son of Abraham—Christ should instead be placed "before"—Christ, Lord of David and Lord of Abraham. Rather, it is a leap from one truth to another, from the truth whose mode of appearance is time and the world itself to the Truth of absolute Life that ignores time as well as the world. The reason for the radical "Before," the nontemporal "Before" of Christ, is given by Christ himself in words of phenomenological apodicity: "because you loved me *before the creation of the world*" (John 17:24); "the glory I had with you *before the creation of the world*" (John 17:5; my emphasis).

The rejection by the Arch-Son of any human genealogy that pertains to him should be thought through. It implies the pulverization of all possible representations of the link between a father and a son, whether naive, taking place on the plane of immediate perception, or scientific, resulting from the reduction of the Galilean approach to this perception. Because all these cases concern a worldly representation, the father/son relation is reversible in the sense that, in the world, each son can recreate the state that was his father's, becoming a father himself and engendering his own son in turn. There are as many fathers as sons. Their relation is reversible not because it overcomes temporal irreversibility but because it allows each of them in turn to occupy one of the two places. Moreover, this relation is not only reversible; it is external, with each would-be father engendering a son situated outside him and thus separated from him, different from him. This externality is merely a mode of apparition in the world, or rather the mode of apparition of the world itself. To be born assuredly means to come into the world and be manifested in it. This is the case with the son as it was with the father. Thus, this conception of birth, which science will simply reproduce in its own language of numbers, is in effect its phenomenological description within the world's truth.

This description has only one fault, albeit a major one: it knows nothing of Life, which never shows itself in the world, everywhere replacing Life with the living, but in a most naive way. On the one hand, the living is no longer considered in himself, within the interiority of its transcendental living state. It is now no more than an organism perceived from the outside, in terms of the world's truth, a bundle of objective processes. On the other hand, this organism that has been abandoned to the world is still apprehended as signifying a "living," a signification whose origin, which is nothing other than transcendental life itself, remains mysterious as long as it is not related to this life. This in turn obscures the very phenomenon of birth, once this phenomenon is reduced to an objective succession of the living—scientifically paralleled by an objective succession of chemical processes. *Birth does not consist of a succession of livings, in each of whom life is presupposed, but rather consists in the coming of each living into life out of Life itself.* Nor can birth be understood except on the basis of this Life and its own essence—on the basis of Life's self-generation as its self-revelation in the essential Ipseity of the First Living.

It is this genuine birth, the only one possible as the Arch-generation of the Arch-Son, that is expounded in John's stunning prologue. John knows nothing of human generation, or rather he knows that such a form of generation is not really a form of generation at all. This is why he addresses only those "not born of blood, or by carnal desire or human will" (John 1:12), not because blood or carnal desire or human desires are bad, but for the much more radical reason that neither blood nor any such desires are capable of engendering life. On the contrary, they presuppose it. Engendering life is an act of Life alone, inasmuch as it engenders itself—an act of God. John addresses those "not born . . . but the offspring of God," to speak not of themselves but of the One who is originally engendered in Life inasmuch as it engenders itself, namely, the Arch-Son whom he calls the Word—Logos, or "Revelation." The revelation at issue is that of Life, and it belongs to Life as its very essence, inasmuch as there is no life except as a revelation of itself, as its self-revelation. The Word designates Life's self-generation since the latter takes place in the form of a self-revelation inasmuch as this self-revelation takes place in the form of an essential Ipseity and thus of the First Living. Because there is no Life that does not occur in this way, in the essential Ipseity of the First Living, the latter is as old as Life itself. To begin with John 1:1 and its three parts: "In the beginning was the Word." Because the Truth of Life (this truth that is Life) is radically alien to the world, then that which Life engenders in the initial embrace of its essential Ipseity—namely, the First Living—does not move outside Life but remains within it, in life's embrace: "And the Word was with God." Because this embrace of Life in which the Word dwells is that very life in its self-revelation, then this Word is no different from the essence of that life: "And the Word was God." The second verse is already a summary of the essential implications that we have just recalled with John, which constitute the kernel of Christianity—what we have called the essential tautologies of Life: "He was with God in the beginning" (1:2). What this "with" [*auprès de*] means is already separated from the long series of misinterpretations that Western thought will impose right up to the Hegelian *bei sich* in the notably dense text of verse 4: "In Him was Life." Here the reciprocal phenomenological interiority of Father and Son is affirmed—if it is true that life is not cast into itself except in the Ipseity of the First Living in such a way that that former carries the latter within it, and vice versa.

The extent to which the transcendental Arch-generation of the Word explained in John's illuminating prologue is opposed to any human genealogy—and especially to the supposed human genealogy of Christ, which it shatters into pieces—is something the following few characteristics among many others will suffice to establish here. The first characteristic of the relation established between the human father and his son is that the latter is exterior to the former, such that the son can go away and leave home. As we have seen, the exteriority of this relation is merely the exteriority of the world, and thus the very appearance of this son is as a human and worldly son—as a son of this world. Since the world's exteriority includes time, its ek-stasy, then to say that the son is exterior to the father is to say that he comes after him. No human son comes at the beginning, nor claims to—and no human father either, which is why he is only a pseudo-father. By beginning his Gospel with "in the beginning" but paradoxically placing a Son there, John explodes the very concept of birth, which always assumes a "before." Similarly, he explodes the concept of son, which, in the language of the world, always presupposes a father who came before him.

Here is the second characteristic upon which rests the radical opposition between the Arch-generation of the Word and any human generation. Despite this Arch-generation that places it at the beginning, does the Word not presuppose the Father who came before it? Does the First Living not imply, like living, that life has accomplished its work in him—this Life without which no living would live? Did Christ himself not say, "The Father is greater than I am" (John 14:28)? However, Life has no need of having accomplished its work in Christ, as in any other living, in order for the First Living to be living, *if the generation of the Son co-belongs to the self-generation of Life as that without which this self-generation could not come about, inasmuch as it does so only by embracing itself in the essential Ipseity whose phenomenological effectivity is none other than the Word.* The Word is not the First Living engendered by life in the course of a process that might have begun without it; rather, it lies within life's self-engendering, by which and as which this absolute self-engendering is realized. Then is the Word, the First Living, not contingent in relation to Life, as is the case with all other livings, in such a way that life could come about without it just as life can also come about without livings—without people? On the contrary, the first among all the livings engendered by life, being interior to and consubstantial with the self-engendering of this life, and as its self-revelation—this life cannot come about without that self-engendering just as it cannot come about without self-revelation. Thus they are—according to what will constitute the major theme of the Johannine texts—one within the other, the Father within the Son, and the Son within the Father. But in human generation, this reciprocal interiority never exists: the two are outside of each other, separated from each other—although in truth neither of them is father, the father of this son, and neither of them is son, the son of this father, except in the illusory appearance of the world.

It is this illusion that Christ destroys in remarkably abrupt terms, not out of ethical or existential motives, as it first appears on casual reflection, but by reason of the very nature of the phenomenon of birth. This is because the latter, which is never intelligible according to the laws of the world and can neither ground nor justify them, inevitably refers back to the radical concept of a transcendental Arch-birth within Life and thus to Christ's own condition.

In these awesome and magnificent texts, the rejection of any human genealogy, and the whole set of relations founded on it, cannot be understood without a return to its basic principle: "'Who is my mother and who are my brothers?' Pointing to his disciples, [Christ] said: 'Here are my mother and my brothers. For whoever does the will of my Father in heaven is my brother and sister and mother'" (Matthew 12:48–50). The subversion of the human order founded on human genealogy is complete, and no less evidently refers to another order, that of true genealogy: "Do not suppose that I have come to bring peace to the earth. I came not to bring peace but a sword. For I have come to turn a man against his father, a daughter against her mother, a daughter-in-law against her mother-in-law—a man's enemies will be the members of his own household. Anyone who loves his father or mother more than me is not worthy of me, anyone who loves his son or daughter more than me is not worthy of me" (Matthew 10:34–37). Beneath the apparently ethical nature of these prescriptions a phenomenology is being affirmed: it is because the human father, along with the constellation of relations constructed around him, is only just an apparent father that this network of relations is itself only an appearance, one that will eventually fall apart. But the human father is only an apparent father because he is a worldly one: it is because life does not show itself in the world that no generation is produced there and that in the world no father is really a father, nor any son a son.

The phenomenology of Christ that we have been elucidating here, of which John's exposition is unrivaled, can be elaborated as follows. No true Father (Life) giving itself to be seen in the world, the coming of Christ into this world—according to what we are calling the thesis of Christianity—aims to make the Father manifest to people, and thus to save them, those who have forgotten their true father and the true Life, who are living only with a view to the world and the things of the world, being interested solely in them and expecting their salvation solely from them. The religious meaning of Christianity—as offering salvation to humankind—is therefore caught up in a phenomenology, since it requires making the father manifest in the world, and thus to people—and yet the world is itself a form of manifestation. It is with this precise phenomenological demand that John explains the dogmatic content of Christianity, and from this arises the radical meaning of his Gospel for philosophy, as much as for religion.

The coming of Christ into the world to save people by revealing to them his Father who is also their Father: this is the thesis of Christianity as formulated phenomenologically by John, in two passages from his Gospel and at least one of his Epistles. Let us briefly recall them:

1. "The Word became flesh and made his dwelling among us. We have seen his glory" (John 1:14).
2. "No one has ever seen God, but the Son the One and Only, who is in the Father's bosom, has made him known" (John 1:18).
3. "That which was from the beginning, which we have heard, which we have seen with our eyes, which we have looked at and our hands have touched" (1 John 1:1).

God's Revelation, which is condition for the salvation of men, must be Christ incarnate, made flesh. And thus it is really Christ's coming into this world that must be God's Revelation and people's salvation. But Christ incarnate, made a man, is like any man. Standing in the presence of this man named Jesus, how can one know that he is not a man but the Christ, the Arch-Son consubstantial with the Father, present with him at the beginning, and in fact God himself? Or, to put it in rigorously phenomenological terms, how can a Life that holds its Living only in its own interior embrace, a Life whose Living consists in its self-revelation—this revelation of itself that it owes only to itself and expresses only to itself—a Life that lived before the creation of the world and thus before anything that could conceivably be visible: How can this Life, which nobody has ever seen, really ask and await the visible to provide its revelation, a revelation that is possible only in and through that Life itself?

Like the idea of the Word become flesh, the thesis that Christ as a man and therefore as a man of this world, visible in it, is equally a condition of God's Revelation and is this very Revelation is similarly belied by the context of each of the statements in which one might believe to have found it. Consider the context of the first: "The Word became flesh and made his dwelling among us. We have seen his glory, the glory of the One and Only Son, who came from the Father, full of grace and truth" (John 1:14). In the Johannine context, "glory" means the same thing as Truth, or as Revelation.

The Revelation that allows us to contemplate Christ, in which he is revealed and can henceforth be recognized as such, is his Glory as the Only Son that he receives from his Father, his glory as Arch-Son—specifically, his own revelation as God's self-revelation. Because "glory" designates precisely this revelation specific to the Arch-Son as self- and arch-revelation of God himself, that is, as the original essence of life, the problematic of glory is the same as that of testimony. I have shown that Christ heeds the testimony of no man, but that of his Father alone, because, as we shall see, his glory is the glory of the Father himself—because, as Arch-Son, his revelation is God's self-revelation and is possible only as such.

The very content of the second text suffices to rule out an interpretation to the effect that the apparition of a man in the world, in this case Jesus, is capable of making God known. The one who makes God known, "the One and Only Son," is precisely the Arch-Son in his transcendental state as Arch-Son, a state that consists of living in the bosom of God. But the bosom of God is the invisible life that is prior to any conceivable visible world: one who, invisible himself, is placed in the invisible bosom of God, can make God known only within the invisible, where God reveals himself in the Arch-Son and as the latter. It is there, in effect, that the only Son makes the Father known. And if we turn now to the context, we find that it reiterates this idea. Within Life lie grace and plenitude, inasmuch as Life embraces itself as well as Truth, inasmuch as this embrace of life is its self-revelation. It is within the Arch-Son and only through him that this grace and this Truth of Life come into themselves, far from being able to do so in the truth of the world and through that Truth: "Grace and truth came through Jesus Christ" (John 1:17).

What immediately follows the second text is the prophecy of John the Baptist in which human genealogy is broken at least twice. This occurs first when John inverts the temporal order of this genealogy, an inversion whose significance we have already noted. "He who comes after me has surpassed me because he was before me" (John 1:15). Second, when formulating his decisive testimony that Jesus is the Christ, John the Baptist does not rest content with what he has seen—"'I saw the Spirit come down from Heaven as a dove and remain on him'" (1:33)—but refers as well to *what God had told him*, that the one on whom he saw the dove rest was the Christ. Here again, and in an exemplary manner, it is evidently not the visible manifestation, the descent of the dove onto the man and remaining there, that can bear witness to and constitute the revelation in which the Arch-Son is revealed as the Word. Rather, this revelation belongs only to Life: it is its self-revelation, in this case the Word of God.

In the third text, from John's Epistle, the shift from the worldly manifestation—"that which we have heard . . . and our hands have touched"—to what is said to be manifested in this way, in the world, is still more striking and more disturbing. It is not simply a shift to what is said to be manifested in this way, in the world; rather, this shift is itself a radical break—an abrupt substitution for what is supposedly made manifest in the visibility of the world, which would be the Word, of another mode of revelation that is specifically that of the Word and in which the Word reveals itself, the Word of Life. Let us recall the text: "That which was from the beginning . . . which we have looked at and our hands have touched, *this we proclaim concerning the Word of Life.* Life has manifest itself . . . " (John 1:1-2). And it is only because this Life—which, according to the context, is "eternal Life" or "what was with the Father and has manifest itself to us"—was made manifest in itself and through it that it is possible to know that the One that bears within itself the Life of the Father is the Word. It is within the self-revelation of this Life, and only through it, that we reach Life and thus the Word—inasmuch as the Word carries Life within itself, inasmuch as it is the Word—and certainly not through its appearance as a man visible in a world. This is what the Johannine problematic and all of Christianity will establish.

John the Baptist's prophecy would suffice to demonstrate that one cannot really discern from a man's visible appearance that he is the Word of Life. To the envoys from the Pharisees who ask if he is himself the Messiah, he declares: "Among you stands one you do not know" (John 1:26). However, we have to recognize that John the Baptist finds himself in the same situation as they do—"I would not have known him" (1:31)—*until the One who had sent him forth to baptize tells him so.* Only God's revelation can reveal the Word, which is, moreover, nothing other than God's self-revelation.

A situation in which it transpires that the mere visible appearance of a man, even if he be Christ, is actually incapable of revealing that he is the Christ is constantly reproduced in the Gospels. Such is the case with the one born blind who is cured by Jesus and thrown out by the Pharisees: "When he found him, [Jesus] said, 'Do you believe in the Son of Man?' 'Who is he, sir?' the man asked. 'Tell me so that I may believe in him.' Je-

sus said, 'You have now seen him, in fact, he is the one speaking with you.'
Then the man said, 'Lord, I believe,' and he worshiped him" (John 9:35–
38). It is remarkable here that although he sees Christ, the blind man, once
cured, still has to believe in him, believe that he is the Christ, as if the fact
of seeing him were yet incapable of giving access to him.

The same thing happens again in the extraordinary conversation
with Philip, after the critical declaration in which Jesus refers to his reciprocal phenomenological interiority with God, presenting his own appearance as that of God himself: "No one comes to the Father except through
me. If you really knew me, you would know my Father as well. From now
on, you do know him, and you have seen him." Now comes Philip's demand, the demand of a world that relies upon seeing—"Show us the Father"—and then Christ's response, which reaffirms his identity with the
Father and thus his state as Christ, inasmuch as appearance in the world
has been replaced by the revelation of Life, or by the Arch-Son's Revelation
as the self-revelation of this Life and thus of God himself: "Don't you
know me, Philip, even after I have been among you such a long time?
Anyone who has seen me has seen the Father. How can you say, 'Show us
the Father?' *Don't you believe that I am in the Father, and that the Father is
in me?*" (John 14:6–10; my emphasis).

Linked to seeing the Father transformed into the reciprocal phenomenological interiority between Father and Son, and to this interiority, whose
radical nature we have demonstrated, is the concept of belief—and here
is what gives belief the hitherto unforeseen meaning that it will receive
throughout Christianity. To believe does not imply a lesser knowledge, homogeneous with the world's but still incomplete or imperfect, so that what
one believes in would still have to prove its reality or its truth by showing
itself once and for all. To believe is not a substitute for a still-absent seeing.
To believe does not refer to a waiting, a waiting for something not yet seen
but that will be seen someday, in a specific sight, within the world's truth. To
believe, *when what is seen is already present, already visible while remaining
incapable of making visible that which matters*, that is to say, the Word in its
state as Word, precisely because the latter is in itself invisible and no kind of
seeing will ever behold it—"to believe" can, then, refer only to the substitution, for a mode of manifestation that is fundamentally inadequate, of a
more essential revelation belonging to another order, that of the Word itself,
of Life itself, since Life reveals itself in this Word and in the form of it. If this

is so, then only in this Word and through it can one arrive at it. Or, more precisely, the Word lies within life itself and in the process of its self-revelation, inasmuch as this process is accomplished as the Word itself, the Word being nothing other than the effective working out of this process. This is why, according to a hidden but inescapable logic, what follows in the text calls not on the Word but on God, whose Word is *the* Word, the revelation. So these are the very words of God—of the one who is present within the Christ, who as God's self-revelation is also present within him—when Christ declares: "The words I say to you are not just my own. Rather, it is the Father, dwelling in me, who is doing his work. Believe me when I say that I am in the Father, and the Father is in me" (John 14:10–11).

The disqualification of the power of showing proper to the world, along with the substitution for this power of a mode of revelation that is entirely unlike seeing and owes nothing to it, nevertheless alone capable of revealing the divine essence being revealed in the Word and as this Word— this critical transformation in phenomenology, to a phenomenology whose phenomenality is Life and no longer the world, is contained in the words that give access to the content of Christianity, to God, albeit at the price of a complete overturning of the presuppositions guiding the course of Western thought since its origins with the Greeks: "Before long the world will not see me anymore, but *you will see me because I live and because you also will live*" (John 14:19; my emphasis).

Substituting one phenomenology for another, that of Life or Logos for that of the world, is not to misunderstand the power of manifestation that belongs to the latter, but rather strictly to circumscribe its domain and thus its capability. For traditional thought as for classical philosophy, for common sense as for science, the pertinence of concepts related to knowledge is founded exclusively on the world's phenomenality and the ways of seeing it delivers. In contrast, by situating original Truth within the original form of revelation that belongs only to life and consists in its self-revelation—life drawing its essence from this capacity to reveal itself and alone being able to do so—Christianity inverts the phenomenological concepts that form the basis for any mode of thought, but especially for the experience on which this thought models itself.

The traditional metaphor for speaking of truth is that of light. But truth is only understood as light because it is already assumed that the truth at issue is the world's. What is true in an immediate sense is what one sees or what one can see. But what one sees is seen only in the world's light, inasmuch as one sees only what is held before one's gaze, what is "outside," and the world is this "outside" as such. It is this equivalence between light, world, and truth, an equivalence that goes without saying and is straightaway adopted by nearly all conceptions of knowledge, of scholarship, of science and the truth itself, until it transpires that the truth must be considered in and for itself, as is the case with philosophy—it is this equivalence that is torn apart in John's prologue.

It is quite remarkable that it is precisely at the moment when it is a question of Christ's coming into the world, a coming-into-the-world that signifies in Greek thought a coming-into-the-light, that the worldly concept of light is struck out—this light of the world being reversed and absorbed into its contrary: darkness. The light of the world, which now designates darkness, is contrasted with the "true light," which is Christ in his own revelation. A series of crucial implications follows, which it is impossible to misunderstand or obscure. In coming to the world, as long as this is a coming-into-the-light, what comes into the world, or into the light, is shown in that light as it is and is thus illuminated by it. Being illuminated in it, finding there its proper place, it is received by that light and received by the world. It would be impossible to oppose to this coming-into-the-world with light itself, since that light is constituted by this coming-into-the-world and is identified with it. With regard to light, then, there is only one kind, that of the world, and precisely for this reason truth and the world are identical.

The ground of this series of implications—the equivalence light/truth/world—wavers when, in verse 9 of the prologue, John declares: "The true light that gives light to every man was coming into the world." That this light comes into the world presupposes that the light does not belong to it. Or else how, belonging to this world, being illuminated in the ek-stasy of its "outside" and being produced at the same time as the latter—how, if this light is identical with and as ancient as the world, could it really come about? But what comes into the world is a light different from the world's, and John shatters any possible equivalence between light and world at a single stroke when he contrasts the light of the world with a true light, a light that at once thrusts the world's light into the shadows and reduces it to darkness.

In this overturning of the fundamental concepts of phenomenality, and because of it, the drama of which all Christianity is the history bursts forth. Because the true light is alien to the world's, in fact it is not able to be recognized there, and, more to the point, *it cannot be recognized.* Therefore, this light that is incapable of showing itself in the world's light overrules the world and its own kind of light, turning it into its opposite, darkness. The world's light is not inherently shadow: it makes things manifest in its way, exhibiting stones, water, trees, and even people as they, too, appear lit by it, as beings in this world. But because the world's light is incapable of lighting with its light, of exhibiting in that light and thus of receiving the true Light whose essence is Life in its self-revelation, its power of making manifest is changed into an utter powerlessness to do so with respect to the Essential: this self-revelation of Life that is the Word—the Word of Life. This sudden transformation of the world's light into Darkness when Life is revealed in the Word is described very concisely in verses 4 and 5 of the prologue: "In him was Life, and that Life was the light of men. The light shines in the darkness, but the darkness has not understood it." This sudden dislocation of the power of worldly light to illuminate, its being changed into darkness when the true light appears, whose essence is Christ's revelation as the self-revelation of absolute Life, is something of which Christ himself speaks: "I have come into the world as a light, so that no one who believes in me should stay in darkness" (John 12:46).

The radical phenomenological irreducibility of these two kinds of revelation—the one of Life and its self-revelation in the Word of Life (the Johannine Logos). and the one that finds its essence in the light of the world, in the ek-stasy of "outside" (the Greek *logos*)—lies at the origin of John's problematic and of the Christian drama in general. In the light of this world this man who appeared in the world and is named Jesus cannot be known or recognized by anyone for what he truly is, the Word of Life: "You have seen me, and still you do not believe" (John 6:36). Indeed, for Christ to appear in the light of the world as this man Jesus, simply in the form of a man whom others recognize as a man and nothing more, *it is absolutely necessary that he be deprived of his divine condition,* of his own revelation in order to become nothing other than this objective and worldly appearance as a man. This is what Paul declares with astounding rigor in his Epistle to the Philippians: "[Christ Jesus,] though of divine condition, did not consider equality with God something to be grasped, but deprived himself, by assuming the condition of a slave becoming like men; *and once recognized as man . . .* " (2:6–7; my emphasis).

But if Christ sheds his divine condition in order to assume the aspect of a man and reveal himself as such within the world's truth, then where and how does he reveal himself in his true state as the very Word of God, as God's revelation? Where and how can one know and recognize him in the condition that is truly his own—as Christ, the revelatory Word of the Father?

The phenomenology of Christ that we have just sketched out supplies the elements of an answer: within the world's truth, Christ is merely a man among others, and nothing permits us to distinguish between them. In the world's truth, Christ's claim to be something other than a man is incomprehensible and absurd, it is a blasphemy and will be treated as such. In the world's truth, Christ's condition, if he is the Christ, takes on a disguise that nothing will ever remove. This is because *access to Christ can be had only in life and in the truth proper to it.* We recall once more that Christ is not in life as things are in the world. Not only is Christ not separated from the life in which he lives while it also lives in him, but he is the essential reason for this original co-belonging of Life and the First Living. The Son's generation co-belongs to Life's self-generation as what this self-generation accomplishes, as the essential Ipseity in which Life, in its self-embrace, becomes Life. Thus there is no way of reaching the Son other than in the course of Life's self-embrace, in the same way as there is no other way for life to embrace itself except in this essential Ipseity of the First Living—no other way for it to reveal itself except in the Word.

The Johannine texts give voice decisively to an endless movement in which the Father and Son embrace each other—the eternal generation of the Word in the eternal self-generation of the Father. But they express this movement from point of view of the Word, in what we have called Christ's discourse about himself. This is why Christ's analysis of his own condition as the Word always proceeds from his "Me," engendered as the essential Ipseity in which Life experiences itself and reveals itself, back to the activity of this life that experiences itself and reveals itself in him. In this way he experiences himself as traversed by this Life, as the site in which it experiences itself in him—who is himself merely the self-experience of this divine Life. Thus he is nothing other than the realization of this life; what reveals itself in him is the self-revelation of this Life, which is his own Revelation, his "glory"—for the revelation of life is the glory of the Father. What is done in him, what he does, is what this life does; thus he does nothing himself, but everything is transmitted through him. What is said in him, what he says, is what this life says. What is willed in him, what he wills, is what this life wills, and he wills only what life wills.

Within this radical belonging of the Son to Life, a belonging relating to the fact that he is this life's self-realization, there truly resides a singular reversal. Totally subject to this life, identifying himself with the movement of its self-realization and even co-realizing in his essential Ipseity life's self-realization, the Son is inside Life as that without which its movement could not be realized—interior to the Father, consubstantial with and equal to him. This reversal takes place in one of the most radical texts in which Christ reaffirms his condition against those who are accusing him of healing on the Sabbath and, what's more, of making himself God's equal by calling God "Father." The extreme modesty of the reply, the on-tological humility that says the Son is nothing outside the Father, able to do nothing without him—"The Son can do nothing by himself, he can do only what he sees his Father doing"—is abruptly reversed in the extreme proposition that everything the Father does, the Son does also—"because whatever the Father does the Son does also" (John 5:19). From this stem the momentous declarations: "All that belongs to the Father is mine" (John 16:15) and "I and the Father are one" (John 10:30).

But we have just recalled these critical implications, constitutive of the authentic content of Christianity, which John announces in an apodic-tic fashion: that inasmuch as Christ is nothing other than the coming-into-itself of Life in its essential Ipseity, everything that is in Christ comes to him from the Father—"All things have been committed to me by my Father" (Luke 10:22)—in such a way that nothing happens in him that is not made to happen by the Father. Thus Christ is never alone, not even at the hour of his abandon: "Yet I am not alone, for my Father is with me" (John 16:32), because, more profoundly, "the Father is in me . . . " (John 10:38). How is the Father in Christ? As the Life of which Christ is, in his essential Ipseity (that is, in his person), the self-revelation. In the same way, Christ is in the Father: " . . . and I in the Father" (John 10:38).

All this is realized in Christ as his own essence, inasmuch as he comes from Life as the Arch-Son co-engendered by Life in its absolute self-engendering. Hence Christ's constant reference, constantly recalled by John, to "the One who sent me." It is in the name of the one who sent him that Christ does everything he does, says everything he says, in the same way that it is from the one who sent him that he draws his own condition as God's envoy, the envoy of Life as its Word. This reference explains the inexplicable, something initially very mysterious: How can Christ, who never studied, know everything he knows and, in fact, know everything? "How did this man get such learning without having studied?" (John 7:15). Christ's reply can only be understood in light of his Arch-condition: "My teaching is not my own. It comes from him who sent me" (7:16). This proposition is reiterated with extraordinary insistence: "For I did not speak of my own accord, but the Father who sent me commanded me what to say and how to say it. . . . So whatever I say is just what the Father has told me to say" (John 12:49–50). And again: "These words you hear are not my own; they belong to the Father who sent me" (John 14:24); "The words I say to you are not just my own. Rather, it is the Father, living in me, who is doing his work" (John 14:10); "I do nothing on my own but speak just what the Father has taught me" (John 8:28).

How is what Christ is saying here, just as his Father said to him, a kind of teaching, and what does this teaching say to us? To teach is to speak the Truth. If what Christ says, saying what was said to him by the one who sent him, is true, it is because the one who sent him speaks true, says the truth: "He who sent me is truthful, and what I have heard from him I tell the world" (John 8:26). But what is this truth spoken by someone who is truthful and has sent Christ? He speaks a very particular truth, not the truth of the world or the things of the world, but the Truth of Life. The Truth of Life is Life itself. Life is the Truth as it is self-revealed. To speak the Truth, for the Truthful who has sent Christ, is to reveal Himself; it is for Life to realize its essence in the essential Ipseity of the First Living, in which it embraces itself and reveals itself, and which is the very Speech of Life, its Word. In this way, God's envoy says nothing other than what is said by the one who sent him, since his speech, the speech of the Word, identical with the Word, is none other than the speech of God—his self-revelation, accomplishing itself in this Word and in its guise.

The phenomenology of Christ—a phenomenology that responds to the question of knowing where and how Christ reveals himself, not as a man whom nothing differentiates from another man, but rather in his condition as Christ and the Word—relates precisely to this condition, to the Arch-generation of the Word in the self-generation of absolute Life. It is in the process of life's self-revelation that the Word reveals himself, and only in this way. But this revelation of the Word as God's self-revelation is also what we have called the reciprocal phenomenological interiority of Father and Son. This interiority is phenomenological in its very essence, being nothing other than the mode in which phenomenality originally phenomenalizes itself—as the original phenomenality that is Life.

As we have noted in passing, John discusses this original phenomenalization of Life specifically in terms of "glory." The reciprocal interiority of Father and Son, that is, the Son's Arch-generation as the Father's self-generation, means in phenomenological terms that each receives his glory only from the other—the Father's self-revelation accomplishing itself in the revelation of the Word, which is nothing other than the self-revelation of absolute Life: "Glorify your Son, that your Son may glorify you" (John 17:1). These two "glories," internal to one another, seem to present themselves as one outside the other in the transcendental story of Christ's mission on earth and of his passion. It is immediately before the Passion story is told that Jesus says: "Now is the Son of Man glorified, and God is glorified in him. If God is glorified in him, God will glorify the Son in himself" (John 13:31).

This reciprocal situation of the two glories will be taken up in Christ's final prayer: "I have brought you glory on earth by completing the work you gave me to do. And now, Father, glorify me in your presence with the glory *I had with you before the world began*" (John 17:4–5; my emphasis). That this glory always refers to Life and to its phenomenological essence in its radical opposition to the world's "glory"—which designates only the stage lights of this grand theater where people parade their qualities and struggle for prestige—can be directly inferred from the passage I have emphasized above. But it is also the explicit content of another passage, a model of conciseness, in which the opposition between the glory that people passionately seek and that of God himself echoes the fundamental phenomenological categories on which all of Christianity is founded—the crucial opposition between the world's truth and Life's truth. "I have not received glory from men. . . . I have come in my Father's name, and you do not accept me. . . . How can you believe, you who accept glory from one another, yet make no effort to obtain the glory that comes from the only God?" (John 5:41–44). That Christ is concerned solely with the Father's glory, and that as the Word he is its pure and absolute self-revelation, is also something that emerges from one of many passages in which Christ, affirming once again that he is not speaking "on his own account" and claiming anew his condition as Arch-Son, identifies himself with the absolute truth: "He who speaks on his own does so to gain glory for himself, but he who works for the glory of the one who sent him is a man of truth; there is nothing false about him" (John 7:17–18).

The reciprocal phenomenological interiority of Father and Son provides the ultimate foundation for a statement like this: "When [a man] looks at me, he sees the one who sent me" (John 12:45). But you cannot see the Father—nor, for that matter, the Son, since you cannot see the Son unless you see the Father in him. The statement just quoted is thus formulated more specifically in the immediately preceding one: "When a man believes in me, he does not believe in me only, but in the one who sent me" (12:44). But how can one believe either in Christ or in the one who sent him? Neither Christ nor the one who sent him is shown in the world's truth. In the world's truth there is Jesus, and the problem is essentially that of knowing whether he is the Christ. Seeing Jesus and wanting to know if he is the Messiah, the Son of God, the disciples demand: "Show us the Father!" (4:8). And again: "What miraculous sign then will you perform that we may see it and believe you?" (6:30). They could equally well demand: Show us the Son!

The reciprocal phenomenological interiority of Father and Son, the autarkic system constituted by the relation between Life and the First Living, signifies that there is no access to Christ except within Life and, as we have seen, in the process by which life eternally engenders itself by experiencing itself in the essential Ipseity of the First Living and thus in revealing itself in that which is its revelation, its Word. In this way Life knows itself in the Word, which also knows Life, being merely its self-revelation. What does not belong to this autarkic phenomenological system of Life and the First Living knows nothing of either one: "No one knows who the Son is except the Father, and no one knows who the Father is except the Son" (Luke 10:22). We have encountered this crucial proposition in several variants: "You do not know him, but I know him" (John 7:28); "No one has seen the Father except the one who is from God; only he has seen the Father" (John 6:46).

In the presence of the autarkic system constituted by the reciprocal phenomenological interiority of absolute phenomenological life and its Word—a system in which nothing belonging to it ever separates itself from it, into which nothing that is external to it can ever penetrate—does not the very teaching of Christianity suddenly become a problem? What does it teach apart from the coming of Christ into the world to save people? But the phenomenology of Christ has established that Christ cannot show himself to people in the world and that, for this reason, despite his acts and his extraordinary words, they do not believe in him.

The phenomenological aporia whereby it is impossible for Christ to show himself in the world *as Christ*, as the Word of God, destroys any possibility of man having access to Christ, of knowing him as Christ and thus knowing God, as long as man himself continues to be understood as a Being of this world. This is doubly true: in the sense that he appears in this world, there taking on the aspect of a man and being recognized in this aspect, to borrow Paul's words; and in the sense that everything that appears to him appears to him in this world and in its light—in the sense, therefore, that the truth to which man has access, and which allows him access to everything that is, is the truth of this world.

It is this conception of a person as a being of the world that Christianity pulls apart. It does so inasmuch as it understands man on the basis of his transcendental birth as a Son of Life and consequently, if Life is God, as the Son of God. First of all, the interpretation of man as a Son of God overturns the standard Western conception of man. Second, it introduces man into the autarkic system of absolute phenomenological Life and its Word, thereby making possible his access to Christ as such and at the same time his access to God, his salvation. It is this interpretation of man as the Son of God that we must now examine.

6

Man as "Son of God"

The central affirmation of Christianity regarding man is that he is the son of God. This definition breaks decisively not only with the customary representations of man, whether those of common sense, philosophy, or science (meaning modern science), but also with most religious definitions. Common sense considers man an inhabitant of this world, a living being, although one endowed with faculties superior to those of other animals. Therefore, the commonsense conception is akin to the philosophical conception that sees man as an animal endowed with reason, that is to say, as capable of forming meanings and thus of expressing himself in a spoken or a conceptual language. For modern science issuing out of the Galilean revolution, what is proper to man has been largely obscured, as we have had occasion to observe. Nevertheless, what unites scientific theses that treat man as part of the material universe—ultimately reducing him to physical and chemical elements, to the conceptions to which I have just alluded—is man's belonging to the world. Nor is this belonging-to-the-world absent from religious conceptions, at least as long as they understand man on the basis of the concept of creation. Creation means the creation of the world, and inasmuch as man himself is created, is himself *ens creatum*, then he, too, belongs to this world. From a theological standpoint, this means especially that, in relation to God, man finds himself in the same situation as does the world in general, that is, as something exterior to divine essence, different from it, separate from it, such that the religious problem consists principally of knowing how man, thus distanced from God, is capable of finding him again, and so of saving himself.

To conceive of man as a Being-of-the-world is not simple. At least two interpretations at work in the definitions we have recalled must be separated from each other, if not contrasted. According to the interpretation of naive realism, which is also that of scientific objectivism, man belongs to the universe in the very precise sense that he is a material part of it, even if this part proves capable of being grasped at different levels—biological, chemical, or physical. Such a conception generally goes by the name "materialist." Its great weakness is to blur the crucial differences that exist between phenomena of a material order and those specific to the human order, so as to establish a continuity between them. Unfortunately, any progress in the analysis of what is specifically human undermines this supposed continuity. This continuity—or, to put it another way, the presupposition of homogeneity between material and human phenomena— poses an obstacle for any truly scientific analysis, that is to say, one free of prejudice. In leading to a reductionism that is today more alive than ever, what was proposed as a principle for understanding is revealed to be merely a principle of misunderstanding.

It is precisely the concern to escape reductionism, by methodologically setting aside scientific knowledge, that has allowed twentieth-century phenomenology to make immense progress in understanding what is specific to man. Regarding the problem that concerns us here, it is a matter of arriving at a definition of man that rejects as basically improper a naive realism that inserts man into the world as a real element, an element homogeneous with the substance of which this world is made and consequently subject to the same laws. But man is in fact not in the world in the manner of some object or, in philosophical terms, in the manner of an intraworldly entity. What is specific to him, to the point of constituting his *humanitas*, is that he is open to the world in such a way that he relates to it within the context of specific experiences: feeling it and perceiving it, imagining it, conceiving it, thinking of it in various ways, fearing it or loving it, for example, whereas no other thing in this world is capable of experiences of this kind, or, for that matter, of experience in general. Although situated in the world, the ordinary being remains closed to it: it does not "have" the world, whereas man is essentially open to the world. Man is thus no longer a Being in the world in the manner of a natural Being, like a stone, air, fire. He is a being of the world in the transcendental sense that he is unto the world, relating to it, never ceasing to experience it. That man is also a natural being—a set of nerves and muscles, and, in the final analysis, neurons, molecules and particles—can no longer define him in his specific condition as a man who relates to the world, as a transcendental man. This is because none of the natural elements of which he is said to consist is capable of "having" a world, of opening itself to what surrounds it by having an experience of it. The natural man of common sense and of science is therefore decisively opposed to the transcendental man that modern philosophy, from Descartes to Heidegger by way of Kant and Husserl (to mention only the most influential), was able to recognize in that which is proper to him. That a transcendental Being-in-the-world—Descartes's *cogito/cogitatum*, Kant's relation to the object, Husserl's intentionality, Heidegger's *In-der-Welt-sein*—defines the very essence of man and is what ultimately distinguishes him from any other thing may be seen in the fact that man cannot turn away from the world, flee it, for example, but is fundamentally linked to it, against the background of an experience of the world that for him does not cease. Always relating to the world, being open to it in multiple ways, in sensation or perception as in forgetting or flight, man has the capacity to do so only insofar as the world shows itself to him, appears to him. It is the primordial appearing and presupposition of the world that precedes and makes possible all the ways in which man relates to it. But the appearing of the world is what constitutes the world's truth.

Here arises the revolutionary character of Christianity—its total originality in comparison to all the problematics deriving from common sense, reiterated to the point of today appearing threadbare. For Christianity, man is not, in effect, a Being-of-the-world, neither in the natural sense nor in the transcendental sense. This is not because, duped by common sense, Christianity is ignorant of transcendental man. On the contrary, no other kind of thought is more foreign to natural appearance than that of Christianity, and none rises more immediately to a transcendental conception of man and of truth. We may recall that, since Kant, "transcendental" has been used for that which refers not to knowledge but to what makes it possible. Thus we are no longer dealing with the ordinary knowledge of things that someone acquires in the course of daily existence but with the a priori possibility that he can arrive at such knowledge. This possibility relates to the fact that these things show themselves to him, that they are "phenomena." The possibility of knowledge does not reside in the things themselves but in the fact that they give themselves to us and appear to us; it resides in their manifestation. By thematizing the way in which things give themselves to us—the mode of their givenness and thus this givenness in itself and for itself—phenomenology turns the transcendental problematic inaugurated by Kant into something extremely radical. At the same time, it exposes the limits of this problematic, since the kind of givenness maintained by Kant and by phenomenology itself is that which is brought to light in the appearing of the world, in its truth.

By defining man as son, Christianity rules out any form of thought—science, philosophy, or religion—that holds man to be a Being of the world, whether in a naive or critical sense. In effect, there are sons only in life. A rigorous phenomenological analysis of life has shown that in itself life is alien to the world. First, the mode by which life phenomenalizes itself, or reveals itself to itself by experiencing itself in its *pathētik* embrace, does not consist of the opening up of a world. Second, in the *pathētik* flesh of life's experience of itself, no world shows itself either, nothing that takes on the aspect of an "outside." Neither the mode of life's giving as self-giving and as self-revelation nor the pure phenomenological substance of which this self-revelation is made, belongs to the world in any shape or form.

Thus the conception of man that arises with Christianity overturns from top to bottom the traditional conception and all its later variants. It does not do so in the sense that it places on high what was down below, and vice versa. Nor does it overturn them as might an axiomatic inversion that proceeds from a new evaluation, privileging the sensible, for example, over the conceptual, or vice versa. We note in passing that an antithesis between the sensible and the conceptual, the valorization or condemnation of one or the other, is totally foreign to Christianity, as is the ethical stance it supposedly expresses with respect to them. This is because neither the sensible nor the intelligible belongs to the essence of man as it is understood by Christianity. They do not belong to this essence because their manner of showing themselves to one another originates in the world's way of showing itself and is borrowed from it. Christianity's overturning of the conception of man, once and for all, does not consist in the inversion of elements included in the reigning conception, but in their exclusion. It is another phenomenological essence that defines the Christian transcendental phenomenological man, another truth. Another mode of the phenomenalization of phenomenality constitutes its substantial reality, the phenomenological flesh that is its flesh. Christianity proceeds to a radical substitution of one mode of truth for another as soon as it posits man as son. Henceforward, it is on the basis of his birth in Life that man must be understood, and thus on the basis of Life itself and the Truth proper to it. But absolute phenomenological Life, on the basis of which man can and must be understood inasmuch as he is a son, is the absolute Life of God himself. To say that man is a son inasmuch as there are sons only in Life and that this sole and unique Life is God's is equally to say that man is the Son of God. So the expression "Son of God" is tautological.

However, if man is the Son, and the Son of God, if he is born of phenomenological Life and draws his essence from it, then everything that has been said (and by the Arch-Son himself) about the phenomenological, and hence ontological, heterogeneity of the transcendental Arch-Son in relation to the world and its truth—all those singular propositions that dispense with an appearance in the world and everything that follows from this appearance (the time, space, and causality that are at play in the world and all the laws said to be those of nature)—all these propositions, we are saying, also concern man himself and place him within the network of fundamental tautologies that they establish. This extension to man himself of the radical arguments that Christ affirmed about himself is something we have discovered from the transcendental analysis of his condition as Arch-Son. We must now delve deeper into this paradoxical extension to man of the extraordinary condition of an Arch-Son born before the world and before historical time. But before attempting this analysis of the implications for man taken as Son of God that derive from the condition of Arch-Son, let us pursue a digression that will add to the phenomenology of Christ.

One of the traditional difficulties of "Christology," meaning the efforts made by theologians and philosophers to conceive of the mysterious being of Christ, is the latter's dual nature. He is both man and God, coming into the world and therefore taking on the condition of a man, but without losing the condition of Only Son and First Born engendered in God himself, consubstantial with him and in the final analysis equal to him. How can we explain the union within Christ of two heterogeneous natures, one human and the other divine? Associated respectively with these two natures, are not all the faculties of Christ's spirit necessarily split in two? For example, is not Christ's human will different from his divine will, and possibly even opposed to it? From the potential conflict between these two wills comes Christ's moral merit, his exceptional virtue, since he constantly subordinates his own will to his Father's, as we see in many of his declarations, in the Lord's Prayer he institutes, and finally in the moment of his ultimate sacrifice in the Passion. It is this constant subordination of his own will to God's that makes Christ the model, whose *imitatio* is the principle of any conduct capable of opening to man the gates of the Kingdom.

But when one tries to understand Christ's being on the basis of the union within him of two contradictory natures, one human and the other divine, one temporal and the other eternal, one must set aside at least two overwhelming prejudices that constantly frustrate any understanding of Christianity. It is presupposed, on the one hand, that there is a preexisting nature of man that occurs as a co-constitutive element in Christ's nature—which is, on the other hand, conjointly explained by his divine origin. One forgets that, as he explicitly states, Christ proceeds from the one who sent him and only from him. Generated in the self-generation of absolute Life and drawing his essence from it, there is nothing in him that is not this Life. The Ipseity in which Christ experiences himself—namely, his subjectivity—is the Ipseity in which absolute phenomenological Life experiences itself—namely, this Life's subjectivity. And it is for this reason that he is consubstantial and contemporaneous with Life, having "come forth" since the beginning, the Arch-Son co-engendered in God's self-engendering and therefore engendered in the same moment. One forgets that man comes too late to intervene, even if only as a constituent element, in Christ's nature. Here lies the aporia: to suppose that Christ can be explained on the basis of a human nature that did not exist when Christ was engendered in Life's self-engendering, in such a way that his essence came about in his total independence from this supposed human nature, and well before something like man saw the light of day. "Before Abraham was, I am." If we turn to the Gospel, even to consider it in the usual anecdotal fashion, how can we fail to notice that Christ never spoke of himself as a man, and never spoke to other people as if he were one of them?

But this Christology founded on the idea of Christ's double nature (accurate in that Christ took on human form, which the Father did not), often hides another unfortunate premise, one that is actually anti-Christian: *What is the nature of this human nature* that is joined with another nature, the divine essence, such that the two together compose Christ's mixed essence? What springs to mind is that the man who mysteriously blends his nature with the divine essence of the Logos consubstantial with the Father is the man of the world, the man of common sense, of empiricism and rationalism, the man who is a rational animal, the natural man who is an integral part of the material universe, or even the transcendental man who opens himself to the world in his experiencing of it—in short, the man rejected by Christianity. To this man Christianity opposes a radically different man, the Son of God, the Son of Life, the new transcendental man born within absolute phenomenological Life, engendered within this Life's self-engendering and drawing his essence from it alone—man resembling Christ, man in the image of God!

Here we uncover not only one of the core intuitions of Christianity but at the same time its devastating power over a Christology bogged down in the pre-supposition of a "human nature." This power is exercised over different traditional conceptions of man that are apparently in competition with one another, yet which all view man as a being of the world. With respect to Christology, these conceptions are inadmissible if within the Arch-Son co-engendered in the self-engendering of absolute phenomenological Life, there is no other essence, nor can there be, than that of this life of which he is the self-realization. As for man, if he is himself a Son, engendered in Life and on its basis, drawing his possibility and his essence from it, then there is nothing else in him either, inasmuch as he is a living, apart from this essence of Life. An essence of man different from that of Christ or God appears impossible as soon as man is understood as Son, and explicitly as Son of God. The idea of a specific and hence autonomous human nature, of an essence of *humanitas* as such, is from the Christian viewpoint an absurdity. To construct a Christology—which means, in the final analysis, to construct Christ himself—by adding to a divine essence, of which we know nothing, a human nature, which from the Christian viewpoint does not exist: this is the paradox of those theologies that believe themselves able to rise from a consideration of worldly and human data to the idea of God, which ultimately means to understand the latter on the basis of the world and its truth. What these speculative constructions are missing, in the absence of a phenomenology of life, is the very notion of what is at issue in Christianity with regard to God, Christ, or man. A dualist Christology is obliged to remove any form of naturalism, any naive expression of the world's thinking and its persistence where a world no longer exists. Therefore, far from understanding Christ (or even just a part of his being) on the basis of man and his condition, it is man who must be understood on the basis of Christ, and can be so only in this way.

To understand man on the basis of Christ, who is himself understood on the basis of God, in turn rests on the crucial intuition of a radical phenomenology of Life, which is precisely that of Christianity: namely, that *Life has the same meaning for God, for Christ, and for man.* This is so because there is but a single and selfsame essence of Life, and, more radically, a single and selfsame Life. This Life—that self-generates itself in God and that, in its self-generation, generates the transcendental Arch-Son as the essential Ipseity in which this self-generation comes about—is the Life from which man himself takes his transcendental birth, precisely since he is Life and is explicitly defined as such within Christianity. He is the Son of this unique and absolute Life, and thus the Son of God. The tautological expression "Son of God"—tautological in that there are no sons except in Life and thus in God—conceals the profound truth that man's essence, that which makes him possible as what he really is, is not man as we understand him, and still less some *humanitas* or other. Rather, it is the essence of divine life—that which makes him one of the living, and that alone.

The thesis of man as the "son of God" thus has a dual significance, part negative and part positive. In a negative sense, it prevents man from being understood as a natural Being, as do common sense and the sciences. But it also prevents him from being understood, from the transcendental viewpoint, as a Being for whom the world would constitute the horizon of all experiences, or the mode of appearing common to each of these experiences. Thus it is Christ's sweeping assertion about himself that must be reconsidered with regard to man and his true essence: "They are not of the world any more than I am" (John 17:14). Just like Christ, as a man I am not of the world in the radical phenomenological sense that the appearing out of which my phenomenological flesh is made, and which constitutes my true essence, is not the appearing of the world. This is not due to the effect of some supposed credo, philosophical or theological; it is rather because the world has no flesh, because in the "outside-itself" of the world no flesh and no living are possible—they cannot take shape anywhere other than in Life's *pathētik* and a-cosmic embrace.

Thus a man must adopt all Christ's polemical and passionate denials concerning his condition if he wants to understand some part of what he is. He is not of the world, nor, consequently, is he a natural Being; he is not the son of his father. No matter the level on which it is constructed, any worldly explanation of *humanitas* is instantly henceforth stripped of its claim to reach the first and final reality on the basis of which alone is anything like a man possible. Character traits and specific psychological behavior are things we can trace to the first relation of the child to the person it considered to be its father: its first traumas, the Oedipus complex, and so forth. But since this father is not its father—and since, being incapable of giving life to himself, he is certainly in no position to bestow it on anyone else—it appears, in the privileged and decisive example of birth, that no worldly sequence of events could account for the Being of a person, inasmuch as he or she proceeds from a birth.

Philosophy has tried to define what a man truly is. In modern times, this grand effort has found expression in the transcendental phenomenological reduction practiced by Husserl. Taking up the Cartesian project that aspires to get at the heart of what we truly are, the reduction in fact brackets the world. In so doing, Husserl is aware of discovering fields of experience that had gone unnoticed by man throughout his history. In these as yet unexplored fields of experience, those of the ego's transcendental life, the essence of man unfolds. Transcendental man, not natural man, is what the phenomenological reduction places in the hands of phenomenology, not as the outcome of a risky discovery but owing to research systematically pursued in the light of conscious premises. But as soon as this transcendental man is reduced to "consciousness of something," to *In-der-Welt-sein* —reduced, in short, to his phenomenological opening up to the world, meaning to the phenomenological opening *of* the world—what constitutes his transcendental essence becomes distorted and is lost. This is because the original mode of phenomenalization by which "man" comes into his condition as Son, that is to say, as Living in Life, as the original mode of phenomenalization of Life itself, has nothing whatsoever to do with a "consciousness of something," with the phenomenological opening of a world —with the ek-stasy of an "outside."

If transcendental man grasped as Son draws his phenomenological essence from Life's self-phenomenalization, a process inherently foreign to the opening of a world, then the thesis of man as "Son of God" is clarified in its many implications. In effect, being engendered in Life, the engendered has the characteristics of this Life. What is valid for the Arch-Son is valid for the Son, and what is valid for them both is the essence of life, or God himself. This is the meaning of the thesis that "God created man in his image": that he gave man his own essence. He did not give it to him as one gives an object to someone, like a gift passing from one hand to another. He gave him his own essence in the sense that, his own essence being the self-engendering of Life in which is engendered the Ipseity of all the living, then in giving his own essence God gave man the living condition, the happiness of experiencing himself in this experiencing of self that is Life and in the radical immanence of this experiencing, where there is neither "outside" nor "world." To engender means everything except to create, if creation refers to the creation of the world, the phenomenological opening up of a first "Outside" where the entire reign of the visible is revealed to us.

Here opens up the abyss that separates birth and creation. For man to be the Son means, for him as for the Arch-Son, that he is not created. The thesis that God created man in his image therefore signifies two things: first, that man was in fact *not* created—and this is why he is not a Being-of-the-world; and, second, that man is not an image, because in fact images exist only in the world, against the background of this original putting-into-image that is the horizon of the world in its ek-static phenomenalization. If man were an image, if he were created in the way that the world was created, he would no longer be the "image" of God and carry in him the same essence, the essence of Life: he would no longer be, and could no longer be, a living. The requirements of a phenomenology of birth suffer no exceptions; what they imply or exclude is universally valid. There are no more Sons in the world than there is an Arch-Son. To make sense of man's essence, the phenomenology of the world must be dismissed, as it was for Christ—and through him.

Or, if you prefer, it is the idea of man in the usual sense that must be renounced. We think there is something like a man because we are looking at the world. It is within this gaze, formed by it, that the silhouette of a man is traced, against the horizon of visibility that is the world's truth. Because the man one sees takes his appearance from the world's appearance, the laws of this appearance also apply to him: space, time, causality, the multiple determinations woven each day by the natural sciences and the so-called sciences of man, in whose web he is caught. This man is brother to the automata that can be constructed according to the same laws—and will be. What this specter lacks in order to be similar to what we are is to be living—not the kind of living foreign to life of which biology speaks but the living that carries within itself absolute phenomenological Life, the man we do not see, any more than we see Christ, the man who was born into Life and takes from his transcendental birth all its *pathētik* characteristics, the transcendental man of Christianity, the Son of God.

Having outlined what the interpretation of man as Son of God rules out, we should now explore its positive meaning thoroughly. An inevitable question arises here: If man carries in himself Life's divine essence, is he not God himself or Christ? What is the difference between them? We must pursue the analysis of the transcendental birth of the Son of Life much further if the transcendental characteristics that define man's essence are to be firmly grounded, and thereby intelligible enough to be grasped. We have seen how, in the self-generation of absolute Life, an essential Ipseity is engendered whose phenomenological effectivity is a singular Self—that of the Arch-Son co-engendered in life as its self-accomplishment and thus identical with the latter. Analogously, true man as conceived by Christianity under the title "Son of God—what we will now be calling the living transcendental Self—is engendered in Life. Inasmuch as, in the self-movement by which Life ceaselessly comes into itself and experiences itself, is erected an Ipseity and thus a Self (because to experience oneself is effectively the same as that self, is necessarily that self), then the Self engendered in this self-movement of Life is effectively the same as that Self, too, and is necessarily this one or that one, a singular Self, in essence different from any other. I myself am this singular Self engendered in the self-engendering of absolute Life, and only that. *Life self-engenders itself as me.* If, along with Meister Eckhart—and with Christianity—we call Life God, we might say: "God engenders himself as me."[1] The generation of this singular Self that I myself am—the living transcendental Me, in the self-generation of absolute Life: this is my transcendental birth, the one that makes me a true man, the transcendental Christian man.

But inasmuch as this transcendental birth is accomplished on the basis of Life, in the process of this Life's coming-into-itself, then the singular Self that I am comes into itself only in absolute Life's coming-into-itself and carries it within itself as its never-abolished premise, as its condition. Thus Life traverses each of those it engenders in such a way that there is nothing in him that is not living, nothing that does not contain this eternal essence of Life. *Life engenders me as itself.* If with Eckhart—and with Christianity— we call Life God, one could say: "God engenders me as himself."[2] But that was precisely the condition of the Arch-Son co-engendered in God's self-engendering, in such a way that his generation was the self-generation of God himself, that he was God. We repeat our question: Me, this living transcendental Self that I am, am I Christ?

Here let me introduce a crucial concept that perhaps ought to have been introduced earlier, since it governs the philosophical understanding of life's essence: the concept of *self-affection.*[3] What is specific to life is, in effect, that it affects itself. This self-affection defines its living, the "experiencing-itself" of which it consists. Affection generally implies a manifestation. If a being of the world affects me, it makes itself felt by me, shows itself to me, gives itself to me, enters into my experience in some way or other. And this is valid for the world itself, which affects me because it is manifests itself to me—this manifestation of the world being, as we have seen, its "truth." Truth and affection are equivalent terms. The concept of affection, designating any affection whatever and thus any manifestation (that affects me via a sound that I hear, an object that I see, an odor I smell, or else that affects my mind via an image or any other representation), contrasts sharply with the concept of self-affection. In self-affection, what affects me is no longer anything foreign or external to me who am affected, and consequently no object belonging to the world or the world itself. What affects in the case of self-affection is the same as what is affected. But this extraordinary situation in which what affects is the same as what is affected occurs nowhere except within life. And such a situation occurs there absolutely, such that it defines the essence of this life. Life is that which itself affects itself in the radical and decisive sense that this life that is affection, and that is affected, is not affected by anything other than itself, by no kind of externality and by nothing exterior to it. In this way, life constitutes the content of its affection. The concept of self-affection as life's essence implies its acosmic character, the fact that being affected by nothing other, nothing external or radically foreign to the world, it comes about in itself in the absolute sufficiency of its radical interiority—experiencing only itself, being affected only by itself, prior to any possible world and independently of it.

Now, this condition of life and of everything that carries within itself life's essence does not result from some speculative assertion. It is a phe-

nomenological condition. As such, it can be discerned in each of the effective modalities of life. A joy may well be explained by an event in the
world or be related to it, and moreover it may itself be related to some
object or cause exterior to it, some cause or object that stands out clearly
in the screen on which the world appears. But the joy itself is not illuminated in the light of any world. Considered in itself, in its pure affectivity
and as joy's pure living in which its reality is exhausted, this joy is merely a
pathētik modality of life, a way in which life experiences itself. And this is
valid for any of life's modalities, starting with the simplest impression.[4]
However, if each modality of life considered in the immanence of its living
carries within it the absolute essence of life, never being other than a mode
of the latter, of its *pathētik* and nonecstatic self-phenomenalization, then
in effect the possibility of a dissociation of this son of life that I am as a
transcendental living ego, on the one hand, from the Arch-Son, on the
other, and finally from the phenomenological essence of this absolute Life,
or God himself—now poses itself as a problem.

Let us distinguish between a strong and a weak concept of
self-affection. According to the strong concept, life affects itself in a double
sense—first, in that it in itself defines the content of its own affection. The
"content" of a joy, for example, is this joy itself. Second, life itself produces
the content of its affection, this content that is itself. It does not produce
this content as it might an exterior creation, casting what is created outside
itself, like something other and alien and external. In fact, life does not create content at all; the content of life is uncreated. Life engenders it, gives to
itself the content that is itself. What matters is the way in which life gives
itself this content that is itself. This self-giving that is a self-revelation is a
transcendental affectivity, a pathos in which every self-experiencing is possible as *pathētik*, as affective in the very depths of its being. However passive
this experiencing that life constantly has of itself in its *pathētik* embrace
may be, it is nonetheless produced by life itself—and it is life's generation
of itself to which the strong concept of self-affection refers. According to
this concept, life is affected by a content that is itself, and, moreover, it lays
down this content by which it is affected—this life that affects and is affected. The strong concept of self-affecting pertains to absolute phenomenological life and is suitable only for it—that is to say, to God.

Me, on the contrary, the living transcendental Ego, I also draw my
essence from self-affection. As far as I am me, I affect myself; I am myself

the affected and what affects it, myself the "subject" of this affection and its content. I experience myself, and constantly, in that, the fact of experiencing myself constitutes my "Me." But I have not brought myself into this condition of experiencing myself. I am myself, but I myself have no part in this "being-myself": I experience myself without being the source of this experience. I am given to myself without this givenness arising from me in any way. I affect myself, and thus I self-affect myself—that is, it's me who is affected and I am so by myself, in the sense that the content that affects me is still me—and not something else, such as the affection felt, touched, willed, desired, thought, and so forth. But this self-affection that defines my essence is not my doing. And thus I do not affect myself absolutely, but, precisely put, I am and I find myself self-affected. Here we find the weak sense of the concept of self-affection, the one proper to comprehending the essence of man, rather than to comprehending God's.

How can we relate the weak and strong senses of the concept of self-affection to each other? How does the former necessarily refer to the latter in such as way as to be founded on it? The singular Self that I am experiences itself only within the movement by which Life is cast into itself and enjoys itself in the eternal process of its absolute self-affecting. The singular Self self-affects itself; it is the identity between the affecting and the affected, but it has not itself laid down this identity. *The Self self-affects itself only inasmuch as absolute Life is self-affected in this Self.* It is Life, in its self-giving, which gives the Self to itself. It is Life, in its self-revelation, that reveals the Self to itself. It is Life, in its *pathētik* embrace, that gives to the Self the possibility of pathetically embracing itself and of being a Self.

Thus we see the passivity of this singular Self that I am, a passivity that determines it from top to bottom. The Self is not only passive with respect to itself and each of the modalities of its life, as each suffering is passive with respect to itself and is only possible as such, taking its affective tenor solely from this passivity whose pure phenomenological tenor is affectivity as such. Above all, the Self is passive with respect to the eternal process of Life's self-affecting that engenders it and never ceases to do so. This passivity of the singular Self within Life is what puts it into the accusative case and makes of it a "me" and not an "I," this Self that is passive about itself only because it is passive to begin with about Life and its absolute self-affection.

But this passivity of the singular Self in Life—the passivity making of it a "me"—is not a metaphysical attribute posited by thought. It is phenomenologically determined such that it is constitutive of the Self's life and is therefore continually lived by that Self. This determination is so essential, the proof of it so constant, that our life becomes confused with this feeling of being lived. If the Self expresses itself spontaneously in the accusative case, it is because it holds fast to its own experience, which is not that of being affected but of being constantly self-affected, within itself, in a self-affection that is independent of external affecting or any relation with the world.

Now, the specific mode of the singular Self's passivity as self-affected in Life's absolute self-affecting not only defines one of its general traits but also engenders the whole set of its essential, and thus *pathētik*, modalities. Thus anxiety is born in the self as if it comes from within. It takes its possibility from the very essence of this Self, from this feeling the Self has of experiencing what it does without being in any way responsible for it, without being able to change anything in it, without being able to get rid of itself or break the bond that attaches it to itself, which makes it into the Self that it will always be. To escape the self—this burden that the Self constitutes for itself inasmuch as it is constantly affected by itself without this self-affection coming from this self or being somehow imputable to it—to want to escape the self and not be unable to do so: that is what provokes the Self's anxiety and, by the same token, all the behavior that anxiety arouses and through which it tries in turn to flee itself. Thus, drive, also born in anxiety and issuing from it, is nothing other than one of these behaviors, or perhaps the most important of them or else their common source. The drives are the untiring effort of self-affected life—the life that is constantly assailed by itself, crushed under its own weight—to hide from itself, to get rid of itself. Life finds it impossible to sever the tie that attaches it invincibly to itself, so it tries to change itself, to convert—and this is the principle of its action, or of any conceivable action—its suffering into joy.

The essential questions that an empirical psychology believes it can situate on an objective plane and include in its repertoire of worldly explanations all in fact derive solely from man's condition as Son of God, or—as we should put it at the close of this analysis—the status of the singular Self self-affected within the self-affection of absolute Life. As Son, man is predestined, and his destiny is written within the reciprocal relation of the weak and strong concepts of self-affection, or in the relation that is established between a life such as his own, constantly self-affected without ever being the source of this self-affection, and a Life that affects itself absolutely, the Life of God.

With respect to these two concepts of self-affection, *naturans* and *natura*, what, then, is specific to the self-affection characteristic of Christ's life? How can we relate it to the life of God and that of "man"? One of the major themes of Christianity is the effort to comprehend Christ as intermediary between humans and God. What this role of "intermediary" consists of is something that a phenomenology of life allows us to grasp more thoroughly than any other mode of thought has been able to manage, for lack of the appropriate means. The relation of Christ's Life to God's is something the theory of the Arch-Son has clearly laid out. Although he is himself generated in the self-affection of absolute Life, Christ co-belongs to the process of this absolute self-affection as the essential Ipseity and the First Living, without which no self-affection of this kind could be accomplished. Thus he is "consubstantial" with the Father, sharing in the power of this process in which, embracing itself, Life makes itself Life.

By the same token, the relation of transcendental man to Christ is clarified, inasmuch as it is intelligible only in the light of Christ's relation to God, the principle of which we have just recalled. A third relation, though, also enters into the field of our phenomenological elucidation: the relation of this transcendental man to God himself. Here we discover the reason why this relation is not direct but is mediated by Christ. To the thesis common to Judaism and Christianity that transcendental man is the Son of God can be added a more properly Christian thesis (although it is also Judaic insofar as Judaism awaits a Messiah): that he is this Son of God only within the Arch-Son, the "Son within the Son." Here is why.

No livings are possible except within Life. As soon as Life's essence is understood, this assertion follows: no living is living, that is, self-affecting, other than in the process of the self-affection of absolute Life. If the essence of this self-affection is understood in turn, the proposition then becomes: no self-affection is possible that does not generate in itself the essential Ipseity implied in any "experiencing-itself" and presupposed by it. But the phenomenological realization of this Ipseity is a Self, itself phenomenologically realized and therefore singular—in other words, the transcendental Arch-Son co-engendered in the phenomenological realization of the self-affection of absolute Life as this realization itself. That no livings are possible except in life therefore means that they are possible within the Arch-Son, and only in him.

Decisive evidence can be brought forward: If we ponder a living, in this case the transcendental Self that I am, then it is not simply on the basis of Life's essence and because the self carries within itself this essence that we are able to understand this living. Only the analysis of the essence of Life, inasmuch as this essence implies the Ipseity of a first Self, allows us to grasp how and why a place is opened up in it, in the Ipseity of this First Self, for any and all conceivable livings—since the latter is possible only as a Self. Thus the Arch-Son precedes any Son, but not in a factual anteriority that could readily be verified. On the contrary, the Arch-Son precedes any Son as the preexisting and preestablished essence without which and outside of which nothing could be constructed that is anything like a Son, like a living Self—like this transcendental ego that I am. And, in fact, if by means of thought we plunge into the life of one of these transcendental egos born in Life, it is clear that, no more than any of them has (or ever had) the capacity to set itself in motion and establish itself in Life, to make itself living, none of them has, or could have, the power to unite this Life with itself—presupposing that Life had flowed into it like a wave—and, uniting itself in this way, to construct in Life this Ipseity on the basis of which alone is it possible as a Self, as this transcendental "me" that I am.

Now let us return to the most extraordinary and reckless of Christ's words in order to perceive their apodictic truth—a truth such that whoever understands it cannot avoid accepting it: "Before Abraham was . . . Me, I am." These words signify that no transcendental living "me" is possible except within an Ipseity that it presupposes (far from having the power to create it, any more than it could have created its own life)—an Ipseity co-generated in the self-affection of absolute Life and whose phenomenological effectivity is precisely the Arch-Son. The First Born within Life and the First Living, the Arch-Son holds the essential Ipseity in which life's self-affection comes to be effective. But it is only within this Ipseity, and on its basis, that any other Self, and thus any transcendental ego such as ours, will be possible. Thus, the Arch-Son holds in his Ipseity the condition of all other sons. No son, no transcendental living ego born in life, would be born in this life had life not previously taken shape as transcendental Ipseity in the Arch-Son. Therefore, the latter necessarily precedes any imaginable Son: he is "the firstborn among many brothers" (Romans 8:29).

This is because only in his Ipseity and in the originary Self that belongs to him can life come to each living, by making of him a "me"—*never coming to him except by making of him a "me"*—this transcendental "me" that I myself am. "Before Abraham was [but this means "before any transcendental 'me' whatever, whether it be Abraham's or David's"], I am."

That a living comes to life only as a living "me" and thus only on the condition that this life has already constructed the originary Ipseity that makes it possible for that living person to be a Self and a "me"—this is what Christianity's fundamental assertions regarding man imply: that man can be the "Son of God" only as the "Son within the Son." We must now delve into this crucial argument.

Man as "Son Within the Son"

The assertion that man comes into his condition as a transcendental living me[1] as a Son of Life, only insofar as Life, in generating itself, has generated the originary Ipseity of the First Living—an assertion that confers on Christianity its very particular physiognomy among other monotheisms—can be formulated in many ways. Sometimes it is an idea underlying propositions that explicitly bear on other subjects, as in the case of prayers or spiritual instructions whose aim is to transform a faithful person's life with a view to his sanctification, and ultimately his participation in divine life. Sometimes, on the contrary, the thesis is articulated more bluntly, in one of the surprising declarations that offer what we have called the essential kernel of Christianity. Understanding the transcendental birth of man as his generation within the First Living, and not merely within Life, is so important that even when that understanding is veiled by edifying discourse, the meaning of that discourse is disclosed only by reference to the generation of the Arch-Son. The latter appears to be the condition of any modification coming along to affect the history or destiny of a transcendental living me.

If we consider the opening of the Letter to the Ephesians (1:3–6), which seems a typically religious text addressed to believers, simultaneously a prayer to God and an exhortation of the faithful, we cannot fail to recognize the theme inherent in this thanksgiving to the Father who has given man his condition as a living me, a me in Christ—having "chosen us in him," in this Firstborn Son. Thus the Arch-Son appears as the site where the gift of Life to the living is made, such that, imbued with an ipseity and receiving from it the phenomenological realization of Life that it transmits, this gift determines a priori any living as a me. The ipseity of a Self and of a me is not conveyed by this gift as something that somehow still remains outside it; rather, it is inherent in this givenness. The givenness of life is never anything other than a self-givenness, and it can be achieved solely in that form, in the original Ipseity that inhabits any conceivable self-givenness. It is not only the gift of God, nor only the site where the gift is given, but the originary co-belonging and reciprocal interiority of Ipseity and of Life that is unveiled and exalted in Paul's lyrical address: "Praise be to the God and Father of our Lord Jesus Christ, who has blessed us in the heavenly realms with every spiritual blessing *in Christ*. For he chose us *in him* before the creation of the world . . . having predestined us to be adopted as his sons *through Jesus Christ*, in accordance with his pleasure and will—to the praise of his glorious grace, which he has freely given us *in the Beloved*. . . . In him we were made heirs" (Ephesians 1:3–6 and 13–14; my emphasis). "Heirs" means the heirs of Life, the fulfillment of grace and all benedictions: outside of it there is nothing, but within it lies the infinite joy of the self, the magnificence of living. We are the heirs of Life, however, only in the Arch-Son; it is in him and through him alone that we ourselves become sons, the adopted "children" of Life, made children in its essential Ipseity and through it.

From Paul come shorter but no less incisive passages that unequivocally designate Christ as the transcendental condition of any possible "me," itself understood as a transcendental living "me," a bearer of Life's essence, and which can henceforth be defined in the striking language of the Apostle to the Gentiles as "God's temple." That Christ is the foundation necessary for a person to become God's temple emerges unambiguously: "For no one can lay any foundation other than the one already laid, which is Jesus Christ. . . . Don't you know that you yourselves are God's temple and that God's Spirit lives in you? . . . for God's temple is sacred, and you are that temple" (1 Corinthians 3:11 and 16–17).

In the Letter to the Ephesians, Paul even more concisely refers our transcendental birth to Christ, as the conjoined birth of a "me" and a living person, a "me" bearing Life within it, and thus God's "temple" or "dwelling": "And in him you too are being built together to become a dwelling in which God lives by his Spirit" (2:22). In this way, these transcendental me's that are "created in Christ" (2:10), taking their Self from his Ipseity, finding their foundation in it and being impossible without it, are called "heirs" (3:6). They share in Life's heritage as Sons of God only because they receive this inheritance from the Arch-Son and from his essential Ipseity, from what the sacraments call his flesh. This intermingling, in the transcendental birth of transcendental egos, of Christ's inheritance in God's inheritance, an intermingling in which "the unsearchable riches of Christ" (3:8) can be discerned, is what the Apostle offers as the mystery hidden throughout the generations (3:21).

Paul's brilliant interpretation of Christianity, so in accord with Christianity that it fuses with the definition of it, nevertheless yields to Johannine texts, which no longer constitute an interpretation, truly speaking, so far do they seem to resonate with the very words of Christ. The Pauline intermingling finds a more original expression there, in the form of a triple implication. On the one hand is the immense crowd of the living, and on the other an only Son, as John constantly refers to him. The many sons are in the Son, and this is why they will be saved only by identifying themselves with this Son, who is himself identified with the Father within their reciprocal interiority. It is this dual identification, the eternal birth of the Son and the birth of sons within the Son, that constitutes the foundation of Christian salvation. We have already covered the explanation of this dual identification with respect to the reciprocal interiority of the Father and the Son, but we have yet to cover that of the sons and the Son, and thus of the sons and God. Like the first, the second receives a thoroughgoing elucidation in John.

We turn our attention first to what is proposed in the guise of a parable. It seems a very simple and easily understood parable, about a pen that holds a flock of sheep. Christ appears in the form of a shepherd, or a good pastor, who has an extraordinary rapport with his flock. Naturally, this allegory makes this rapport comprehensible by referring to that which actually exists between a shepherd and his flock: the sheep know his voice and follow him, and, as for the shepherd, "he calls his own sheep by name" (John 10:3). The sort of relations that anyone can observe in rural life are then abruptly torn from their familiar frame, so that they no longer derive from it the principle of their intelligibility. Rather, John situates this principle in the acosmic and atemporal relation that exists between absolute phenomenological Life and the originary Ipseity that it generates in its eternal self-generation and as the condition for that. No longer does any worldly archetype—nor consequently any metaphor—help us to understand what is now at issue: the relation of sons to the Arch-Son, which cannot be understood except in the light of the more original relation of the Arch-Son to absolute Life. The reciprocal phenomenological interiority of Christ and God—this is the key John uses in turn to understand the relation of the sons to the Son, and it is the only key that fits. If we now suppose that the relation among the sons can itself be comprehended only in the light of their relation to the Arch-Son, it is the totality of relations among the living in general—humans, Christ, and God—that is called into question. But this overall questioning of the relations among the living, which takes its principle not from the world but from the Arch-generation of Life, is something we must provisionally set aside in order to concentrate on a single one of its aspects, albeit an essential one: the relation of the sons to the Arch-Son.

But this relation is exactly the theme hidden in John's parable, where Christ appears not only as the shepherd of the flock but also as the gate of the pen where the flock is kept: "I am the gate" (John 10:9). If Christ is the gate of the sheepfold, it is because access to any conceivable transcendental me resides in the original ipseity in which something like a Self and a me is alone possible. A proposition that situates access to the me within an Ipseity older than it is, however, should unnerve anyone capable of perceiving its profound implications, for this proposition applies to any transcendental me, my own as well as that of any other man, to speak here only of sons.

Regarding my own me, the proposition means that I do not have access to myself and thus that I cannot be myself except by passing through the gate of the sheepfold. I am not myself, and cannot be, except by way of Life's original Ipseity. The *pathētik* flesh of this Ipseity, in which Life is joined to itself, is what joins me to myself such that I may be, and can be, this me that I am. Therefore, I cannot join me to myself except through Christ, since he has joined eternal Life to itself, creating in it the first Self. The relation to self that makes any me a me is what makes that me possible; in philosophical language, it is its transcendental condition. Since it draws its possibility from this relation of self to self, the me is itself a transcendental me. And, as the gate through which the sheep pass, Christ is the transcendental condition of these transcendental me's. Never would a transcendental me be given to itself—nor come into itself so as to be capable, in this continual coming-into-itself, of being a Self—if the original phenomenological Ipseity of the First Self of Life did not furnish it with the substance of its own ipseity. Thus, there is no Self, no relation to self, except in Life's first relation to self and in the Self of this first relation. No self is possible that does not have as its phenomenological substance, as its flesh, the phenomenological substance and flesh of the Arch-Son.

This is the meaning of the parable about Christ as the gate of the sheepfold. Christ is not foremost the one who mediates between humans and God. Christ is foremost the one who mediates between each me and itself, the relation to self that allows each "me" to be a me. This relation is not an abstract relation, however, one that can be reduced to a formal conceptualization. As I have said, it has a phenomenological concreteness, a flesh. If the connection to self wherein any conceivable me is constructed is the original Ipseity of the Arch-Son who joins each me to itself, then such a connection is by the same token the grass on which the sheep graze, the grass that nourishes them and allows them to grow. Any me that relates to itself grows by itself, swells with its own content. This growth of the self in any possible me, this self-affection in which the self touches itself at every point of its being, is its flesh, its phenomenological flesh, its living flesh. In my living flesh I am given to myself and thus I am a me—I am myself. But it is not me who has given me to myself; it is not me who joins me to myself. I am not the gate, the gate that opens me to myself, nor am I the grass, the grass that allows my flesh to grow. In my flesh I am given to myself, but I am not my own flesh. My flesh, my living flesh, is Christ's. As the One whom John quotes says: "I am the gate, whoever enters through me . . . will come in and go out, and find pasture" (John 10:9).

But the gate of the sheepfold, which according to this strange parable provides access to the place where the sheep graze—thus founding the transcendental Ipseity from which each me, being connected to itself and growing in itself, draws the possibility of being a me—this gate provides access to all transcendental living me's, not to only one of them, to the one I am myself. Christ is not within me solely as the force that, crushing me against myself, ceaselessly makes me a me. Each me comes into itself only in this way, in the formidable power of this embrace in which it continuously self-affects itself. This is why the gate opens onto all living things: access to each of them is possible only through Christ. We must understand precisely what such a proposition means. If access to any conceivable me presupposes its coming-into-itself thanks to an a priori Ipseity that does not flow from it but from which it flows, then, in effect, to accede to this me means to follow the path of this prior coming-into-itself from which it results—to go through the gate, to cross the incandescent threshold of this original Ipseity in which the fire of Life burns. It is impossible to come to someone, to reach someone, except through Christ, through the original Ipseity that connects that person to himself, making him a Self, the me that he is. It is impossible to touch flesh except through the original Flesh, which in its essential Ipseity gives this flesh the ability to feel itself and experience itself, allows it to be flesh. It is impossible to touch this flesh without touching the other flesh that has made it flesh. It is impossible to strike someone without striking Christ. And it is Christ who says: "Whatever you did for one of the least of these brothers of mine, you did for me" (Matthew 25:40).

This is not a metaphor. It does not mean: whatever you do to one of your brothers, it is as if you did it to me. In Christianity there are no metaphors, nothing of the order "as if." This is because Christianity has to do only with reality, not with the imaginary or with symbols. A me is not "as if" it were a "me." This me that I am is not "as if" it were my own. In that case it would as well be "as if" it were that of another, another me. These imaginary deviations derive from the fevered representations of illness, especially the sickness of life in which each individual turns against himself and no longer wants to be what he is, identifying with another, if necessary, to accomplish this. Far from questioning what is irremediable about a me forever anchored to itself, these imaginary deviations presuppose it. But the me is not anchored in itself forever except by force of the essential Ipseity that, giving it to itself, binding it to itself in its *pathētik* embrace, has made of it this me that it forever is. Thus, before this me ever existed, the original Ipseity of the Arch-Son cast it into itself. Without this Ipseity that preceded it, no me would ever be. So if I have something to do with me, I first have to do with Christ. And if I have to do with another, I first have to do with him in Christ. And everything I do to him, I first do to Christ. The significance of these implications underlying the Christian ethic will emerge later on.

Next, the parable puts forward an extraordinary hypothesis: that it is possible to arrive at any me whatsover, whether my own or another's, without passing through the essential Ipseity from which this me derives its possibility. What such a hypothesis questions, we must note, is nothing less than the whole set of Christianity's fundamental intuitions, those which concern life's self-generation as the generation of an original Ipseity alone in which any transcendental living me is, in its turn, erected as Son of God and "Son within the Son." *Could there be a living person, a me, who dispenses with life, a me without the original Ipseity of a Self within him?*

John's text now experiences its greatest moments of tension as Christ's anger explodes, a scene depicted by Rubens in the Brussels altarpiece. Bounding into the clouds, holding a lightning bolt in his hand and brandishing it over the world, Christ prepares to destroy it: "I tell you the truth, the man who does not enter the sheep pen by the gate, but climbs in by some other way, is a thief and a robber" (John 10:1). And then comes the astonishing declaration: "All who ever came before me were thieves and robbers" (John 10:8). But no one came before Christ: "In the beginning was the Word"; "Before Abraham was born, I am"; "David called him Lord." Let us bear in mind that these are not straightforward statements but phenomenological propositions of an apodictic validity, and, as I have pointed out, whoever perceives what it is they aim to describe is obliged to accept them. That nobody came before Christ means that nobody could have come before him, because no me is possible unless in the Ipseity engendered by absolute Life in experiencing itself in its original self-affection. There is no self-affection that does not bear an ipseity within it, without which it would never come about. Likewise, *me's who accede to themselves and take possession of their own being*, or else those who accede to others and enter into relation with them—at no time do any of them circumvent the ipseity that gives them to themselves, thus allowing them to be me's. Whatever it may say or do, each me has already made use within itself of an ipseity into whose power it did not enter for nothing; it has already appropriated what does not belong to it: it is a thief and a robber. Thieves and robbers are all those who have not bent their knees before what within them has given them to themselves, who have entered the sheepfold without passing under the triumphal Arch, scaling the fence in shame, in the dark of their blindness. Under what conditions could such a theft take place —in what dark night? What sort of blindness occurs that makes it possible? This will be the question we must ask. For the time being, and for the purpose of this phenomenological analysis, it is crucial that we take the measure of Christianity's formidable body of thought about the individual—even if, especially if, from a philosophical viewpoint this contribution has remained largely unexplored.

We will now use the term "Individual," with a capital letter, for the real essence of what common language refers to under this name. This real essence is to be a living transcendental me: this is the real essence of man. The most original feature of Christian thought about the Individual is that it linked the concepts of the Individual and of Life from the outset. What makes such thinking so limitlessly profound is that this relation between Individual and Life is precisely not a relation in the ordinary sense, that is, some sort of link between two separate terms each of which can exist without the other. Nor is it a "dialectic" relation, as defined by modern thought: a relation between two terms in which the one could not exist without the other, since each can exist only in their conjoined condition, in their "syn-thesis." The dialectic relation leaves undetermined the phenomenological essence in which this relation is produced; but soon thereafter it tacitly interprets this essence in a phenomenological way as the truth of the world, wherein this relation is manifested, along with the terms between which it is established.

The relation between Individual and Life in Christianity is a relation that takes place in Life and proceeds from it, being nothing other than Life's own movement. This movement is that by which Life, constantly coming into itself in its experiencing of itself and thus in its "living," constantly engenders itself by engendering within it the Ipseity without which it would not be possible for this living to experience itself. The relation of the Individual and Life is thus identified with the process of Life's self-generation as the generation of the Arch-Son—with the relation of reciprocal interiority between Father and Son, the primordial relation situated at the heart of Christianity, which we have already examined at length. From this relation of reciprocal interiority between Life and Individual—between Life and the Arch-individual, we should say—the concepts of Life and Individual emerge turned upside down. This overturning acts retrospectively on everything that preceded Christianity, and acts prospectively on everything that will come after it. To act here means to render obsolete, to subvert. Let us consider in succession how Christianity overturns first the concept of life and then that of the individual—it being understood that it is not possible to consider them separately and that it is precisely this impossibility, namely, the originary co-belonging of Life and the Individual, that constitutes one of Christianity's most essential assertions.

As for life, we have had occasion to see how much it has remained a vague concept in the history of Western thought. As long as its definition consists of no more than a simple enumeration of the objective properties that can be discerned in living entities, then life appears as a force whose status is so uncertain that modern science has had no choice but simply to eliminate it. Within philosophy, particularly prior to the developments in twentieth-century biology, the concept of life finds itself in an analogous situation. Other than as the objective properties of living organisms, life appears as an obscure entity, the only difference in this case being that it could be asserted and gradually become the theme of speculative philosophy, instead of simply being repudiated as in modern science.

Romantic thought offers the prime example of a conception of life whose prestige largely rests on the indeterminate character of its subject. The only determination of this indeterminate entity called life derives precisely from the fact that it is thought of independently from the individual, being considered as a force superior to that individual. Life thus appears as an impersonal and anonymous power and, because it excludes the singularity of the individual, as "universal." Inasmuch as it is universal, life is ready to assume the role of a principle—the principle of a global explanation of all phenomena, the principle underlying the world. Universal life is not only superior to the individual but foreign and therefore indifferent to it as well. It is an impersonal flux that submerges what it encounters and is therefore foreign to all it collects, brings along, or sets in motion. "It is a matter of indifference to this stream of life," says Hegel, "what sort of mills it drives."[2]

The separation of Life and the Individual reveals its decisive and devastating consequences as soon as the Individual is returned to his proper essence, the ipseity without which no Individual would be possible. During our initial discussion of life (in Chapter 3), we saw that life's coming to the forefront in Schopenhauer's revolutionary philosophy resulted ultimately in its abasement. Not acknowledged in its own phenomenality, but rather deprived of it, finding itself bound up with representation, that is to say, with the world, life became no more than a blind force. But one reason for this incapacity to think of life as Truth and, moreover, as its original essence is now plain to us: the separation of Life and Individual. A life without the individual in it is a life without ipseity—without Self; it is a life that does not experience itself and that finds it impossible to do so, a life deprived of the essence of living, deprived of its own essence—a life deprived of life, foreign to life. But if the concept of life is to be reserved for designating this absurd entity of a life foreign to the essence of life, a life that does not experience itself, it is only on one condition: that, in one master stroke, this entity is set up as reality and, what's more, as the principle of any reality. A life that does not experience itself is an unconscious life. The concept of unconscious life does not result solely from the opposition between life and the world's truth but must be understood more rigorously as the phenomenological expression of the concept of a life deprived of ipseity, incapable of experiencing itself, foreign to the individual—the concept of an anonymous life.

It is the concept of a Life separate from the Individual that has furnished romanticism with its major themes. It is not that romanticism eliminates the individual from the start. On the contrary, the individual is taken as the point of departure—as a probability, appearance, to be more precise. Romanticism aims at the dissolution of this somewhat provisional individual in a higher reality, in the flow of the boundless river that is universal life. Only by bursting the bounds of his individuality would the individual be able to rejoin the impersonal depth of reality as a whole and fuse with it. The elimination of the individual's individuality, and thus of the individual himself: this is what is proposed, in a variety of conceptual ways, as the condition of salvation.

The profound achievement of the Christian intuition is to shed light on the inanity of these conceptions. The individual can be identified with universal life only on the condition that an essential Ipseity does not disappear but is maintained—in the individual as well as in life itself. Failing that, far from being able to unite with universal life, the individual would be annihilated. Meanwhile, Life can be Life only on the condition that it bears within itself this Ipseity as old as it is. Such is the profound insight of Christianity: transcendental Ipseity as the condition of the Individual as well as of Life. The former is not possible without the latter, any more than the latter is possible without the former's Ipseity. But this crucial connection was not established by Christianity with regard to any particular individual or any particular life. It was grasped from the beginning, in the first dazzling bolt of Life, there where Life self-engenders itself in its essential Ipseity.

To understand the Individual on the basis of the originary co-belonging of Life and Ipseity is to propose an entirely new concept. The individual, individuality, the principle that individualizes and so grounds individuality—all are issues that philosophy has perennially posed. As with any fundamental question, that of individuality arises against the backdrop of a phenomenological horizon of questioning that, consciously or not, determines the answer. The radical originality of Christianity is to have viewed the individual within Life's Truth, whereas traditional thought has never viewed him other than in the world's. Thus, the problem of the individual was not so much misunderstood but was more often the object of complex and explicit problematics. Since the essence of the Individual resides in his Ipseity, which is only realized within Life's self-realization, then any thinking about the individual that tries to grasp him on the basis of the world's truth must inevitably meet with failure.

Let us be content here with a brief return to Schopenhauer. For him, the problem of individuality plays a decisive role because, conceiving as he does of life as an anonymous and unconscious life—unconscious because anonymous, because it is deprived of individuality and the individual—he must at least offer a specific theory of life. Schopenhauer had no idea of the traditional Ipseity in which life's self-givenness and thus its originary revelation are accomplished. Nor did Western philosophy as a whole. Consequently, individuality could be understood only in the light of the sole kind of phenomenality that was known, that of representation or, if you prefer, of the world. In other words, Schopenhauer could only take up the standard interpretation of individuality, formulating it in accordance with the conceptual system and terminology he had just inherited from Kant. His conception of individuality was not elaborated merely in the light of a theory of the world's truth; it coincided with it, being but its application to the problem of the individual or, rather, a reformulation of this problem.

The individuality of what is posed as "individual" applies to all that manifests itself in the world, whatever it may be, and consequently to anything whatsoever. What individualizes something showing itself in the world is that it appears at this point in space, at this moment in time. Thus, two totally identical objects still differ by reason of the different places they occupy. And two sounds similar in their aural qualities—in their pitch, their intensity, their timber—even two notes that are ultimately identical by virtue of the likeness of their properties, would still differ by the fact that they are sounded at two different moments in time. In the final instance, it is not the properties of things that individualize them, since these properties could be identical and the things still be different. What individualizes, the principle of individuation, is space and time. But space and time are ways of showing. In Kant, space and time are specifically a priori forms of intuition, that is to say, ways of appearing and making appear that together constitute the way of appearing and of making appear that is the world. The principle that confers on each thing its individuality, and thus differentiates it from all others, is the appearing of the world, its truth.

This is true for people as well as for things. What individualizes a person, what makes him this individual and not another one, is the place he occupies in the world, the moment at which he occurs in the time of this world and in its history. And each of his acts, each grasping motion of his hand, and likewise each of his thoughts, receives from the position it occupies in time a mark that individualizes it absolutely—making it this one or that, different from any other. We now see the absurdity of any thought that reduces the essence of truth to the world's. Inasmuch as the principle that individualizes is identified with the emergence of this world, a person's individuality is identical with that of every entity shown in this world and cannot be understood otherwise—other than in the same way as that of any being whatsoever, whether a historical event, a tool, or a simple "thing." Personal individuality is not understood in any other way, and cannot be, because the principle that individualizes is the same in all cases.

Here we should debunk the so-called unity of the principle that individualizes. This unity is impossible if the phenomenological principle as such refers back to the essence of phenomenality and of truth—or, more precisely, to the major antinomy into which phenomenality divides according to the two modes of phenomenalization, that of the world's truth and that of Life's Truth. What individualizes something like the Individual that each of us is, different from every other—each "me" and each transcendental ego forever distinct and irreplaceable—is not found in the world at all. The individuality of the Individual has nothing to do with that of a being, which in any case does not exist, never resulting from anything other than the anthropomorphic projection of that which finds its condition in the unique essence of individuality. This is ultimately why the principle that individualizes is as unique as each being that it leads into the condition that is its own. A being has no individuality but only an external spatio-temporal designation that makes possible a subsequent parametric determination. There is no Individuality except the Individual. The individuality of the Individual never exists except as its ipseity. There is Ipseity only in life. But Ipseity is not found in life like grass in a field or a stone in the road. Ipseity belongs to the essence of Life and to its phenomenality as well. It is born in the process of life's phenomenalization, in the process of its *pathētik* self-affection, and as the very mode in which that self-affecting comes about. Ipseity belongs to the transcendental Arch-Son and exists only in him, as what life necessarily engenders by engendering itself. Ipseity is with life from the first; it belongs to the first birth. It is contained in this Arch-birth, makes it possible, is only intelligible within its phenomenology. Ipseity is the Logos of Life, that in which and as which Life reveals itself by revealing itself to itself. Ipseity is there in the beginning and comes before any transcendental "me," before any Individual. Before Abraham. But all Individuals proceed from this Ipseity and are possible only within it, in this Ipseity that is prior to the world, in this Ipseity as old as life, eternal as life. If by man we usually mean the empirical individual, one whose individuality relates to the world's categories—space, time, causality—in short, if a man is a being of the world intelligible in the truth of the world, then we must come to terms with him: this man is not an Ipseity, he bears within him no Self, no me. The empirical individual is not an Individual and cannot be. And a man who is not an Individual and who is not a Self is not a man. *The man of the world is merely an optical illusion. "Man" does not exist.*

The collapse of any worldly conception of a man restores to the initially disconcerting theses of Christianity's radical phenomenology of life their depthless profundity. In effect, here is a man who can be a man—who is an Individual, a Self, a me—only in Christ, in the original Ipseity co-engendered by Life in its self-engendering. This understanding of man as the Son of Life within the Arch-Son and within the original Ipseity of this Life renders obsolete, and even somewhat ridiculous, the conception of man proper to modern objectivist ideology, whether that of common sense or of scientism, with the former largely perverted by the latter.

How far the essential and originary connection between Ipseity and Life extends is something that John's parable, in which Christ declares he is the gate of the sheepfold, allows us to understand. In the first place, Ipseity is born in life; it is by being cast into itself that life generates the Ipseity in which, embracing itself, it comes into itself. But an extraordinary reversal takes place when Christ, identifying himself with the gate that gives access to the sheep, presents himself as the one who enables life to nourish itself, to feed on itself, to grow and enlarge the self and thus to be living: "I am the gate; whoever enters through me . . . will come in and go out, and find pasture." The reversal follows: Christ no longer as engendered in life but as the one who gives life. No longer as the Son—even if he is indeed the First, the Arch-Son. Nor as a living being—even if he is indeed the First, the First Living Being. Nor as a living being who presupposes life and is possible only on the basis of it, but now as the One who, superior here to life in a way, has power over it, the power to give it and thus to engender it. This generation is, unquestionably, no longer formulated in terms of the transmission of Life to the Living, but in some fashion from the Living to Life. And thus, after Christ calls himself the gate, come the most astonishing words of the parable: "I have come that they may have life" (John 10:10).

In what sense, and how, does Christ give Life? In the sense that no living would be able able to acquire Life had Life not been transmitted to it as Life that had already received into itself the form of Ipseity and been marked with its indelible seal. Only a Life of this kind, a Life originally ipseized, is able to make living the livings that we are—livings who are transcendental me's capable of growing in their own flesh, of expanding at each moment in their being, in this Self that they received at the same time as Life. Only one who has passed under the triumphal Arch of Arch-Ipseity can come and go out and find pasture, be one of those sheep grazing in the fold.

The transcendental birth of the living here explicitly receives its precise characterization: to be, without doubt, a Living in Life and only through it. Life makes room for any conceivable living. It contains a priori in its essence the vast multitude of all those whom it can call to life: "In my Father's house are many rooms" (John 14:2). But each of these rooms is similar to the enclosure where the sheep graze in that entry to each of them is impossible except through the Arch of Arch-Ipseity. Ipseized Life in the Arch-Ipseity of the Arch-Son prepares a place in such a way that a place is ready for every conceivable living as a living me—as coming into itself into the Ipseity of this me, and that because it is living from a Life come into itself in the original Ipseity of the First Living. "I am going there to prepare a place for you. And if I go and prepare a place for you, I will come back and take you to be with me that you also may be where I am" (John 14:2–3). Thus, there is no place for a living in life unless life has previously been laid down within it as an Ipseity in which only the living who draws life from this ipseized life is henceforth possible as a living me. Ultimately, there is a place somewhere only for such a me.

The parable leads beyond itself. It lets us hear words that speak without parable, prior to any parable, words that take hold of and gather together the crucial tautologies of Christianity: "I am the way and the truth and the life" [in French: C'est Moi la Voie, la Vérité, et la Vie; or in a more literal English: It's me the Way, the Truth, and the Life] (John 14:6). The identity of the four terms is posed: I, or rather Me=Way=Truth=Life [*Moi= Voie=Verité=Vie*]. The final identity, Truth=Life, is something we have established at length: it is the fundamental thesis of a phenomenology of life. According to this phenomenology, phenomenality is originally phenomenalized in a *pathētik* self-affection that defines the only conceivable form of self-revelation, the self-revelation of which the essence of life consists. So Life—and not the opening of a world into the ek-stasy of "outsideness"— constitutes the original Truth, the original phenomenality. Truth=Life.

The second term of the tautological sequence—the Way—can be related to the third and fourth terms and to the identity established between them, or to the first term: I. In relation to the third term—Truth—the Way expresses a general thesis of phenomenology, that the means of access to something consists in the manifestation of that thing. That is, more generally, it is the phenomenality of a phenomenon that constitutes the means of access to this phenomenon. This decisive thesis of phenomenology remains entirely without meaning, however, as long as we do not know what phenomenality consists of, or, more precisely, the way in which it is phenomenalized. Indeed, the study of the way in which phenomenality is phenomenalized ought to be the very theme of phenomenology, its primary and most essential task. Even when it believed itself devoted to this task, phenomenology failed utterly. Duped by the presupposition that rules Western philosophy, phenomenology merely adopted that philosophy, notably by way of classical thought, and therefore interpreted the phenomenality of the phenomenon as the world's. Hence, saying that the Way is the Truth means saying that *all to which we can accede shows itself to us in the world*, in a manifestation that is the very Truth of the world. But when, in revolutionary fashion, Christianity interprets truth as Life (this is, of course, a metatemporal and metahistorical revolution), then the Way that leads, that clears the way, is precisely Life. It is Life that is the Way, a Way totally different from the world's, one that leads to something totally different from what manifests itself in the world. To what does the Way lead when it is Life? It leads to Life. This Way is nothing but Life itself, inasmuch as Life self-reveals itself in the self-affection that constitutes its own phenomenality—its phenomenological substance, its flesh, the flesh of all that is living.

And now, relating the second term to the first, the statement reads: "I am the Way" ("*C'est Moi la Voie*"). I=Way. This fundamental identity has no meaning unless it is related to the two other tautologies contained in the sentence—and so to two conditions. The first is that the Way is constituted by the Truth, which it assuredly is, according to the most general thesis of phenomenology. But the second condition, and final tautology, is decisive: it is that the Truth is constituted by Life. If it were constituted by the world, as it is according to traditional philosophy and even according to popular belief, then the world would constitute the way, the means of access, to all that can be shown to us. But if that were the case, there would for us be neither Life nor I (nor, for that matter, any truth, nor any world—although this is not the place to establish that).

The question is how this I can be the Way when the Way that leads to Life is life itself, its self-revelation. But remember that this I that is the Way is not just any transcendental me, anyone among us. This I (*Moi*) is that of the Arch-Son, and he alone is the Way. What is the essence of this Way that is the Arch-Son—to what does it lead? Its essence is the original transcendental Ipseity generated by Life in its self-generation. Thus *it is the Way that leads to life itself*, the Father's self-embrace as his embrace of the Son and as the Son's embrace of his Father. We have already discussed this relation of reciprocal interiority, but that is not what we are concerned with here. The sentence we are studying is very obviously addressed to people. It is to them that Christ says: "I am the Way." It is for them that he is the Way, *the Way that leads them to life*, as we have seen. Life does not come to them, does not come into them to make them living people, except insofar as life has made itself Ipseity in the Arch-Son. It is not a savage, anonymous, unconscious life—which in fact does not and could not exist in this form—that can be transmitted to each living person. Rather, it is a life that, having embraced itself in its original Ipseity, can then give itself as a life that is phenomenologically effective, a life bearing its ipseity to all livings, who, on account of this ipseized life, and only in this way, will be able to live as a living "me." Thus the Way that leads the livings to Life is this life rendered living in its original Ipseity, the Life of the Arch-Son. It is this life in its original Ipseity that is referred to in the sentence as "I."

However, the Arch-Son is not merely the Way that leads the living to Life. Truly speaking, he is not this Way except insofar as he is and was the Way in another, still more original sense. Before leading the living to Life, he led Life to the living, and it is only because he has led Life to the living that he has led them to Life. How has Christ led Life to the living, such that he is able to utter the most extraordinary, seemingly crazy, sentence, one in which he more or less positions himself before Life: "I have come that they may have life"? He led Life to the living *by first leading it to itself in him*, in and through his essential Ipseity—and then by making a gift of this ipseity to any living being so that, within that ipseity, each of them becomes possible as a living Self. The generation of the Arch-Son in the self-generation of absolute Life makes possible the generation of any conceivable living. It is in this way that Christ is the Way: because, having led Life to each living, he finds himself, by the same token, the one who leads each living to Life.

In the parable, Christ refers to himself as the gate of the sheepfold. We have called this gate a triumphal Arch, because it is the Way that leads to Life. One does not pass under this Arch on two occasions. It is not that there are two trajectories, one leading from Life to the livings—since Life affects itself in an essential Ipseity in which it now engenders each living— and the other leading from each living to Life—since in the Self that makes it living and in the original ipseity of this Self, it is in fact Life that affects itself. These two trajectories are congruent: there is but a single gate, a single Arch, a unique Rapture in which Life blazes forth. The generation of the Arch-Son in the self-generation of absolute Life inhabits the coming-into-itself of each living person in such a way that the coming-into-itself of each person bears within it the generation of the Arch-Son in the self-generation of absolute Life and is possible only in this way.

But the intersection of these two pathways under the Arch where Life radiates—the pathway that leads from Life to the living and the one that leads the living to Life—does not produce a reciprocity between these two terms, between Life and the living. Reciprocity involves only the relation of interiority between absolute Life and the Arch-Son, inasmuch as the Ipseity in which God eternally embraces himself is also that of the Arch-Son who finds himself generated in this way. The relation between the Ipseity of absolute Life and the me of each living implies no reciprocity of this kind: the path cannot be traveled in both directions. God could just as well live eternally in his Son and the latter in his Father without any other living ever coming to Life. On the contrary, the coming of any other living to Life, the transcendental birth of any me, implies Ipseity and thus the generation of the Arch-Son in absolute Life.

This asymmetry marks the infinite distance that separates Christ from other people. It is this distance, moreover, that Christ constantly re-calls to them behind each of his statements—in effect, throughout the Gospels. The asymmetry does not, however, admit its real meaning at first sight. Christ seems to contrast himself with people understood as natural Beings. The natural filiation that is appropriate to them and that situates them in the world's time according to the order of generations—Joseph, son of Heli, son of Matthat, son of Amos—is abruptly broken off and re-jected by Christ as far as he himself is concerned, as we have explained at some length. "Before . . . Abraham . . . I." Lord of David. It is as the Arch-Son engendered before the creation of the world that Christ, it seems, sharply separates himself from people who "come into the world" and thus appear in the world alone. But Christianity teaches that when a man is in turn understood as Son and his essence is thus torn from the world's truth and reinterpreted as Life's, then the opposition between Christ and people can no longer rest on the natural character of people. They are, in fact, no longer natural beings; they no longer belong to the world and are no longer manifested in it. *Natural man is ruled out from the very moment when his condition as Son is posited.* It is thus on the plane of life itself that the abyss separating Christ from people opens up, and it must likewise be under-stood on this plane. This is what the analysis of man as son within the Son has established. Something like a living "me," a transcendental living me, as we have called it, exists only in, and through, the original Ipseity of abso-lute Life. "You did not choose me, but I chose you" (John 15:16)—or, as John will formulate it in his First Epistle: "We love because He first loved us" (4:19). That Life does not come to any living being except through the original Ipseity in which Life is given to itself is something the context makes equally clear: "Then the Father will give you whatever you ask in my name" (John 15:16).

Thus, to the reversibility of Life and its Ipseity—of Father and Son, in their reciprocal interiority—is starkly contrasted the irreversibility of the relation of the Arch-Son with all those who receive from him and his original Ipseity the possibility of their Self and their me. This irreversibility, however, is not something negative. Instead, it carries within itself an extraordinary event, the marvel of marvels. It is not merely that in this Arch-Ipseity of Life there occurs the potential for each living to become a living transcendental me. What's more, thanks to this ipseity in which a living relates to itself, touches every point of its Being, experiences itself and enjoys itself, this living is not merely a me but is irreducible to any other, experiencing what it experiences and feeling what it feels, unlike any other—not because what this "me" experiences is different from what another experiences, or because what it feels is different from what another feels, but simply because it is the one experiencing it and feeling it. In the bosom of the single and same Life, the single and same Ipseity, it is irreducibly different. This is because *such is the essence of the Arch-Ipseity generated in absolute Life that, giving to every thing whatever it is to which Life is given in order to experience itself, Life makes that thing, in the phenomenological realization of experiencing itself, into a Self that is absolutely singular and different from any other.*

Thus, the generation of the Arch-Son in the self-generation of absolute Life is to some extent reproduced in each transcendental birth, since therein a single and same Life, experiencing itself in and by means of its original Ipseity, gives birth to howsoever many *moi's* that are irreducibly different and new—to howsoever many Individuals, none of whom is even remotely similar to any other, none of whom has been preceded by an Individual who could be compared to him in some way, none of whom will be followed by another who might encroach even slightly on, or cast doubt on, his irreducibility to and difference from any other Individual— the one who is this singular Self, forever different, forever new.[3]

No worldly cause can explain this Ipseity of a Self that is radically individualized in the act by which Ipseity joins it to itself and makes it a Self. This is because this Ipseity does not itself proceed from a world, being possible nowhere except in Life and in its essence. Life thus produces in its Ipseity the infinity of all livings in such a way that each is itself irrevocably itself from the moment it becomes living, from its very birth. It is the Self's coming-into-itself in the Ipseity generated in the self-generation of Life that makes it a singular and incomparable Self. Because in its Ipseity that is prior to the world Life has prepared this "space" for Individuals who are irreducibly singular and new, one may read, in the absolute Here managed by this Ipseity of Life, what the confused hero of Kafka's *Amerika* deciphers on the poster of the Grand Theater of Oklahoma: "Everyone is welcome! . . . Our Theater can find employment for everyone, a place for everyone!"[4] Each of these places is marked by a white stone, the one that the Apocalypse destines for the conqueror, "a white stone with a new name written on it, known only to him who receives it" (Revelation 2:17). Here are those "whose names are in the book of life" (Philippians 4:3).

That in his Arch-Ipseity the Arch-Son transmits Life to all possible livings—possible inasmuch as it is not only a living but a Self unlike any other, one who exists as something absolutely new, whom nothing has preceded or will replace—is something that explains the very particular place occupied by Christ in the New Testament. In fact, he awards this place to himself at the expense of, if not out of contempt for, everybody else. For someone who listens to him with sufficient detachment, it appears that the Word of Christ is by no means limited to moral teaching. Precepts and prescriptions do not seem to be worthwhile in themselves, or to define what is at all events essential. A purpose overtakes them, moving toward what alone matters. To the ethical question, What should I do? comes a perplexing answer: "Then they asked him, 'What must we do to do the works God requires?' Jesus answered: 'The work of God is this: to believe in the one he has sent'" (John 6:28–29). But as we have demonstrated, the question soon bounces back. To believe in the one who sent him is to believe that the one who is speaking is precisely the one who has been sent, that Jesus is the Messiah, the Christ. "What miraculous sign then will you give that we may see it and believe you? What will you do?" (John 6:30). Once Moses' giving of manna has been set aside as purely symbolic, the true work, the miracle, receives its true name: the giving of life in its phenomenological flesh, the "bread of life." It is finally a matter of knowing what this bread is: "'Sir,' they said, 'from now on give us this bread.' Then Jesus declared, 'I am the bread of life'" (6:34–35). The reason behind the immeasurable and blatant egocentrism that pervades the New Testament is at last clear. It is because Life is given to each in the Ipseity of the Arch-Son that no one matters other than That One. Once again, the commentary of the Apostle Paul hits home: "For I resolved to know nothing while I was with you except Jesus Christ" (1 Corinthians 2:2).

The interpretation of man as "Son of God," or, more precisely, as "Son within the Son," has many weighty implications. But before we pursue them, there is one question that cannot be deferred. If men are really Sons of God within Christ, how can we explain that so few of them know this and remember it? If they bear within them this divine Life in all its immensity—because there is no other Life but that, and the living can only bow before its profusion—how can we understand why they are so unhappy? In the end, it is not the tribulations visited upon them by the world that oppress them; rather, it is with themselves that they are so discontented. It is their own incapacity to achieve their desires and plans, it is their hesitations, their weakness and lack of courage, that provoke the deep malaise that accompanies them throughout their miserable existence. If they never tire of attributing the cause of their failure to circumstances or to others, it is only to fool themselves and to forget that the real cause lies within themselves. As Kierkegaard puts it: "Consequently he does not despair because he did not get to be Caesar but despairs over himself because he did not get to be Caesar."[5] But how can one despair of this me if it is nothing less than the coming into us of God within Christ? Such despair is possible only if, one way or another, man has forgotten the splendor of his initial condition, his condition as Son of God—his condition as "Son within the Son."

It is this forgetting that we must now attempt to understand.

Forgetting the Condition of Son:
"Me, I" / "Me, Ego"

Speaking of ourselves on any subject, and therefore constantly, we say "I," "me." People spontaneously using the personal pronoun, whether in the nominative or accusative case, are scarcely concerned with why they refer to themselves consistently in this way, nor with what knowledge allows them to do so. But *such knowledge must really exist somewhere*, since if people did not know that there is a "me," and more precisely this particular "me," how could they think of themselves and present themselves as such? In a sense, this knowledge is so common that it appears almost ridiculous to speak of it. Why do you say "me" in speaking of yourself, and what do you have in mind when you say that and think of yourself? As trivial as this question may be, put like this, no one is capable of answering it. No doubt this is why it is dismissed with a shrug. As for philosophers, they know hardly any more. Their remarks on this subject—we cannot call them analyses—appear brief and precarious, if not derisory. What is striking in those rare texts in which the question of "me" is directly tackled is that this "me" and the knowledge one has of it are always purely and simply presupposed. But this presupposition is so lacking in foundation that the existence of this "me" might just as well be denied; or else the knowledge one has of it, and hence the knowledge it has of itself, are contested and considered uncertain, if not purely fallacious. In truth, philosophy knows nothing about what concerns the me and the problems linked to it. We shall see why.

Of this singular me that I am, that each person is found to be, the only knowledge humanity possesses does not in fact derive from itself. It is not man who knows that he is a me, nor in general what a me is; it is not man who knows what makes him a man. This knowledge is possessed by Life and Life alone. On the plane of thought, it is paradoxically Christianity that brings it. Among religious beliefs more than two thousand years old, not to mention superstitions, Christianity is today the only belief that instructs man about himself. At the same time, the laborious conceptual system of philosophies, on the one hand, and research in the positive sciences (with their complex and elaborate methodologies), on the other, can only turn man aside from what he truly is, to the point that he loses any notion of what he is and, by the same token, all confidence in himself, all form of certainty. Confidence and certainty have been replaced by dismay and despair. The more the positive sciences develop and boast of their epistemological breaks, their revolutionary problematics and deconstructions of all kinds, the less man has any idea of what he is. This is because what makes him a man—specifically, *the fact of being a me*—is precisely what has become totally unintelligible to thinkers and scholars these days.

How man is a me and first of all a self, more precisely this self and this me that he is—unlike and to the exclusion of any other—is what the Christian thesis of man as Son has established: a Son generated in absolute phenomenological Life, which is that of God himself. It is because modern thought and science, notably biology, know nothing of this transcendental Life—the only Life that exists—that they know nothing of man's me either. People do know it if, despite the terrorist expertise that smothers them, and by means of which attempts are made to condition their minds from schooldays onward, they continue to say "I," "me." But they no longer know *why* they say it; they would lower their eyes if by chance one of these experts or enlightened psychologists were to ask them—which is unlikely, moreover, since these scholars have no idea themselves. The possibility of saying "me," "I"—more radically, the possibility that there exists something like a "me" and an "I," a living "me" and "I" who are always a particular one, mine or yours—this possibility is only intelligible within absolute phenomenological Life, in the Ipseity of which is engendered any conceivable Self and me. This is Christianity's thesis about man: that he is a man only insofar as he is a Son, a Son of Life, that is, of God.

But what we now have to understand is no longer the generation of this me in the Life of God, but rather why man has lost the notion of his true essence: in Plotinus's phrase, *why the sons no longer know they are sons.* Does the origin of this ignorance of man about himself lie in some perverse ideology or does it have some deeper reason (of which this ideology is merely one expression among others)? The second hypothesis is the right one. Man's ignorance about his true condition does not issue from an external or transitory cause. Rather, it is rooted in the very process by which life generates in itself the me of all conceivable livings. It is inside this process of life making Ipseity, Self, and me that we should perceive and grasp it. Thus the occultation of the condition of Son coincides apparently paradoxically with the very genesis of this condition. Within the movement of this genesis is hidden that in which, and for which, each person is this ego that he or she is. The birth of the me contains the hidden reason why this me unceasingly forgets this birth, or precisely his condition of Son.

Therefore, the process by which sons are born must be studied more closely to bring to light the remarkable dissociation between two concepts man constantly uses to define himself: "me" and "ego." "Me" and "ego," in effect, are not the same thing, even if classical thought slides from one to the other in the most extreme confusion and without even seeing that in this double designation of the Self, as constant as it is, there is at least one problem. "Me," says the Self generated in the original Ipseity of Life, but it says it in the accusative (not nominative) case. That the singular Self speaks of itself in the first place and must use the accusative precisely translates the fact that it is engendered, not bringing itself into the condition that is its own, not experiencing itself as a Self, and not having this experience of self, except in the eternal self-affection of Life and of its original Ipseity. Because this engendering of the me in Life's self-affection is phenomenological in a radical sense, the coming of the me into itself, which rests on the coming of Life into itself, is lived as basically passive with respect to this primitive coming of Life. We have seen that the me is what self-affects itself, but since this self-affection is imposed on it by Life and is just like that of Life, one could say, more exactly, that the "me" is constantly self-affected. This character of the Self's being self-affected is designated by its being put into the accusative: "me." In the end, "me" signifies this: *for each me, its ipseity does not come from it, but inversely, it comes from its ipseity.*

Here we must follow up on the process of the transcendental birth of the "me" in the Ipseity of absolute Life in order to understand how, by a mutation as decisive as it is imperceptible, this generation of the "me" becomes that of an ego. The "me" is engendered in the self-affecting of absolute Life and experiences itself passively against the background of the original Ipseity of Life, which gives the "me" to itself and makes of it what it is at every moment; therefore this "me" finds itself at the same time much more than what is designated as a "me." Experiencing itself in Life's Ipseity, *it enters into possession of itself at the same time as it enters into possession of each of its powers. Entering into possession of these powers, it is able to exercise them.* A new capacity is conferred on it, no less extraordinary than that of being a "me," even though it is a simple consequence. It is the capacity of the "me" to be in possession of itself, to be one with it and with everything it carries inside, which belongs to it as so many components of its real Being. Among these components are bodily powers: the power to hold, to move, to touch, to strike, to get up, to control its limbs from inside itself, to turn its eyes, etc. There are also powers of the mind: the power to form ideas and images, the power to desire, etc. There is no difference in kind between these sorts of powers: both belong to "me" *because it is a me.* It is in the *pathētik* experience it has of each of these powers that it coincides with them. It is because it coincides with them that it is able to put them into operation and thus to act. To act, to exercise each of the powers that compose its being, is only possible for a "me" that has entered into possession of each of its powers—which can only take place because it has first entered into possession of itself, which in turn can only take place thanks to the *pathētik* proof it has of itself in the original Ipseity of absolute Life. All this is accomplished in the transcendental genesis of the "me." At the end of this genesis, there comes a "me" put into possession of itself and all of its capacities. Then, since it advances armed with all its powers at its disposition, this "me," which has taken hold of itself and of all that it carries within, is an "I."

"I" means "I Can." The proposition "I Can" does not bring any particular property to the essence of "I" but simply defines it. Phenomenological analysis allows us to recognize in the "I" a certain number of concrete powers as we have just done, powers that it is then possible to list and to classify under various headings, such as "powers of the body" or "powers of the mind." But the "I" is by no means the sum of these sorts of powers. Whatever their importance (inasmuch as each of them opens up a new field of experiences—experiences that in the first place are purely interior, those of exercising these powers, and therefore spiritual experiences), however, each is a power only if it is at man's disposition. This is precisely what characterizes and defines the ego: to be in possession of such powers and have them at one's disposal.

If "I" means "I Can"—"I Can" deploy each of the powers that I find in me, because, coinciding with that power and placed inside it in some way, I have it at my disposal and can exercise it whenever I care to and for as often as I want—then an essential distinction is necessary. The relation of the "I" to each of its powers cannot remain in the obscurity and indeterminacy of an identity that has been hastily asserted. Two sorts of powers are at issue—powers not only opposed to each other, but really quite different. On the one hand are those powers we call, for example, holding, moving, feeling, imagining, wanting—which are in effect in our possession, at our disposal. Since the "I" exercises it, each of them is lived by that "I" as its own. There is an incontestable experience that leads the "I" to say, specifically: *I* take, *I* walk, *I* feel, *I* imagine, *I* want, *I* do not want. Each of these powers is at the "I"'s disposal, in its possession, because this "I" coincides with them and can exercise them when and as often as it wants. *This is something over which the "I" has no power whatsoever, which is allocated to it quite apart from its will.* Each power it calls its own (as the very condition of its exercise) is therefore radically opposed to a nonpower. This nonpower is much more decisive than the power that it makes possible: *it is the absolute powerlessness of the "I" with respect to the fact that it finds itself in possession of this power, able to exercise it.* In possession of this power, able to exercise it, the "I" is only an "I" inasmuch as this power is given to it. But this power is only given to it inasmuch as the "I" is given to itself. And the "I" is only given to itself inasmuch as it is a "me," a living transcendental me given to itself in the self-givenness of absolute Life. The self-givenness of Life is, of course, its original Ipseity in the phenomenological effectivity of the singular Self of the First Living.

This is what is said in an abrupt way in New Testament texts, and specifically by Christ himself, the First Self of whom we have just spoken: "Apart from me you can do nothing" (John 15:5). The blinding significance here is that the possibility of any conceivable power is presented not as residing in a greater power, an infinite power like that of an all-powerful Being—contrasted with the limited powers and forces belonging to humankind and finite creatures in general. This sort of external and superficial hierarchy, worthy of a natural theology, totally leaves out the decisive intuition of Christianity, which John starkly reaffirms. The source of all power consists in the Self of the Arch-Son, that is, the original Ipseity of absolute Life. It is only the coming into itself of any power whatsoever that allows this power to unite with the self and to act—a coming into itself that is the coming of the me into itself, that is, the coming of Life into itself in the Self of the Arch-Son.

Any power the ego possesses is given to it in the very process by which it is engendered as "me" in the Ipseity of the Arch-Son. This is something that appears no less clearly in the final argument with Pontius Pilate. Faced with an obstinately silent Christ, in order to persuade him to speak and no doubt to defend and save himself, Pilate makes the threat: "Don't you realize I have the power either to free you or to crucify you?" The answer is radical: "You would have no power over me if it were not given to you from above" (John 19:10–11). From these devastating replies emerge once again the decisive arguments of Christianity. Any possibility of power implies that this power is in possession of itself, given to itself—where any self-givenness occurs, in the original Ipseity of Life. The originality of Christianity is demonstrated once more: as we have seen, within it is neither an obscure force, nor an anonymous power, nor unconscious action. This is because force, power, and action cannot be deployed unless previously given to themselves in the self-givenness of absolute Life. Here again Paul goes straight to the crux: "For it is God who works in you to will and to act according to his good purpose" (Philippians 2:13).

We find ourselves at the heart of the Christian theory of the ego. There is no ego but that of the Son, that is to say, a living transcendental "me" generated in absolute phenomenological Life, experiencing itself in the experience of self and thus in the Ipseity of this Life. It is only because such a "me" exists that such an ego is in turn possible, experiencing itself in the experience of the self and of this "me." The ego is not the double of the "me," its exact copy—and, still less, another name for it. The ego adds to the "me" whose ego it is that, given to itself in the experience of self and of this "me," it enters into possession of its own being, as well as the various powers that constitute it, such that it is able to exercise them—when and as it wants. The "me" given to itself in the Ipseity of Life, and only through that Ipseity, has become the center, the source, the home, of a multiplicity of powers, and thus of a multitude of acts that it performs when it pleases. It has gone from passive to active. Whereas previously nothing depended on it because its own condition as living transcendental "me" did not depend on it either, now everything depends on it, because it is a collection of powers and it disposes of these powers freely and unreservedly. This is what "power" means: not the exterior designation of a simple particular power, but the fact of being in its possession, as of a potentiality that resides in you and depends on you as to whether it is acted upon at any moment. And this is also what being "free" means: to be able to utilize at any moment this collection of powers, which constitute your very being. This "me"—generated passively in life but becoming in this generation the center of a multitude of powers that it exercises freely, becoming in the first place one who can exercise them, this fundamental "I Can" so brilliantly described by Maine de Biran—is the ego.

The condition of the ego, when understood as the center of initiative and action, appears paradoxical. On the one hand, the ego's operation of each of its powers is an incontestable fact, and even more than that: a permanent possibility that is only given to it at any moment because it is identified with that possibility, because it is nothing other than the giving to itself of this possibility. Thus this possibility belongs to the ego as its very being. And because this possibility is that of utilizing each of its powers, it is free to do so. All freedom rests on preexisting power and is merely its operation. Because the ego finds itself in possession of this power, it is free. But to be in possession of this power is the reason why it is an ego given to itself in its "me." It is from being a "me" that the ego is an ego, and it is from being an ego that the ego is free. Thus there is no ego that is not free. Arguments that deny the ego's freedom treat it as a worldly entity subject to worldly laws. By that reasoning, humans are only the product of the many determinisms that compose the weft of the objective universe. But nothing of what is shown in the world arises from its appearance or its laws, or could ever have the least relation with what makes the ego an ego, in some way acting on it or determining it. It is the mode of givenness of the ego to itself, and thus its manner of possessing each of its powers and using them, that nullifies the whole set of discourses usually made on the subject—today more than ever.[1]

The ego that is free to exercise each of its powers when it wants to experiences itself as such. It experiences its freedom, or more exactly, this power which is its own to exercise each of the powers given to it. It experiences this power because, let us say, the givenness that granted it each of these powers is none other than its own givenness to itself, the self-givenness constitutive of its Ipseity. Experiencing each of its powers while it exercises it—and in the first place, the power it has of exercising them—the ego now assumes it is their source, their origin. It imagines that it possesses these powers, that they are its own in a radical way—produced by itself, and which it could produce each moment it is exercising them. As somehow the absolute source and origin of the powers that compose its being (the effective and acting being with which it identifies and by which it defines itself), the ego considers itself also the source and origin of this very being.

Thus is born the transcendental illusion of the ego, whereby this ego takes itself as the ground of its Being. To be itself, to be this Self that it is, is something it henceforth considers its own responsibility, as something arising from itself and, in the end, having reference only to itself. To be able, to be able to do, to want, to freely want what it wants (meaning what it can want), is now something the ego attributes to its own power, to its own will. Exercising its power and taking itself as its source, as the ground of its Being, the ego believes it perceives its true condition and so suffers under the similar illusions of forgetting and of falsifying that condition. It forgets Life, which in its Ipseity gives it to itself and at the same time gives it all its powers and capacities; it forgets its condition as Son. It falsifies by taking the givenness of the ego and all its powers to itself as the work of this same ego. In the transcendental illusion, the ego lives the hyperpower of Life— self-generation as self-givenness—as its very own, and transforms the latter into the former.

Paul strikes at the heart of the ego's transcendental illusion: "What do you have that you did not receive? And if you did receive it, why do you boast as though you did not?" (1 Corinthians 4:7). And the Epistle to the Galatians also makes it clear that this is really an illusion: "If anyone thinks he is something when he is nothing, he deceives himself" (6:3). The denunciation of the ego's transcendental illusion uttered in total clarity by Paul restates Christ's own, specifically in the parable related by John that we have already examined—except he used a more violent tone: "Liars, thieves!"[2] For it is not some kind of lie, some distortion of the facts, that is exposed here. It is its own condition that the ego deforms in the very word it uses to enunciate it. *Ego* implies that it is due to itself that the ego does what it does, is what it is. This implication is so immediate that it is produced well before the ego dreams of formulating it, as soon as it experiences itself as the I Can we have discussed. Who, in fact, lifting a weight, does not think that he is the one lifting it; or, taking an object, does not think that his own strength is doing so? Liar! How could he exercise this power if Life had not given it to him along with all his capacities? Liar, and hence a thief, too! Properly speaking, to attribute to yourself what does not belong to you is a theft. And when the theft concerns not a particular object but the very nature of the power that is acting, then the theft is permanent.

Therefore, the first cause of people's forgetting their condition as Sons is the transcendental illusion of the ego. But this first cause immediately leads to the second. The ego's transcendental illusion is not totally illusory, in fact. In carries a portion of "reality" and "truth," which we have to deal with—simply because it is essential. The gift by which Life (self-giving) gives the ego to itself is in reality one with it. Once given to itself, the ego is really in possession of itself and of each of these powers, able to exercise them: it is really free. In making the ego a living person, Life has not made a pseudo-person. It does not take back with one hand what it has given with the other. "If you knew the gift of God!" (John 4:10): this phrase of Christ's means that this gift is that of Life—the extraordinary gift through which a person who by himself would be nothing (particularly not any self) instead, coming into himself in life, rises up in the unpardonable proof and the intoxication of self and thus as a living and as a Self—and simultaneously as one who, plunging into himself through life's transparence, has at his disposal each of the powers put in him by life. I Can—the activation of each of my powers—is the contrary of an illusion, as is the "I am" born of this "I Can." Thus the effectiveness of this "I Can" / "I am" overrides the fact that this living "I can," this living "I am," has come about only thanks to the endless work of Life in it. Thus the positive quality of an indisputable experience constantly masks what makes it possible. "Me, I" —I constantly superimpose myself on my condition as Son, without which there would be neither "me" nor "I," nor any kind of power.

Still, the active power of the ego could not conceal that it is not the source of this power if this source did not constantly conceal itself. This source is the self-givenness of absolute Life that, in giving this ego to itself and in making it an ego, also gives it the disposition and use of its powers. Only that phenomenological status of absolute Life explains the ego's transcendental illusion. It is only because, naturally invisible, radically imma-nent, and never exposing itself in the world's "outside," this Life holds itself entirely within that the ego is ignorant of it, even when it exercises the power life gives it and attributes this power to itself. But with respect to itself, its own being and all its activities, the ego is the first dupe of its illusion. From this results the following situation: the more the ego exercises its power, the more profound the experience it has, in the concreteness of its effort, of effecting this power, the more it attributes this power to itself, and the more it forgets the Life that gave it. Superimposing itself on the transcendental illusion by which the ego lives itself in the exercise of its power as the cause of that power, Life's dissimulation pushes to the limit this ego's forgetting of its most essential possibility: its generation in the original Ipseity consubstantial with Life—the forgetting of its condition as Son.

But another consequence is immediately tied to this: invisible Life's dissimulation within the ego, even when Life is conjoined with it, opens up the whole space of the world and leaves the ego free before the world, and for it. The more hidden Life stays within the ego, the more open and available is the world. The ego throws itself on it, or rather it projects itself toward everything shown in this world, toward all the things, whatever they may be, that have suddenly become the sole object of its preoccupation. Forgetful of its "me," the ego is concerned with the world. Thus an extraordinary situation is created: once it loses sight of its condition as Son, the ego is only interested in what lies outside. Everything shown, the entire realm of the visible, has value in its eyes and merits effort and perseverance. Nothing is desirable except what is accessed in the world's "outside," and the desire to take hold of what it covets must also follow this same path, the one leading outside itself—to "worldly goods."

In truth, even if the ego concentrates its interest on them, making them the constant object of its covetousness, the goods of this world are not considered in themselves and for themselves, but only in relation to itself. It is in their relation to the ego that they arouse interest, and it is for the ego that they become "good" and valued. In the world, there is no value. In the end, it is not the things of this world that the ego is concerned with but rather itself. What it wants is not wealth in itself but to become rich; not power but to become powerful. Not respect or prestige but to be respected and crowned with prestige. Moreover, it is as an ego that the ego is concerned with all that; "as an ego" means as this fundamental I Can that possesses as such the capacity to propel itself toward all these goods and acquire them and, at the extreme, to identify with them and enjoy them.

We are now in the presence of a circle or a system, if it is true that in the daily bustle in which people are constantly preoccupied with this or that, never dropping one preoccupation except for another *ad infinitum*, then it is the ego itself that holds the power to undertake all these activities at the same time as it defines their sole goal. To such a system, of which the ego constitutes the alpha and omega, we can give the name "egoism"—and because it draws its possibility from the ego itself, "transcendental egoism." But with regard to such a system, in which the ego, concerned with this world's goods, is really concerned with itself, how can we say that the ego—living in this way, relating everything to itself and thus only thinking of itself—constantly forgets its own condition, and itself?

The answer is that this relation to self—the background against which the ego relates everything to itself, the world and its goods—assumes the form of Care. To relate to oneself in and through the care of oneself is to throw oneself forward toward oneself, project oneself ahead, open toward oneself a path that is "outside oneself," that is "outside" the world. It is to be projected toward an exterior self, a self that is to-come and unreal: unreal not because the exterior self is still to-come, in the mode of not-yet, but because it is exhibited in the world's truth, where there is no Life, no Ipseity, and consequently no possible Self.

Thus two radically different ways for the ego to relate to itself, two different modes of this relation, confront each other. One is *the relation to itself of the ego in care for itself*, in which the ego, throwing itself outside itself toward itself, never reaches anything but a phantom, some possibility (to become rich, powerful, prestigious) it gives itself as a task "to realize," but which is precisely never real, as long as it relates to this task in Care. The other is *the relation to itself of the ego in life*, a relation generated in the original Ipseity of Life and only possible within it. The ego's relation to itself in Being-careful-of itself is not only radically opposed to the relation to itself of the ego in Life's Ipseity, but in fact they are mutually exclusive. The relation to itself of the ego in Life's Ipseity determines the real Self, the absolutely immanent Self, grasped in the *pathētik* embrace of Life and constituted by it, which never leaves that embrace yet cannot be observed by the eye. On the contrary, the relation to self of the ego in care of itself in the world liberates only a ghostly and unreal Self. It constantly occupies the stage, lies behind all projects; all projects bring it back to itself. Whether occupied with its own business or another's, with things, or directly with itself, this ego never really stops being occupied with its own self. But because the true Self that ultimately makes this ego possible, which gives it to itself in Life's Ipseity, never appears in the foreground but keeps itself outside the performance, the ego is not concerned with it. It is due not to simple distraction or some sort of futility, but for a more profound reason that it is impossible for the ego to care for its true Self. This reason lies in the very structure of the Care projected into this "outsideness" where no real Self ever lies. Due to the transcendental system of egoism, in which, in its bustling activity, the ego never stops relating to itself in the world, the Self generated in Life is absent in principle. Thus arises the mutual exclusion upon which Christian ethics will be founded. The more the ego is concerned with itself, the more its true essence escapes it. The more it thinks of itself, the more it forgets its condition of Son.

This crucial situation results in the passionate polemic Christianity directs against Care. That people have to be concerned with goods necessary to their existence is certainly not what Christ condemns. The very short prayer to God in which he formulates the requests speaks of "daily bread" (a request that sounds less archaic than was asserted not so long ago). How else can you celebrate life except by putting first the most elementary needs? The critique of Care cannot be understood unless you refer to the fundamental presupposition of Christianity concerning Truth. Refusing to define humankind by Care means eliminating the reduction of phenomenality to that of this world, and consequently, eliminating the definition of humankind as Being-in-the-world. That man is not primarily Care and does not have to behave as such results directly from the argument that, as Son, he has his essence in Life. In Life there is no world whatever, no place for care, which always projects itself "outside" and is never preoccupied except with what is other, is preoccupied with itself only as something other. "The rose [a metaphor for life] has no care of itself," goes a famous line by Angelus Silesius.[3] It has no care of itself because it never relates to itself in the distancing of a world, in the "outside" of seeing. "The rose has no care of itself nor does it desire to be seen," the text continues. Living in conformity with its essence of Life has removed in principle the very possibility of Concern, as well as everything Concern is concerned with.

This correlation between the setting aside of Care and the definition of man as Son is expressed in Christianity's opposition between two kinds of men. On the one hand, there is the *man of the world*, who is only concerned with the world and can only be so against the background of his previously conceived essence as being-in-the-world. On the other hand, there is the *man who is not of the world* because, Son of Life, he finds himself originarily determined in himself by Life's a-cosmic character. The opposition between these two men primarily relates not to a difference in behavior, but to the phenomenological structures to which they refer. It is not people's situations and gestures that bring them to hate those who act otherwise. It is their very nature—belonging to the world in Concern—that makes them rebel against the Sons of Life, the ones who demand from Life and it alone the principle of their actions, as what they feel and experience. "And the world has hated them, for they are not of the world any more than I am of the world" (John 17:14).

The opposition between belonging-to-the-world and belonging-to-Life is so essential that Scripture, too, is determined by it—precisely because, as we have seen, it always has a phenomenological basis. "They are from the world and therefore speak from the viewpoint of the world, and the world listens to them. We are from God, and whoever knows God listens to us, but whoever is not from God does not listen to us" (1 John 4:5–6). Once again, Paul makes this essential contrast reverberate: "Set your minds on things above, not on earthly things," thus preserving the phenomenological motivation by which life, even that of a person, only comes about in Life, whereas in the world's "outside itself," into which Care throws itself, humans encounter only death. "For you died, and your life is now hidden with Christ in God" (Colossians 3:2 and 3). Then there is his imposing declaration to the Galatians, which explicitly links the condemnation of Care to the phenomenalization of the world and its concrete temporal modes: "You are observing special days and months and seasons and years! I fear for you, that somehow I have wasted my efforts on you" (4:10–11).

Because Care is care for the world, it finds that its capacity to give what it cares for has been dislocated. What it gives is suppressed in the very movement by which it cares for it. Care gives something only in destroying it, in the form of what is not yet or no longer and consequently will never be. It gives only in the form of an unreal, whatever the form taken by it: memory, expectation, image, or simple concept. This unreality of everything Care cares for resides not in Care as a particular mode of life but in the kind of phenomenality to which it has entrusted from the beginning everything it cares for. This phenomenality, that of the world, as we have seen, makes unreal a priori everything it makes visible, making it visible only in the act by which, posing it outside itself, it empties it of reality.

Christianity had the profound intuition of this primary derealization that Care performs. It calls this derealizing Care "covetousness." "You want something but don't get it. You kill and covet but you cannot have what you want" (James 4:2). The reason for failure lies not in what is demanded but in the mode of the demand, in the mode of manifestation of what Care cares for, since this mode of manifestation derealizes what it makes manifest. "When you ask, you do not receive, because you ask with wrong motives" (4:3). The critique of covetousness occurs constantly in the New Testament: "Do not conform to the evil desires you had . . . for evil human desires" (1 Peter 1:14 and 4:2). Throughout this critique, the significance is transparent: it refers the ontological dissolution of the object of this Care to the milieu onto which Care opens. Hence it often takes the form of a critique of the future: "You who say, 'Today or tomorrow we will go to this or that city, spend a year there, carry on business and make money.' Why, you do not even know what will happen tomorrow" (James 4:13–14). It results in the assertion of Life's self-sufficiency in its independence from everything arising in the world: "Watch out! Be on your guard against all kinds of greed; a man's life does not consist in the abundance of his possessions" (Luke 12:15). And hence the contrast between two treasures, one amassed in the world instead of being built in life. The opposition Life/Concern is baldly formulated: "Who of you by worrying can add a single hour to his life?" (Luke 12:25). It achieves its paroxysmal form in the words of Christ himself, praying not for the world (John 17:9), refusing kingship in the world (John 6:15), and placing humankind in a position to choose: "He who is not with me is against me, and he who does not gather with me, scatters" (Luke 11:23). It is the phenomenological status of Care, then, that falls prey to a strange dialectic. As a way of living, Care arises from the mode of phenomenality proper to the way of living, experiencing itself as what it is, as the suffering from an empty desire. However, inasmuch as it is cast outside itself toward what it is concerned with, it is the outsideness of what it is concerned with that fascinates it, the phenomenality of the world invades its gaze and so then, according to phenomenology's inversion of concepts—an inversion culminating in the idea that Life means Light and the world means darkness—it must be said that "If the light within you is darkness, how great is that darkness!" (Matthew 6:23).

In Care, man's forgetting of his condition of Son takes drastic form. In this respect, forgetting follows directly from the system of egoism, which follows from the transcendental illusion of the ego. Thanks to this illusion, inside this system, in Care, the ego, relying on itself and aware of acting from within, throws itself into goals that are its own possibilities to come—it throws itself outside itself and toward itself, in such a way that it never attains itself, never attains this goal that it is for itself in the guise of various possibilities. This is because outside itself, in the world's outside, there is no Self at all. The ego's transcendental illusion, the system of egoism, and Care—these three superimposed and related forms of forgetting of self have a common premise, however: that the Self allows itself to be forgotten when, in Care, the ego cares only of itself, or when, in egoism, it thinks only of itself. This premise was mentioned concerning the ego's transcendental illusion, precisely as its condition: it is Life's phenomenological status, its original and essential dissimulation that plunges it into an apparently insurmountable forgetting. It is this forgetting of Life that we must try to elucidate.

We usually understand forgetting as a mode of thinking. We forget what we are not thinking about or not thinking about any longer. To think of something is to relate oneself intentionally to it, to direct one's gaze to it in such a way that what we are thinking about rises up before this gaze, in the "outsideness" that is the truth of the world. As long as we keep our gaze on this object, we are thinking about it and not forgetting it. But as soon as the focus of our thought turns away from it we forget it. However, what we forget in this way we can always remember. All that is shows itself to us in the world's truth we remember and forget in turn.

This is not the case with Life. In Life there is no "outside," no space of light into which thought's gaze could slip and perceive anything before it. Because Life is not separated from itself, because it never places itself at a distance from itself, it is incapable of thinking about itself or even remembering itself. Life is forgetting, the forgetting of self in a radical sense. The forgetting that Life has regarding itself has nothing to do with the forgetting of thinking with respect to what is shown in the world's truth, which, as we have just seen, is always susceptible to being changed into a corresponding memory. In contrast, the forgetting of Life is definitive and insurmountable. Life is without memory, not due to distraction or some unfortunate disposition, but instead because no intentionality, no focus of some *objectum* is capable of taking place in it, of being interposed between Life and itself. Since it escapes any conceivable memory, Life is the Immemorial. It is because Life escapes any possible memory that humankind forgets its condition of Son—albeit this condition is as a living whose essence is Life.

The analysis of the condition of Son lays bare three relations—the relation of the ego to the self, its relation to Life, and Life's relation to itself—because the ego relates to its self only inasmuch as it relates to Life, and it relates to Life only inasmuch as Life is related to itself. It is within Life's relation to the self, in effect, and only there, that the ego relates to its self. This relation, in all three cases, draws its essence from Life, from its Immemorial. This is why the Immemorial, which ineradicably marks Life's relation to the self, similarly marks the relation of the ego to Life, its generation, and the relation of the ego to itself, the "self" of man.

Let us begin with the latter. If it is within Life's relation to itself that the ego relates to itself, then is it not extraordinary to realize (as a decisive proof of the implication and the nature of these different relations) that the *dissimulation of Life's relation to itself is identical to the ego's relation to itself, the dissimulation of the ego itself*? It is within the relation to itself, within its very Ipseity, that the ego is invisible—in the same way as the Life that generates this Ipseity, and thus this ego. Just as the forgetting that life has toward itself—life incapable of taking its place before its own gaze, thinking of itself, remembering itself—is insurmountable, so is the forgetting that strikes the relation of the ego to itself, the "Self" of this ego.

Once more, the traditional representations of "I," "me," and "self" are overturned. That the ego is incapable of thinking of itself, and notably of remembering itself, will appear paradoxical—since thinking of and remembering oneself indeed occupy a major part of most people's time. But what ego presents itself to their thoughts, and whom do they remember? Why, an empirical individual born in a specific place at a specific time, leaning over his mirror to count his facial wrinkles, remembering the time when his face was smooth. But such an individual does not exist unless he is perceived as a me, and he is only perceived as a me on the condition of an Ipseity that for its part never shows itself in the world, occurring only in the invisible life and as the phenomenological effectuation of it.

In the relation to the self constitutive of the Ipseity that secretly inhabits any visible man and woman, there is neither thought nor memory, and this is what dislocates the classic conceptions that ground the possibility of me in memory. In effect, they represent the me's life as a succession of "lived moments" [*vécus*] that occur continuously. The possibility of the me appears, then, as the maintaining of its identity through the continual flux of its states. It is precisely memory that is given the task of reunifying these sundered states by apprehending them as those of one identical me whose unity, and thus possibility, are safeguarded in this way. Unfortunately, any attempt to ground the possibility of me in memory immediately turns upon itself because, with respect to our *living* "me," and thus the possibility of life within it, any intrusion of a memory distancing this life from itself in order to allow it to see the past in distance has already destroyed the essence of this life, its self-affection. Crushed against itself, it experiences itself in its *pathētik* immediacy without ever being separated from itself and without being able to be so. Far from gathering life into its "unity with self," which is nothing other than its Ipseity, memory opens up the gap in which no life is possible, but only what is no longer. A life given by memory would be a life in the past. But a life in the past is a phenomenological non-sense, something that excludes the very fact of "living."

The forgetting that the Self maintains regarding itself allows us to better understand its true nature: the self is only possible as pathetically submerged in itself without ever posing itself in front of itself, without pro-posing itself in some visible form (sensory or intelligible) or another. Such a Self, foreign to any apparition of itself in the world, is what we are calling a radically immanent Self, a Self neither constituted by nor the object of thought, without an image of self, with nothing that might assume the aspect of its reality. It is a Self without a face, which never lets itself be envisaged. It is a Self in the absence of any perceptible Self, such that this absence of any perceptible Self or thought constitutes the Self's veritable Ipseity, as well as everything possible on the basis of it. It is only because no Image of itself is interposed between it and itself, in the manner of a screen, that the Self is thrown into itself unprotected and with such violence that nothing can defend it from that violence any more than from itself. It is solely because this violence is done to it of being a living person in Life's forgetting of self, and thus in the forgetting of itself, that the Self is possible—as this Self of which no memory throws back the image, which nothing will separate or deliver from itself, so that it is the Self that it is forever.

Life's forgetting of self has a corollary: the Self's forgetting of self is generated in its self-generation. This is what explains, in the end, man's forgetting of his condition of Son. In this way, *man's forgetting of his condition of Son is not an argument against that condition but rather its consequence, and thus its proof.* But man's forgetting of his condition of Son not only proves this; it also explains the no less extraordinary fact that, despite the ego's constant exercise of its power—which makes it say "I Can"—"I," this ego, no less constantly forgets its condition of ego than the ego forgets its condition of Son. Here we discover a theoretical sequence that is more than essential. Precisely because man has forgotten his condition of Son, his own condition of ego escapes him. And, in effect, as soon the Ipseity in which any me and any "ego" is generated becomes occulted, then the condition of this me and this ego is abolished: the ego is no longer possible. No longer possible, the ego is no more than a phantom, an illusion. From this dissolution results one of the most characteristic traits of modern thought: an extremely serious challenge to man himself, his devaluation and reduction to what subsists when one no longer knows what makes him a man—to wit, an ego and a me. We would have to follow step by step the modes of this theoretical murder from Kant to Heidegger and, on a more superficial level, by Marxism, structuralism, Freudianism, and various human sciences, not to mention the scientism specific to our own era—but that is not our task here; at most, we may grasp the principle of this disaster rather than recount its history.

Even deeper than the forgetting of the ego's relation to itself is the forgetting that permeates its relation to Life. In effect, in its relation to self, the ego can well forget the true Self that establishes it—outside the world, independently of any thought or memory or care. In the night of this absence of thought, the ego is no less given to itself, experiencing itself pathetically in the constantly exercised I Can. Thus it remains submerged in itself and unaware—even when it is concerned only with the world. But the relation that unites the ego, no longer with itself but with Life, is very different. If the ego comes into itself only in the coming into self of absolute Life and in the process of its eternal self-generation, then was this process not accomplished from the start? And has Life not come into itself in its Ipseity before the world so that any ego may be able to come into itself, too? Does Absolute Life not precede all livings as the unsurpassable presupposition, as an "already" that can never be withdrawn, as a past that can never be caught up with—an absolute past? Life's anteriority to every living (and similarly, the First Self's anteriority to any particular Self) corresponds to the most radical forgetting. Forgetting here no longer bears on what one is without knowing it, but rather on what happened before one existed—on the system of autarchic enjoyment constituted by the reciprocal interiority of Father and Son, when there is not yet any me nor any ego such as our own. In the absolute already of Life's autarchic enjoyment lies the Immemorial, the Arch-Ancience that eludes any thought—the always already forgotten, that which lies in Arch-Forgetting.

Nevertheless, Christianity asserts the possibility that someone may surmount this radical Forgetting and rejoin the absolute Life of God—this Life that preceded the world and its time, eternal Life. Such a possibility signifies nothing other than salvation. To rejoin this absolute Life, which has neither beginning nor end, would be to unite with it, identify with it, live anew this Life that is not born and does not die—to live like it does, in the way it lives, and not to die.

To rejoin the absolute Life of God—would that not also be, though, for someone who has forgotten it, to find once again a condition that was once one's own, if it is true that in one's transcendental birth one came into oneself only in the very coming into itself of absolute Life? Would it not mean to be born a second time? But can someone be born a second time? This is Nicodemus's anguished question in his nighttime conversation with Christ: "How can a man be born when he is old? Surely he cannot enter a second time into his mother's womb to be born?" (John 3:4).

9

The Second Birth

Christianity gives itself the explicit task of allowing people to secure their salvation. According to its decisive intuitions, this salvation consists for the ego of finding once again in its own life the absolute Life that does not stop engendering it. This project implies two initiatives. The ego/person lost in the world, preoccupied only with things and thinking of itself only in relation to things—"Martha, Martha, you are worried and upset about many things" (Luke 10:11)—must perceive, by contrast, its true condition, that of a living that does not draw its condition from itself. The true person, we have sufficiently shown, is not the empirical individual perceived in the world, but the transcendental "me" who constantly experiences itself as living, as that ego that leads the life that is its own without ever being the source of this life. This is why it experiences life precisely in the radical passivity specific to any life that does not bear itself inside. To live as a living transcendental me, given to itself in a life that does not itself give but that is given in the self-givenness of the absolute Life that is God's, such is the Christian definition of man, its condition of Son. *This condition of man as Son is precisely what allows his salvation.* If man undergoes the experience of this absolute Life, which has neither beginning nor end, if he coincides with that Life (and no longer with himself), then he will not know death.

How can a person regain this absolute Life of God, so as to live henceforward from this Life that does not die? The way in which Christianity undertakes to answer this crucial question makes manifest its extraordinary logic, the power and coherence of the intuitions on which it is based. *To rediscover in one's own life the absolute Life is something that is only possible in life itself and in the Truth that belongs to it.* In contrast, it is impossible to discover, find, or re-find absolute Life in the world's truth, by means of some kind of knowledge. This is the first presupposition of Christianity's quest for humankind's salvation: the setting aside of everything to which people usually address their demands, if not for salvation in a properly religious sense, then at least for progress, success, or the obtaining of what one desires, especially happiness. If, in traditional philosophical thought, it is wisdom—a wisdom built upon knowledge, careful thought, judgment, and so on—that ought to lead to beatitude, then we must recognize that this beatitude has nothing to do with the Beatitudes of the Sermon on the Mount. But the banishment of knowledge—any form of knowledge, whether philosophical or scientific, intelligible or sensory—in the process of Christian salvation is not gratuitous but rather is motivated by the very nature of the expected salvation. In order to vanquish the Forgetting that renders absolute Life Immemorial, the Forgetting in which thought holds Life, we should precisely not ask that of thought. The salvation that consists of rediscovering this absolute Life escapes all orders of knowledge, expertise, and science. It does not spring from consciousness as understood by classical or modern thought, as in "consciousness of something." It is not some "becoming conscious of" that can liberate a person. It is not consciousness's progress through various kinds of knowledge that will secure salvation.

We must take the measure of what is disqualified regarding the possibility for people to come to God: nothing less than what defines *humanitas* in the eyes of Western thought—thought itself, knowledge, science, Reason. The fact that access to God cannot be achieved in and through thought, and in rational thought less than any other, renders absurd the very project of demanding proof of God's existence. Here we come upon one of the great weaknesses of traditional religious philosophy: the ruinous confusion it creates between, on the one hand, the concrete internal possibility of effective access to God, and on the other, the prior establishment of his existence from a rational standpoint. This confusion between the *pathētik* relation of the living being to absolute Life—a relation achieved in life—and a relation to God that is reduced to a proof of his existence effects a decisive displacement of the question of God, which finds itself posed and shaped on terrain where it has already lost any possible mean- ing—at least if the question concerns the possibility for people of meeting God, of uniting with him and being saved.

It is Saint Anselm of Canterbury who first performed what we may call the denaturation of the question of God, the transformation of an af- fective fusion with divine life into a mediated rational approach. With the substitution of the latter for the former, the Christian project of Individual salvation gave way to speculation on "proofs of the existence of God," and this went on until Kant put a stop to it—without being able to offer hu- mankind any other path toward the foundation of its Being, that is to say, its true essence.

However, it was indeed the possibility of our access to God that pre- occupied Saint Anselm: "Teach my heart where it may seek thee, where and how it may find thee."[1] At lightning speed, the condition of this ac- cess is perceived and posed unequivocally: it is that I place myself where God does, or else that God place himself where I am: "If thou art not here, where shall I seek thee?" And in effect if God does not reside in this Dwell- ing that is also mine, I will never be able to find him, unless I change my- self into something quite other and extraordinary, totally foreign to what I am. But then, once the indispensable condition of access—that is, God's presence—is granted, along comes the disconcerting realization that, with this condition fulfilled, access has not taken place. "But if thou art every- where . . . why do I not see thee present?" Instead of seeking to elucidate this crucial paradox, which lies really at the heart of Christianity, that is, that the essence of God is such that *it may be present without anyone seeing it*, Saint Anselm confines himself to a hasty borrowing from Scripture: "No doubt you reside in an unapproachable light." Here, then, the condi- tion of access to God is suddenly ruined, since the light in which it resides, meaning access to God, is precisely inaccessible. From this follow very logically the lamentations that fill the long first chapter of the *Proslogion*, about the exile in which humankind finds itself now that it is separated from God. This separation is so radical that one cannot comprehend how humankind could even search for God—"Teach my heart how to seek thee"—nor, in truth, comprehend the possibility of this prayer.

At the beginning of chapter 2 comes the faith that stimulates the un- derstanding by which faith opens up to God: "Give me . . . to understand that thou art *as we believe* and that thou art *that which we believe*" (my emphasis). But this faith that arouses and stimulates the understanding *immediately gives way to that very understanding*. The text goes on: "We believe that thou art a being than which nothing greater can be conceived" (ibid.). "We believe that" here means we think that, we judge that, we conceive that God is a being such that one can conceive of nothing greater. Our access to God is now reduced to this. It is no longer a question of a revelation of God, of a revelation revealing God and produced by God himself, a revelation made to Beings capable of receiving it, which ultimately means Beings consubstantial with this self-revelation of God—in short, a revelation of itself that Life makes to livings. It is also not a question of Faith understood in its specificity, as Faith and certitude of life in itself, as we have suggested. Access to God is reduced to a conception of the understanding (of our understanding), which consists of what we henceforth are calling Saint Anselm's proof. This proof is developed in two stages. First one establishes that the content of this conception is incontestable if one reduced it to a pure representative content. It is incontestable that I may represent to myself a being such that one cannot conceive of anything greater. Then one establishes that such a being necessarily exists (if not, then one could conceive a greater one and it would exist). In philosophical terms, such a being does not exist only as the content of the understanding (*in intellectu*), but in reality (*in re*).

Now it behooves us to perceive the massive contradiction implied in the reduction of access to God to a proof of his existence delivered by the understanding. In general, to prove is to prove something, to submit this something to a set of conditions that it must satisfy, conditions that together constitute the proof itself. From the start, the proof appears more lofty than what must be proven; it is erected in the manner of a tribunal, and it is before this tribunal that everything that intends to demonstrate its rights is constrained to offer itself, in the proper manner, conforming to what is expected of it, thereby to receive the approbation that will deliver up its existence. In the case of God's existence, this citation before a power of validation greater than it not only is strange but immediately contradicts Anselm's definition of God, that nothing greater exists.

But it is on the phenomenological plane that the absurdity of any proof of God's existence becomes apparent—and it is impossible to define "proof" other than in a phenomenological way. In effect, to prove is to make seen, such that what is seen in this seeing (it little matters what is actually seen and how it is seen) cannot reasonably be doubted. What is seen in this clear-sighted way and is thus found to be indubitable could be something like 2 + 3 = 5 or else, "If I think, I must indeed exist." Any rational truth rests on such an evident given, on what gives itself to be seen in and of itself. It is in effect by being seen in this way that any content of thought may be recognized and affirmed by any mind—that it becomes "rational." If God could be shown in this way, it would be a rational truth and any reasonable person ought to affirm his existence. There would be a place for a rational theology and for a gradual development of this theology, as for any other rational knowledge.

But what sense is there in demanding a proof of God's existence? When we put into play the rational requirement of any kind of knowledge—that is, evidence—with respect to God, we commit a number of catastrophic confusions, of which some have already been pointed out in the course of this discussion. In the first place, we are confusing what is shown and its way of showing itself. What is shown could be either 2 + 3 = 5 or "If I think, I am." The way it is shown is *obviously*, within sight, in that "outside" that is the world's truth. To demand a proof of God's existence means to put God on trial in the world, to subject him to the obligation to appear according to this mode of appearing that is the light of this world, the ek-stasy of exteriority, where things and ideas are shown. In effect, a criterion of truth preexisting God is applied to him, to which he must conform, at least if he pretends to existence and to truth.

Here are two more absurdities implicated in the project of submitting God to this truth criterion. The first is the presupposition that God is inherently foreign to Revelation and consequently forced to request, from a revelation external to his essence, the possibility of being shown in that revelation, in the place it assigns and the fashion it prescribes: as evidence such as Reason would have it, before consciousness's gaze, as consciousness would have it when it claims rationality. And a second absurdity is to prescribe for God the mode of manifestation implied by any evidence, this horizon of visibility that is the world's "outside." To prescribe to God such a mode of appearing means to prescribe it to absolute phenomenological Life, which is never revealed like this, never elsewhere than in itself. It is not just rational thought, or what calls itself such, that commits the major mistake of wanting to apply the criterion of evidence so as to make divine essence the subject of rigorous knowledge—or to relegate it to meaninglessness if it refuses to conform. Philosophies that strain to break the narrow confines of rationalism—even phenomenology itself—have succumbed to a double contradiction. First, they pretend to subordinate God to a mode of manifestation alien to his proper essence—as if God did not reveal himself, as if his essence did not consist of an original and absolute self-revelation, that of Life. Then, they ignore this original mode of phenomenalization that is Life's self-revelation, and which constitutes God's essence, and submit the latter to the sole mode of manifestation that is known, which is the world's truth.

For Heidegger, the truth of the world is that of Being itself. Here we must restate the necessary subordination of ontology to phenomenology. "The Truth of Being" means there is no Being except in this Truth. It is not Being that dispenses Truth, but the reverse. It is only within Truth, in the appearing and insofar as Truth appears, that anything whatever is in turn capable of Being, since it is shown in this appearing and through it. But this primordial appearing is understood by Heidegger as that of the world. *The absurd subordination of God to Being is the subordination of Life's Truth to the world's.*[2] Even worse is the misrecognition of the former as the latter and its exclusive reign. But misrecognizing Life's Truth also means misrecognizing divine essence. Whether one simply denies it or carries ignorance of Truth to the extreme of absurdly subordinating it to the world's truth is actually of secondary importance. What good is citing the "sacred," "god," or gods, when one has totally lost the divine essence in its proper and irreducible phenomenality? Heidegger comes up with inadmissible propositions: "The experience of God and his manifestness, insofar as the latter can encounter humans, strikes in the dimension of Being";[3] "The sacred . . . does not burst into appearance unless beforehand . . . Being has been illuminated."[4] Far from the illumination of Being unfolding the appearance in which something can be shown to us as "sacred," "god," or "the gods"—the gods of fantasy put there to do good, to conceal the limits and finally the platitude of any worldly thought—this illumination forever forbids access to it.

We must now return to the founding intuitions of Christianity. Access to the living God—access to Life—occurs only in Life, in the eternal process of its self-generation as self-revelation. Nor, truly, is the issue now the process of absolute Life considered in itself, but rather the possibility for people to reach and to have access to God. But here arises the greatest obstacle, on which the problematic of salvation has broken apart. Let us recall the terms of this aporia. Life's self-engendering, in which each living ego is engendered, signifies for that ego an absolute-Before: what is accomplished well before it and without it, before David, before Abraham— "before the world was." How, then, can this ego rejoin a Life that outstrips it in an antecedence that is scarcely thinkable? How can it be that we are not separated from what happened long before us in this absolute-Before, in this Immemorial of which we have no memory? Is not any "Before," for one who comes after, necessarily past and lost? And when this Before is Life, a Life that is always already accomplished, always already living, so that from it can be born all livings, then is not the latter, the one who comes after Life's Before, forever cut off from it, separated from this absolute Life in which alone it could escape death?

What Christianity obliges us to find is an entirely new and unusual conception of temporality—one that is the essence of Life's own temporality. Only this previously inconceivable temporality allows us to grasp the relation of our birth to the Before that absolutely preceded it, which is also to say, the relation of our birth to what is not born. The ordinary conception of temporality is that of the world, which has given rise to different interpretations. Common sense and science understand time as a sort of encompassing milieu in which things appear such that they are caught in the flow that carries them to nonbeing. Contemporary phenomenology has given rise to much more elaborated conceptions of time. Overall, time is identified with the phenomenological upsurge of the world, and thus with its truth. Hence the temporalization of time consists in a coming to the outside, a distancing, the establishing of a gap into which a horizon of visibility is dug, which is precisely the world's horizon, its phenomenality, its light. This is why time and the world are identical, and why the world's truth, consisting of time, is an appearance/disappearance in which all the things of this world are caught.

Regarding the problem at hand, that of the relation of the living to Life's absolute-Before, the presupposition that has just been restated involves the following consequences. Any "before" implies a gap, a distancing, or, as we might call it, an ek-stasy. For something like a "before" to appear in our experience, the one to whom "before" is shown must retrospectively relate to it, such that one's relation to this before consists of a retrospective look that supposes this distancing, this ek-stasy. In the "outside" of this ek-stasy is discovered both the horizon of the before—the phenomenological and ontological dimension of the past as such—and also (inside this horizon of the "before") what was before, what is past. What is past is no longer, but we understand why this is so. Due to its ex-static nature, the horizon of the past is a horizon of unreality because, placing everything outside itself, it has deprived everything of its own reality, emptied it of itself, and reduced it to an empty representation. Thus everything shown on this horizon is unreal because, being shown in that way, given in the past, it is no longer.

This double condition—of opening like a horizon of exteriority within the past's ek-stasy and of giving on that horizon only what is no longer—is avoided by the absolute-Before of birth. This is because, in the process of Life's self-generation, which is its coming into itself, no horizon of exteriority, no ek-stasy, is ever deployed. In this way, *never is what is engendered in the process of Life's self-generation related to what engenders it as a before from which it could be separated by any distance whatever, by the distance of an ek-stasy—specifically by the ek-stasy of the past.* How, then, is what is engendered in Life—the living—related to the power that engenders it, if that power truly remains for it an unending absolute-Before? We have to imagine a form of relation to the Before that is no longer the distance of the past—no distance, no "ek-stasy." *Any form of relation that does not take its possibility from the distancing of an ek-stasy instead draws it from feeling.*

First we have to perceive what is incontestable about the possibility of such a relation. A pure sensation, considered alone, is never ex-statically related to itself, because then it would have ceased to *feel itself* in order to become the sensation of something outside, an object's sensible quality, for example. It would no longer be that pure impression immersed in itself, incapable of taking the least distance from itself, of separating or detaching from itself—that pain that the person who feels it is forced to feel just as long as he feels it. But the *pathētik* relation to oneself that inhabits any sensation and any feeling, any modality of life, is not the doing of that particular modality, that pain, that impression. Rather, it belongs to Life as its *pathētik* flesh, the pure phenomenological substance of which life is made. But life, as we know, is a movement, a process, the process of eternal coming into itself of that which experiences itself without ever being separated from it. This movement of coming into itself that is never separated from itself is life's own temporality, its radically immanent, inex-static, and *pathētik* temporality. In this temporality there is neither before nor after in the sense we understand them, but rather eternal movement, an eternal flux in which life continuously experiences itself in the Self that life eternally generates, and which is never separated from itself. As soon as we understand the possibility of something like "living," we see that in the temporalization of this original immanent temporality there is nothing of the past nor anything that has not yet been—nothing lost and nothing anticipated. In the very movement of living (since it is accomplished as the Self's self-movement), everything is living and continues to be so.

But now the issue is not this movement of life moving and experiencing itself pathetically in the immanent temporality of a self-movement never separated from itself, but rather, we remind ourselves, the possibility for an ego like ours to be inserted into it. This possibility does not reside in the ego itself but in the condition of Son—in the condition of someone who only comes into himself in Life's own coming into itself. Not in the coming into itself of the ego's own life, which it is precisely incapable of bringing about, but in absolute Life's coming into itself, which alone is capable of doing so, of bringing about and giving itself to itself in the power and joy of a self-givenness and an effective self-affection. Thus there is only one Life, and it alone gives the ego to itself. Only because in the self-movement of its immanent temporality this Life is never separated from itself, the ego (given to itself within the self-givenness of absolute Life) is not separated from Life any more than from itself. It is only because this absolute Life is capable of bringing itself about in the hyper-power of its effective self-givenness and thus of living that, given to itself in the hyper-power of this absolute self-givenness, the ego is itself capable of living, not by itself, but thanks to the hyper-power of this absolute Life. Thus the Christian definition of humankind becomes radically clear. There is no living except a Son. But there is no Son except that of this unique and true Life that engenders itself constantly. The Son is not like a simple living emerging somehow in a factual life that lives itself somehow—about which we can establish only one simple fact: this Son is generated in the hyper-power of this absolute Life that brings about its own life, the only possible life, the only one capable of being brought into life and thus of living—the Life of God.

Nevertheless, few of the New Testament passages about man and his condition as Son understand the matter in this way: Son of God most often means not what man is but what he must become. Precisely because he is not that, he must become so. A resulting division is established among human beings, between those who are Sons of God and those who are not—

or not yet. This division is not gratuitous, and its conditions are clearly defined. The Son of God is the one who does not commit sin: "Anyone born of God does not continue to sin" (1 John 5:18). To the extent that he does not commit sin, the Son of God is not separated from God but "keeps him safe" (ibid.). An equivalent to John's proposition is found in Paul's Epistle to the Romans: "Those who are led by the Spirit of God are sons of God" (Romans 8:15). There is also a sort of corollary: "It is not the natural children who are God's children" (9:8), which itself echoes the Prologue by John we have already discussed: "Those who are not born of the flesh . . . "

To be born of God and to keep him within oneself without being separated from him, and thus without falling into sin—this precise and overdetermined meaning of the concept of Son of God is found in many essential passages of the New Testament that deal with salvation. This salvation resides precisely in the condition of Son of God in the sense just stated, which appears repeatedly in John's writings: "Whoever does justice is his child" (1 John 2:29); "Everyone who loves is a child of God and knows God" (1 John 4:7). To carry God within oneself is also, according to a series of implications that have been laid forth, to believe that Jesus is the Christ and that the Christ is consubstantial with the Father. To carry God within oneself in these different ways is thus to be the Son of God in the strong and overdetermined sense that we have been elucidating: "Everyone who believes that Jesus is the Christ is a child of God" (1 John 5:1); "Every spirit which acknowledges that Jesus Christ has come in the flesh is from God" (1 John 4:2). Salvation consists of carrying God within oneself while being his Son in this new sense, according to the amazing declarations in Revelation: "They shall walk with me in white"; "His name I will never strike off the roll of the living, for in the presence of my Father and his angels I will acknowledge him as mine;" "the Lamb . . . will be their shepherd and will guide them to the springs of the water of life" (3:4; 3:5; 7:17). And that this filiation comes from radical becoming, from the transformation of one who in his identification with Life receives his salvation from it, is also stated no less abruptly: "Behold! I am making all things new! . . . I am the Alpha and the Omega, the beginning and the end. A draught from the water-springs of life will be my free gift to the thirsty. All this is the victor's heritage; *and I will be his God and he shall be my son*" (Revelation 21:5–7, my emphasis).

The overdetermination of the concept of Son, as Son of God having a share in the source of life, generated in that place where life self-generates, is obviously linked to the strong concept of self-affection by which life engenders itself as the true and eternal Life. But doesn't this overdetermination of the strong concept of Son, grasped in its connection to the strong concept of self-affection that belongs to absolute Life, also leave indeterminant the weak concept of Son, whose life does not have the ability to bring itself into Life? What, then, is the condition of one who lives his own life, who does not drink from the source of life, who has not received the heritage of the victor, one whose name is not written in the roll of the living—one of whom God has not said "I will be his God and he shall be my son"? To the questions implicitly raised here, the Book of Revelation replies with the same brutality: "Though you have a name for being alive, you are dead" (3:1). Far from attributing this type of declaration to some visionary excess, Paul's systematic construction includes it in his thematic: "Although you were dead because of your sins and because you were morally uncircumcised . . . " (Colossians 2:13). The question posed by Paul, as well as by Revelations, becomes, then, the unavoidable paradox around which a constellation of problems revolves: how is it possible to live in any fashion if one is dead? If that is the case, how is the pure appearance by which one at least passes for living still conceivable? Inversely, if one is really dead, how can one rediscover and drink anew the water of the source of life that watered the stags? How can one suddenly find one's name in the Book?

These questions are linked to the relation that exists between Life and the living, which consists of a series of necessary implications. These define the whole set of equally necessary responses that should be given to such questions. Because the relation of Life to the living has been the subject of a systematic elucidation, we are now in possession of these answers.

Here is the first: a living is living only by the working of Life in him. Consequently, the relation of a living to Life cannot be broken, and cannot be undone. This relation is so essential that the living not only carries Life as his most intimate and ever-present condition; it is his very presupposition, in the sense that Life necessarily precedes any living as the absolute-Before relative to which he is always second. It is only because Life comes into itself in the eternal process of its self-affection that the living (in and through this process) comes into himself. This is shown by the phenomenology of birth, establishing in an apodictic way that any living is the Son of true Life, absolute and eternal, and of it only. "Here and now, dear friends, we are God's children" (1 John 3:2). And again: "How great is the love that the Father has shown to us! We were called God's children, and such we are" (1 John 3:1). The issue is not understanding how people living from an uncertain and ill-assured life, incapable of founding itself—how people similar to the dead—could be capable by some radical transformation in their nature of changing into quite different beings, those Sons dressed in white that are described in Revelation, those "children of God's promise" that Paul speaks of (Galatians 4:28), who are promised to an incorruptible life. Rather, the issue is perceiving how the Sons who are all Sons of God's absolute Life, living only in and through it, can actually lose this condition. And how, having lost it, they can find it again and be reborn in this unique and absolute Life that, from affecting itself and giving itself, does not know death.

It is remarkable that this double possibility, inscribed a priori in the relation of the living to Life as two ways for this relation to be realized, is described by Christ himself in the extraordinary parable of the two sons, usually known as the Prodigal Son (Luke 15:11–32). We recall that the younger one, having asked his father to give him his share of the inheritance and having squandered it in a foreign land, returns to his father: "Father, I have sinned against God and against you; I am no longer fit to be called your son. . . . " (verse 18). The father showers him with gifts: "For this son of mine was dead and has come back to life; he was lost and is found" (24). To the other son, who had remained faithful and is offended by his father's behavior, he declares: "My boy, you are always with me, and everything I have is yours" (31).

Two decisive theses arise here. First, the idea that the spiritual transformation of the Son into his true condition as Son of God, as spoken of in Revelation, into his condition as "child of God's promise" (promised to incorruptible Life), is only possible within the context of the prior condition of living, born of Life in the very movement by which life comes into itself. It is in his capacity as Son and because he is one that the lost Son can regain a condition that was originally his, and that, for this reason, he in fact regains it. The prior character of the condition of living does not merely mean that living precedes any becoming that may occur. Rather, this condition of living itself refers back to its own precondition, to the absolute-Before of Life from which the living person takes his living quality. Any becoming that can happen to him presupposes within the living that absolute-Before, to which this becoming ultimately returns. It is to this radical presupposition of absolute Life, included in the condition of the living and making it possible, that the Christian concept of Son refers. It is due to this absolute presupposition always included in him that the Son can and must regain the condition that is his. This is also one of John's decisive intuitions: "If we know that our requests are heard, we know also that the things we ask for are ours" (1 John 5:15). Thus the return of the prodigal son to his Father's house, the return of the son to his condition of Son, is made possible by his very condition as Son. To come back to Life, to be reborn, is given as a possibility always present to one who is born of Life. A rebirth is thus implied in any birth because the new life to be reached, the second life, is just the first one, the oldest Life, the one that lived at the Beginning and that was given in its transcendental birth to all living people: because, outside it and without it, no living person nor any life would be possible.

A final difficulty remains before us. The possibility of being reborn to this absolute Life, which he had forgotten by losing himself in the world and becoming concerned only with things and himself, subsists in man, who derives it from his transcendental birth and carries it inside as what constantly gives him to himself—this is still only a possibility. In its immanent temporality, absolute Life has in vain joined to itself someone who, coming after it, is not thereby separated from it—any more than separated from himself. Although Life indeed remains in each Son as the interior presupposition of his condition, from which he cannot separate himself, the prodigal son has nonetheless forgotten this. The power, closer to man than himself, that gives him to himself, can continue to work within him without his knowing it; but for him things don't seem that way. *Phenomenologically,* someone who lives only for himself, who cares only about his own feelings and pleasures (as if he gave them to himself and as if the power that really gives them did not exist), who believes he leads an autonomous life and is not the beneficiary or debtor of any heritage or any promise—is that person not the prodigal Son? And why would he come back, guilty and ashamed, to his Father, someone who no longer even knows he has a Father, who no longer knows he is a Son?

There is no access to God in the world (any "proof" of God's existence, any rational theology is ruled out), but only in life. But there are two lives: the one given to itself in its self-generation and the one that is only given to itself in absolute Life's self-generation. Foreign to the world, the Christian problematic of salvation is unfolded exclusively in the field of life, and this is why it finds itself abruptly confronted with the doubling of life. In a sense, it is true, this doubling is merely apparent, since the ego is not given to itself in what becomes its own life except in absolute Life's self-givenness. The immanence of absolute Life within the ego's own singular life is what makes theoretically possible the ego's salvation. But, once again, this possibility remains theoretical, only a simple possibility. Why does the ego that lives from its own life, thoughts, desires, and pleasures (while the power that gives it to itself remains for it insurmountably Forgotten)—why would this ego overcome this Forgetting, suddenly feeling inside *the only life that exists*, the power that in its self-givenness gives any conceivable life?

Here we are offered one of the strongest intuitions of Christianity, linked to all those we have already discussed. Life leads us to something no knowledge allows us to see. But the doubling of the concept of life, the distinction between absolute Life's self-givenness and the life of the ego that is only given to itself in absolute Life's self-givenness—this differentiation is not only theoretical but phenomenological. It is the Forgetting of the former that the ego must defeat if it wants to be reborn and escape death. This second birth only comes about due to a mutation accomplished within life itself, the decisive mutation thanks to which the very life of the ego is changed into Life of the absolute. Inside life, this mutation is not prepared by any theoretical knowledge. It can only find its principle in life, in absolute Life and its movement: it is a self-transformation of life according to its own laws and structure. Willed by life, this self-transformation of life leads to its true essence, to absolute Life. That this transformation of life, owing nothing to the world's truth or its logos, receives its motivation from this life, that it belongs to this movement and concretely accomplishes it, this determines life as an action. *The self-transformation of life that it wills, consisting of an action and leading it back to its true essence, is the Christian ethic.* This ethic is announced in Christ's words: "Not everyone who calls me 'Lord, Lord' will enter into the kingdom of Heaven, but only those who do the will of my heavenly Father." (Matthew 7:21).

Thus the Christian ethic presents itself from the start as a displacement from the realm of the word, meaning also of thought and knowledge, to the realm of action. This displacement is decisive for three reasons. First, it leads the world's truth back to Life's. Second, dissipating all the il-

166 The Second Birth

lusions that traditionally link the truth to representation, to theory, and to their ecstatic foundation, it unequivocally relates Life's Truth to the process of its self-engendering, to the power of an action. Third, in life, it is precisely no longer the ego's power, the I Can constitutive of its will and freedom, that is at issue, but the "Father's Will," or the process of absolute Life's self-engendering. Now the ethic can link the two lives, the ego's and God's, in such a way that it assures the former's salvation in practice. *To do the Father's will designates the mode of life in which the Self's life takes place, so that what is henceforth accomplished in it is absolute Life in its essence and by its requirements.*

The Christian ethic thus rigorously follows the fundamental presuppositions of Christianity and is their application. The presuppositions are that God is Life; that access to God is access to Life in itself, its self-revelation; that man takes the means of reaching God from his condition as Son, as living in Life. He has within him the self's relation to Life, a relation that joins him to himself and alone can join him to God. To do the Heavenly Father's Will is to let the relation to the self that joins the singular Self to itself be accomplished, just like the relation to itself of absolute Life—for the living man it is to let life be accomplished in himself like the very Life of God.

The genius of the Christian ethic is to point out in the simplest of ordinary lives, accessible to all and comprehensible by all, the concrete conditions—the circumstances, as it were—in which the extraordinary event is produced by which the ego's life will be changed into God's. As an example, let us consider the parable of the Good Samaritan (whose good deed is terrifyingly represented by Luca Giordano in the painting in the Rouen Museum). Someone like the priest or Levite, who passes by without helping the man robbed by brigands who has been thrown down and is covered with wounds—that person now advances along the route to perdition without knowing it. By contrast, the Samaritan, setting aside his own business, all preoccupations about himself or his interests, is concerned only with the unfortunate one. Taking him to an inn, having him tended, paying for everything—in short, *practicing mercy*, he has done everything that could be done to "inherit eternal life" (Luke 10:25–37). If such is the metaphysical destiny of the protagonists in the parable, it is good that acts are what count.

Precise behaviors of the kind indicated in the New Testament were summarized by medieval theology as the "seven works of corporal mercy" (to feed those who are hungry, clothe those who are naked, care for the sick, release captives, visit prisoners, and so on) and of spiritual mercy (teach the ignorant, convert sinners, console the afflicted, pardon one's enemies, pray for the living and the dead, and the like). It is not conformity with an external model of conduct that is required. Rather, within each person who performs each of the stated acts of mercy, salvation flows. Salvation is the second birth entry into the new Life. The action of the Christian ethic places the living person into the absolute Life that was before him and, giving him to himself, gave him life in his condition as Son. How that action allows the recovery of that condition remains to be specified. Any action, as we have shown at length, consists in the application of a power that can be exercised only if it is in possession of itself—which means only if given to itself, not by itself but within life. This is the ego-defining condition of the I Can. When the Christian ethic effects the decisive displacement that leads from words to acts—"It is not the one who says . . . but the one who does . . . "—it addresses this ego, draws on a power that is within it. The ethic designates this ego as someone who, in performing an act of mercy, achieves his salvation. At the same time, the ethic disqualifies language as inherently incapable of playing this role, because as a milieu of pure unreality, language is foreign to life. The contrast between acts and words that traverses the Gospels has no meaning unless there is a decisive opposition between what carries life in itself and what is deprived of it in principle. This is because the doing carries life as its irresistible presupposition, because there is no doing unless given to itself in life's self-givenness, unless the work of salvation is entrusted to it.

Entrusted to doing and to action, but not to any old action. If we examine the list of works of mercy, we see that is not a simple enumeration of empirical attitudes and conduct that would be beneficial to people who practice them. A hidden contrast runs through them, but not an opposition between simple precepts still removed from their achievement in practice, which is demanded as the single road that leads to life. Instead, the opposition appears on the level of the action itself. It distinguishes and contrasts two types of action—in effect, one that leads to life and the other to death.

Isn't the one leading to life quite simply mercy? This is what ought to direct our conduct with respect to all those whose situation of need or distress requires us to bring them aid and assistance. So is it not someone who comes up to us, without even speaking or making any sign—a simple face that calls on us in such a way that we can either turn away or respond to the appeal? We know the decisive role played by the other person, more exactly by the neighbor, in the Christian ethic, something to which we shall return. The question of the relation to others, however, cannot be examined by itself until the presuppositions underlying Christianity's approach to it have been clarified. These presuppositions concern precisely the way of acting implied in works of mercy. Paradoxically, it is neither the neighbor nor the mercy with which we should treat him that explains the way of acting required by the Christian ethic. Moreover, if it was really the other person that lay at the principle of this ethic, reduced to a sort of radical altruism, how could it determine a conduct different from one finding its principle within me? Is the other person more than me? Is one person worth more than another?

It is in the essence of action itself, nowhere else, that the Christian ethic perceives the principle of the division of all forms of action between those that save and those that lead to perdition. It is enough to recall the essential link that unites the transcendental illusion of the ego to the problem of action, since the ego finds itself constituted in itself as I Can. Disposing of itself and each of its powers, leaning on itself, by the same token it takes itself as the source of these powers, as we have said. Not content just with attributing everything it does to itself, it even poses itself as the unique goal of all its actions, caring for things, other people, and itself only with itself in view. So it is in its very action and each of its acts that it has lost *the essence of action, if action consists not in the application of determinate powers but in the hyper-power that has given each of these powers to itself*—in the hyper-power of absolute Life. In the action of the ego as action, supposedly issuing from itself and aimed only at itself, the very essence of absolute Life is ruled out. Far from leading to the life outside of which there is neither ego nor action, this action turns away from it, and by the same token turns away from life everything it touches, others as well as itself.

The action implied in merciful works is now quite clear. Whether it involves nourishing those who are hungry, clothing those who are naked, caring for the sick, or another act, *the manner of acting in these various actions has ceased to concern the ego that acts or to relate to it in any fashion; a common trait equally determines them all: forgetting oneself.* In a radical phenomenology of life like that of Christianity, and in the essence of the Ipseity in which life attains itself, the forgetting of self has a double meaning. What is ruled out is not only the empirical and worldly individual (to which the ordinary understanding of a person is reduced) but also, more essentially, the transcendental ego that acts. For this particular ego, which puts into effect the powers of its body and mind, which says "I Can," there is no longer any question of that ego it cared about until then and which was still him. It is the system of transcendental egoism (in which it is the transcendental ego that acts and that acts with a view to itself) that is abolished.

Hence, what kind of action is acting in works of mercy, if it is not a power proper to the transcendental ego that says "I Can"? In this ego there is no power different from its own, different from all the powers it possesses, except for the hyper-power of absolute Life that gave it to itself in giving itself to itself. *In works of mercy—and this is why they are "works"—a decisive transmutation takes place by which the ego's power is extended to the hyper-power of absolute Life in which it is given to itself.* In such a transmutation, the ego forgets itself, so that in and through this forgetting an essential Ipseity is revealed—not its own Self but precisely what gives this self to itself by making it a Self, absolute Life's self-giving in the Ipseity of which this life gives itself. It is no longer me who acts, it is the Arch-Son who acts in me. And this is because "I no longer live, but Christ lives in me" (Galatians 2:20).

Here some of the founding intuitions of Christianity take shape. The analysis of the Self showed that there is no true Self other than a radically immanent Self, whose relation to self excludes any distancing, any putting at a distance, any "outside," any possible "world." Thus this Self has no image, no perception, no memory of self, is not concerned with itself, and does not think of itself. This relation to self is Forgetting, not the forgetting that might be cancelled by the corresponding memory, but the Forgetting that nothing can cancel—the Immemorial of its relation to self in the Ipseity of absolute Life. It is only with the elimination of the worldly self shown in the world and of the worldly relation to self in which the Self sees itself, desires to be seen, is concerned with itself, works with a view to itself, that the advent comes of the true Self, which experiences itself within the Ipseity of absolute Life and is nothing other than that.

But what does "advent" mean here? How does this transformation of the worldly self come about, which (in the forgetting of everything it is for itself) opens up to the original Ipseity of Life? Nothing for which we have established the theoretical possibility—not even the theory we have sketched—can be accomplished by theory. *Only the work of mercy practices the forgetting of self in which, all interest for the Self (right down to the idea of what we call a self or a me) now removed, no obstacle is now posed to the unfurling of life in this Self extended to its original essence.* Forgetful of Itself in merciful actions, in this new action there is only its givenness to itself in the Arch-Givenness of absolute Life and in its Arch-Ipseity. The person has rediscovered the Power with which he is born—and which is itself not born. He is born a second time. In this second birth he has rediscovered Life, so that henceforth he will not be born anymore; it can truly be said in this sense that he is "not born."[5]

Here then is how each work of mercy leads to salvation. Each time, it produces a decisive substitution, by virtue of which the worldly acting of the ego concerned with things, others, and itself, with a view to itself, gives way to the original action of Life that gave this ego to itself. Because action is wholly phenomenological, the process of this substitution is phenomenological, too, and one who practices mercy has felt the eruption in himself of Life.

This phenomenological process, incontestable each time it happens, is not some event arising from magic, the effects of which we can only admire after the fact. One who is born of life finds actions capable of satisfying him only if this action suits his condition. The action can only suit the condition of Son if it comes from that condition and returns to it. *Its coming from the condition of Son is what makes it possible in the first place.* There is no "I Can" except in life. As extraordinary and difficult as the requirements of the Christian ethic appear to people, the no less extraordinary fact remains that they are rooted in their true nature. The requirements offer themselves as safeguard, and thus they return to the Son. The Christian ethic testifies to its own condition, in which is simultaneously designated the only possible ethic for humankind. Outside of it, humankind cannot help but be literally denatured, scorned, destroyed. Here is the reason why the precepts of this ethic are formulated so trenchantly, not as advice or suggestions, but as conditions of life or death.

We should now review this ethic.

10

The Christian Ethic

The Christian ethic aims to allow people to overcome the forgetting of their condition as Son in order to rediscover (thanks to it) the absolute Life into which they were born. The decisive presupposition of the Christian ethic is that the possibility of this second birth consists not in knowledge but in doing. But this process of salvation does not rely on doing (to the point of being identified with it) unless it is totally transformed. To do, to act—this has to be thought of quite differently. How? In life and as the fundamental determination of it, more as a mode of absolute Life. Because, in Christianity, doing is situated in the dimension of life and belongs to it, so its achievement is mixed up with life's movement, to the point—when it has become "thy will be done, on earth as it is in heaven"—of being nothing but the self-achievement of absolute Life. It is only because doing is life's doing that it can ultimately be what makes life: the absolute self-givenness and self-revelation of Life, in which God's revelation is achieved.

We must clearly perceive the extent to which doing, understood by Christianity as action by invisible Life, belongs to Life and, invisible like it, breaks decisively with the usual representations of action that derive from Greece, as well as from classical and modern thought. The principle of the Christian ethic only becomes intelligible in the light of an entirely new philosophy of action. The same is true for all the "commandments" that define this ethic and for the very meaning of what Christianity understands by "commandments." In ancient, classical, or modern thought, to act means to take some interior design, some subjective project, some desire or wish or will (whether or not explicit or conscious), and give it an exterior realization, in such a way that the ontological weight of reality resides in the objective formation in which the action results. It does not matter whether this objective formation is still only a mental content or a thought content (for example a geometric figure), or whether, on the contrary, it is a real object (for example, a vase made by a craftsman). In all cases, reality resides in the product of the action, which appears as a content situated within conscious sight, and therefore objective—a content that can be touched, in the case of the material vase, or at least seen with the mind's eye, in the case of the geometric figure or ideal object.

As for the action that led to this objective result, it consists of the very process that leads in general to something objective: a process of objectification. It is the very movement by which what did not yet exist except in internal virtuality finds itself brought outside, placed within sight, and henceforth perceived by that sight, become visible and thus objective and real. Action consists literally of this passage from interior to exterior, from what is not seen to what is seen, from what is still only a simple subjective intention, in itself deprived of reality, to what, from having emerged into exteriority and become visible as such, now finds itself real. In action more clearly than in any other phenomenon, it appears that phenomenality consists precisely in this coming outside into the world's light: action is like making, it is a making-come-outside.

To act, to make or do [faire], also means to produce. Pro-duce (*producere*) is to lead before, in that outsideness of the world that jointly defines phenomenality and reality, inasmuch as what shows itself is real—what shows itself in the world's truth. In all respects, making or doing [faire] is conceived within Western tradition on the basis of the world's truth. Making or doing [faire] is only understood as a requirement of reality. But it is in the world that any reality is realized. By itself, the realization is just the coming into this world, and finally the coming of the world itself—its emergence into the light, its appearance, its Truth.

Christianity proceeds to overthrow the concept of reality as well as that of action. In tearing action from external Being and from the process of objectification leading to it, Christianity situates action in its rightful place, where to do is to make an effort, take pains, suffer to the point that the suffering of this effort is changed into the joy of satisfaction. To do refers to life's internal *pathētik* self-transformation and finds there its sole motivation, its unique purpose, not to mention the very milieu in which it is accomplished and is possible. So, surprising as it may seem at first glance to the naïve realism of ordinary perception, the subjective conception of action is the only one that preserves its possibility. If we consider action as an objective process similar to a natural process, to a cascade of water that makes a turbine turn, then nothing distinguishes this so-called action from some material process, and there is no longer any action, but only objective phenomena. Human acting and the effort and suffering involved are reducible to causal sequences, to "the action of gravity," for example.

If we consider action as a process of objectification and externalization, the aporia we run up against is no less insurmountable. It would require that in each instant, by an extravagant leap outside his condition as a radically subjective and invisible living person, the agent is transformed into an object situated in front of it, that he himself becomes this object, an inert thing. In reality, the action does not stop being subjective, any more than does the living person who performs it. From beginning to end, it is action by life, which, like life, is never separated from itself. What we call the exterior result of action is always just the global re-presentation in the world's truth of what has its original site in Life's Truth. What is exterior are the objective displacements of an empirical individual who is himself objective—this individual whom one may see. But a person is never this, but rather an invisible transcendental me, and it is this me who acts. If it is its body that acts, it is its living body, its invisible transcendental body. The exterior "action" is just the representation of this originally subjective and living interior action. The genius of Christianity is to have understood from the start, apart from and long before any philosophical presupposition or analysis, that action is life's, and only possible as such.

To situate action within life has a rigorous phenomenological meaning, however. *To say paradoxically that action is invisible is to assign it a mode of radical revelation, that of Life itself, ultimately of God Himself.* Action, doing, practice, and the body are torn from the absurdity of positivism, which would reduce them to objective phenomena analogous to all phenomena in the universe. They are also torn from the absurdity of classical philosophies, which see in them a passage or, rather, an unintelligible leap between two irreducible orders. They are torn, finally, from the confusion of a vitalism that, making action the basis of determining human existence, nevertheless proves incapable of assigning it any phenomenological status whatever, making it the expression, denuded of meaning, of a blind and anonymous force. The fact that action is of life and belongs to it leads, by contrast, to relating phenomenological analysis of the former to the latter, with decisive consequences for the ethic, which will be apparent to us. Among these consequences, the most important is to transform a naturalistic or humanistic ethic into a general conceptualization of action, on the basis of the interpretation of a person as the transcendental "me" born of God—a conceptualization that is consequently only intelligible on the basis of God himself, and not of "man" or "nature."

The phenomenological analysis of life has shown that life's givenness to self in the transcendental "me" is founded in absolute Life's givenness to self and is only possible through it. If absolute Life's self-givenness is God's self-revelation, then the latter is implicated in the life of the transcendental "me," which is only self-revealed in this absolute Life's self-revelation—that of God himself. Any life is now accomplished "before God." God is like an Omni-seeing Eye that sees what happens in each individual life; once again, this is because life's self-revelation carries within it God's self-revelation. This decisive and almost unthinkable situation, which ensures that our life is accomplished in God's sight, a sight that is not a gaze but rather absolute Life's feeling itself inside any individual life, involves all our actions, to the extent that they are no longer dissociable from our life, any more than our life is from the self-revelation of absolute Life.

Thus, whereas in the world's truth my action is manifest in the guise of objective external conduct accessible to all, in Life's Truth grasped as one of its modalities (even better, as its very action), this action reveals itself not just to itself in the transcendental me that accomplishes it. In this revelation to itself of my action is included life's self-revelation and thus God's. So each of my actions is revealed to God at the same time as it is revealed to me, and in the very act by which it does so. "When you fast, put oil on your head and wash your face, so that it will not be obvious to men that you are fasting, but only to your Father, who is unseen, and your Father, who sees what is done in secret, will reward you" (Matthew 6:17).

The extraordinary phenomenology of action that results from Christianity's linking of it to the phenomenology of life finds in this stupefying passage its irresistible formulation. The radical opposition set up between the world's truth and Life's Truth corresponds to a duality of action: between, on the one hand, its exterior appearance in the form of a visible objective process accessible to all and, on the other hand, the secret character of this action, since, belonging to life in its very movement, it is as invisible as life. But the phenomenology of life practiced spontaneously by Christianity is by no means limited to the opposition, as decisive as it may be, between two heterogeneous modes of revelation: that of the world, in which everything is seen from the outside, and that of life, in which everything is lived from the inside. More secret than life itself (because operating within it) is the ultimate division between the absolute self-revelation in which life gives itself to itself and the passive self-givenness in which the transcendental me is given to itself—such that the latter is never separated from the former, from God's self-revelation. This is the Omni-seeing Eye that scrutinizes all of my actions, the ineluctable "before God" to whom a person owes the fact of living—this Son of Life who is given to himself only in the self-revelation of absolute Life.

The modification of action when it is transferred from the sphere of the world's truth to Life's is so important that we must differentiate its stages and meanings. According to a belief that is as widespread as it is naive, as long as action takes place in the world, it obeys its laws. These are partly laws of things and partly laws that make these things manifest (for example, space and time) and constitute the phenomenological structure of the world properly speaking, "outsideness" as such. The laws of things are not only physical laws. Among these "things" are social and cultural ones, and even people as empirical individuals appearing in the world. This is why there are alongside natural laws social and finally moral laws, laws relating to the conduct of these individuals and supposedly regulating them. Unlike natural laws, which are as necessary as the facts they govern, moral laws are presented as prescriptions or commands: they carry an obligation for people to conform their acts to them. Although this obligation is felt by individuals, the overall belonging to the world's truth by the system of actions means that everything within this worldly system is objective: actions, of course, but also the individuals who perform them, and finally the laws—the Law to which they submit themselves. This Law, which governs the ethical and religious system of a people, is exterior to the individuals who compose it, transcendent to them. This exteriority is the world's, and in its truth the Law is manifest.

At the same time as action is torn from the world's truth to be immersed in life's pathos, Christianity throws the whole worldly system of actions into its abyssal subjectivity. It calls into question the objective character of action itself, which is *stripped of its pretension to contain the reality of action and acting as such* it is only an appearance, and a fallacious one. Therefore, what is presented as the exterior conduct of fasting is not what fasts. How can the conduct of fasting, shown before us as a conduct that the whole world sees as external and objective, at the same time not be the action of fasting? Because the action of fasting does not appear itself in the world's truth and cannot appear there, and this in turn is because no action (particularly not this one) reveals itself, except to itself in life's self-revelation.

"Woe to you, teachers of the law and Pharisees, you hypocrites! You clean the outside of the cup and dish, but inside they are full of greed and self-indulgence!" Then comes the terrible judgment: "Woe to you, teachers of the law and Pharisees, you hypocrites! You are like whitewashed tombs, which look beautiful on the outside but on the inside are full of dead men's bones and everything unclean" (Matthew 23:25,27). The implacable and untiring denunciation of hypocrisy is not foremost a judgment, but rather presupposes a schism within appearance between two irreducible modes of phenomenalization. Luke explicitly refers the Pharisees to a preexisting phenomenological dualism: "You are the ones who justify yourselves in the eyes of men, but God knows your hearts" (Luke 16:15). This dualism of phenomenality is radicalized in all the Gospels; it appears in John, for example, as the dualism of two kinds of "praise" when it is said of the Pharisees: "Many even among the leaders believed in him. But because of the Pharisees they would not confess their faith . . . for they loved praise from men more than praise from God" (John 12:42).

It is not only action that Christianity removes from objectivity. The law that should govern action undergoes a displacement that is no less decisive. Leaving the sphere of exteriority, in which the law was given to people in the guise of an ethical or religious proposition—a transcendent Law that is alien to living subjectivity and supposedly regulates it from the outside, like an imperative or an objective statement—the law, too, is assigned in a paradoxical way to another phenomenological site—that of Life, of which it is just the self-movement of absolute Life, from which any particular life receives its own impulse.

Here arises a critique of the Law within Christianity, formulated with rare violence by Christ, and for which Paul finds and wonderfully explains the ultimate motivation, which relates it to Christianity's central thesis, which places reality within life. It is precisely because the Law is transcendent and exterior to life and perceived by life as beyond it that it is deprived of reality. And by the same token, it is deprived of what finds in life's reality the possibility of being fulfilled: action. The Law is thus unreal and powerless. Because it unites powerlessness with unreality, the Law places the whole system organized around it (especially the people to whom it is addressed) in an untenable situation. On the one hand, it prescribes, in the form of injunctions that are perceived quite clearly and thus indubitably: "Thou shalt not kill, thou shalt not commit adultery," and so on. On the other hand, however, this clearly enunciated commandment (not susceptible to being used for trickery) is by itself incapable of producing the action that suits it. "Has not Moses given you the law? Yet not one of you keeps the law" (John 7:19).

The basic powerlessness of the Law to produce by itself the action it prescribes confers onto the world built upon it, onto the ethical world in general, a contradictory feature. To the extent that the Law is given by Moses (and consequently the world is not only ethical but, more profoundly, religious), it is religion that is struck by this contradiction. On the one hand, the world of the Old Law is riddled with commandments, prescriptions, prohibitions. On the other hand, those who inhabit it and constantly run up against the Law in the course of their daily existence find themselves unable to observe it, lacking the force necessary to accomplish it. This force resides neither in them—or they would not have need of the Law—nor in the law, whose unreality deprives it of all efficacy. Thus the Law projects before action the path it should follow to approach God, without granting it the least bit of the power it would need to commit to following this path.

To see what ought to be done without possessing the power to do so, to see what ought to be done while finding oneself deprived (in and through this seeing, in and through this commandment) of the ability to execute it—this is the dramatic and desperate situation in which the Law has placed each person, despite the fact that it is addressed to him from outside as a transcendent Law. A Law that defines the infraction and the crime, that opens before people the gaping possibility without giving them the power to avoid either, is a cursed Law. An absence of Law would be better, a state of innocence in which the possibility of crime was not every moment within sight. The Law, on the contrary, curses all those who do not put it into practice—in fact, it curses everybody, since it gives nobody the power to follow it. The Law multiplies crime, as the Apostle says in a striking phrase: "The law was added so that trespass might increase" (Romans 5:20).

We must recall why the Law is powerless: it is not located in the life where any conceivable action takes place, and thus it is incapable of putting that action to work. The Law is foreign to life in the double sense Christianity gives to this concept. It is foreign to my life and resides beyond it. Moreover, it is foreign to absolute Life, which generates each living by making him a Son. The Christian ethic lies in the interplay of these two lives: to the degenerate son, who takes himself for his own master and the reason for everything he does, everything that comes into his head, it assigns concrete modes of action that alone might return him to the splendor of his initial condition, that is to say, to righteousness. Righteousness occurs when everything is restored to its place and man is reestablished in his dignity as Son. But this interior transformation, this re-birth, this re-generation, at the end of which comes righteousness, cannot be produced by a Law that is foreign to action and thus to any transformation. "For if a law had been given that could impart life, then righteousness would certainly have come by the law" (Galatians 3:21).

Paul's analysis goes further. The Law as an ideal archetype for all actions conforming to this model is revealed as nevertheless incapable (due to its basic unreality) of producing them. But one might be tempted to limit the scope of this objection with an important observation. The Law at least aims to offer this model, rather than leave action in uncertainty about what it should do. In this way, the Law does not make only transgression (and thus crime) possible, but also observance and submission. At least this is what happens in a religious society when, in conformity to the Law, priests offer sacrifices in expiation of sins, their own as well as those of the faithful. In these sacrifices, made according to the Law and thus thanks to it, expiation and purification are actualized; they enter into reality's effectivity and engage in the world of salvation.

This is what Paul is contesting. According to him, the inefficacy of sacrifice and offerings relates precisely to the fact that these ritual acts are patterned on the Law. Everything happens as if the Law's unreality were communicated to the acts it motivates, determining their own unreality and, by the same token, their inefficacy. "For there are already men who offer the gifts prescribed by the law. They serve at a sanctuary that is a copy and shadow of what is in heaven. This is why Moses was warned when he was about to build the tabernacle: 'See to it that you make everything according to the pattern shown you on the mountain'" (Hebrews 8:4–5). The inefficacy of action guided by the Law's pattern is twice affirmed. The first is an assertion: "For if there had been nothing wrong with that first covenant, no place would have been sought for another" (Hebrews 8:7). To this first reason, still just a statement, is added a more decisive one: the indefinite repetition of ritual sacrifices suffices to prove their vanity. For if a single one of them erased sin, then there would be no need for another one. "[The law] can never, by the same sacrifices repeated endlessly year after year, make perfect those who draw near to worship. If it could, would they not have stopped being offered? For the worshipers would have been cleansed once for all, and would no longer have felt guilty for their sins" (Hebrews 10:1–2).

But if sacrifices have been effectively offered, if the sacrificial act has been really accomplished, how could it be ineffective? Does the fact of being based on the ideal (and hence unreal) pattern of the Law suffice to strip action of its own reality and make it inoperative? Could the powerlessness of the Law, which comes from its unreal status, flow back onto the action itself, to the point of distorting it? Has the action of the Old Covenant ceased to work? Here the Christian theory of action abruptly illuminates the critique of the Law and makes it both possible and necessary. The critique of the Law is never only a critique of the Law, but really implies a critique of action tied to the Law, and this is what it is ultimately aiming at— action conforming to the Law and whose essence is to be ruled by it. So an action's conformity to the Law is objective conduct's conformity to an ideal model, to the Law's pattern. This objective conduct merely offers the exterior appearance of action within the world's truth and not real action, revealed to itself in the *pathētik*, invisible testing of life. Thus one may offer sacrifices without life itself being offered in sacrifice, in the sole place where sacrifice is possible, where true action, Christian action, takes place—where life is given to itself and where, thus given to itself, it acquires the power to give itself. The duplicity of appearance—the dual character of truth— forcefully explains how the external appearance of an objective conduct showing itself in the world's truth (for example, a conduct conforming to the representative model of the Law) by no means involves real action that acts in the secrecy of life under the all-seeing Eye of God. And this is why external conduct that conforms to the Law means nothing—no more in the case of sacrifice than in that of fasting. In its overall relation with the transcendental Law and in the Law's view, in the world's truth, external conduct (ultimately identifiable with an objective process) betrays its difference from real action and manifests its total powerlessness. As Paul says: "It is impossible for the blood of bulls and goats to take away sins" (Hebrews 10:3; see Psalms 40:6–8).

But it is not in the same fashion as in Paul's creating and unfolding of a complex (and sumptuous) problematic that the critique of the Law occurs in the Gospels, where it is no longer truly a critique but rather a total rejection that occurs in the critical situation created by that rejection. It is not even a rejection, properly speaking, since rejection looks at what it rejects and is still defined in relation to it. It is not a sort of contesting of the Law: rejection presupposes the Law after all, and in some manner follows upon it. In the Gospel, by contrast, an action arises that no longer takes account of the Law and quite simply ignores it. Christ heals the paralytic on the Sabbath. Among the many implications of this extraordinary act is above all this one: the Law does not count, it is not a Law for action and to which he should submit, since in this act, precisely, he does not submit to it. The Law of the Old Covenant is dismissed. This is why a problematic of the Law, accounting for the Law and reflecting on it, only occurs after the fact, in a retroactive look back at what has been superseded. Hence the scandal for all those who still live under the Law and want to define their actions by it—even though, in practice, this is something they never do: "So because Jesus was doing these things on the Sabbath, the Jew persecuted him." This annulment of the old Law and thus of an ethic, and even a religion, that had reigned until then, must have a powerful motive, one which concentrates within it the cardinal theses of Christianity. This motive is put forward all at once: "My Father is always at his work to this very day, and I, too, am working" (John 5:16–17).

By this abrupt reply (at first glance unsuitable, since it does not address the nonobservance of the Law that has provoked this scandal), Christ in effect displaces the object of the debate, transferring it from one domain of reality to another: from the domain of the Law (which is precisely not that of reality) to the domain of Life. Still, he does not call upon an artificial life that, depending on the course it follows and the vicissitudes it traverses, could still (considered from outside and as one conduct among others) find itself in accord or not with said Law. What is addressed, in a sort of unexpected leap, is not such a life (even less such acting) but the essence of phenomenological Life and, by the same token, its original acting, which is itself absolute: the process of self-generation of this Life, which does not stop engendering itself, or, as John puts it, the "Father" who "is always at his work."

As for Christ, he has justified his act of healing on the Sabbath by identifying it with the original essence of acting, itself identical with the original essence of Life, that is to say, with the process of its unceasing self-generation. It is because the process of absolute Life's self-generation does not cease, because "the Father is always at his work," that Christ, too, does not cease working, not even on the Sabbath day: "I, too, am working." By identifying his acting with God's absolute acting, with the unceasing process of self-engendering of absolute Life, Christ refers to himself unequivocally and, once more, as consubstantial in his acting with the action of this process. He is the transcendental Arch-Son cogenerated in the process of self-generation of Life as the essential Ipseity, and the First Living, in which (and in the form of which) this process is alone accomplished. This is why it is given to him, as to the Father, to work—and work without cease. *Life does not know rest on Sunday or Saturday*—which is better for all livings, moreover.

The violent displacement of the principle of acting, its transfer from the unreal universe of the Law to the essence of Life, which defines reality at the same time as it overthrows the reigning concept of ethics, determines the Christian ethic from top to bottom. That it has rejected the Old Law, or, more simply, that it has ceased to maintain it as the directing principle of acting, does not mean abandoning action to contingency or to the arbitrariness of the subjective attempt of the moment, at the whim of the acting subject—as if that were possible! It is not the idea of the Law, in truth, that is at issue, but the representation made of it. Precisely, *the Law is no longer a representation and cannot be so, because the Law that commands acting cannot be of another order than acting itself, which belongs to Life and only deploys its essence within it.* Because acting has its site in Life, no contact with it is possible, no manner of acting upon it so as to put it into operation or modify it is conceivable—unless within Life and because of it. Therefore, if there must be a principle of acting, unless it be given over to uncertainty or chance, then this principle (lacking which, one is left with radical impotence) cannot help but be homogeneous with it, with Life itself. The principle, the New Law, the Commandment, is thus this authority of Life and none other. This is the decisive displacement Christ effects, having grasped and placed the Commandment within Life and as the Commandment of Life itself.

But if Life now constitutes the Commandment, if it is the New Law, then the whole Christian analysis of life has to be considered anew, if only very briefly, if the ethic that it professes is to be understood and perceived in its principle. What, then, in the light of the fundamental intuitions of Christianity, is the meaning of the thesis that Life itself constitutes the Commandment, the sole principle of the ethic? Of course, this: that the Commandment is no longer in any way external to life, alien to what it must submit to as to a transcendental authority that might constrain it—from the outside. This is a scholastic hypothesis, as Paul has shown, if it is true that the transcendent Law, external to life, foreign to its reality and thus to action, finds itself to be in principle an unreal entity, incapable of acting. If it is, on the contrary, Life itself that is the Commandment, then the status of the latter has completely changed: it is a radically immanent Commandment, inside life, merely one with it and with its movement. The relation between Life and the Law is thus inverted. It is no longer the Law that determines Life, something the Law proves itself precisely incapable of. One might say that it is now Life that determines the Law, since there is no more Law in the ordinary meaning of this word, in the sense of an ideal norm. This is because the Law is now inside life, one with it. But this entirely new situation must be elucidated. The identification of the Commandment with Life places us outside the Old Law without yet saying what the New Law is, except that, unlike the former, it carries Power within it. But how does the Commandment command, how does it exercise its power, what does it command and to whom? This is what we can ask only of Life—if it is Life that commands.

In the light of the Christian concept of life, the relation of Commandment to the one who is commanded is exposed in extraordinary clarity: it is the relation of Life to the living person. The relation that opens the Christian ethic is the transcendental birth of the ego. What is commanded takes the form it does because the Commandment is that of Life. The relation that opens the Christian ethic is the relation of filiation. The one to whom the Christian ethic is addressed is not man such as he most often and primarily understands himself, such as he has been understood since Greece—a man who is a particular being, endowed with signifying properties. The one to whom the Christian ethic is addressed is a living transcendental me, this one, this living Self generated in Life's Ipseity—a man, if you wish, but the transcendental Christian man, transcendentally defined by his condition as Son and by it alone. This is the first commandment of the Christian ethic: you will live, or, more precisely, you will be this living Self, this one and none other.

Here opens up an abyss that separates the Old Law from the New Law: whereas the Old Law is incapable of positing what it commands, the acting it prescribes, so that those to whom it is addressed remain both unchanged in their real being and yet cursed by the Law that they do not apply, by contrast the New Law has already accomplished its prescription—it has already thrown into Life those to whom the injunction is made to be livings. This is a strange Commandment if it is already accomplished in them in the form of this living self that each person discovers himself to be and which has made of each, without that person wanting or even knowing it, what he or she is. Can one even say that this is a Commandment? A sort of contingency is linked in principle with the idea of commandment: the fact that it may or may not be observed. The one to whom it is addressed is separate from the commandment, distinct in his being from what the commandment itself is. This separation acquires a decisive meaning, both ethical and ontological, if the acting prescribed by the Law, but which must be added to it, contains reality in such a way that, if deprived of it, the Law remains merely an empty representation, whose sole power is to curse and condemn. But if in the New Law the Commandment is Life, if it carries within it reality and realization, and is already realized in each living person, then can we still give it that name? Is an ethic even conceivable if everything is accomplished once and for all, if no task remains, no Law to indicate what it is, no liberty to submit to?

But as we have recalled, the relation of the Commandment to the one who is commanded is identical in the Christian ethic to the transcendental birth of the ego, the institution of the transcendental Christian person in his condition as Son. The Commandment of Life, which is Life, thus generates the ego to whom it is addressed, whom it addresses inasmuch as it generates and establishes it in its condition of living ego. Therefore, it also contains the freedom required by any ethical commandment that addresses and can only address free will. We have seen how, given to itself in life's self-givenness and thus given possession of its powers, the ego finds itself free to exercise them. The task prescribed by the Commandment has also been defined: it is to live. Thus, the Christian ethic, whose Commandment is Life, contains at its core all the elements of an ethic, even though it overturns their nature and meaning. The New Law is no longer an ideal norm, an empty noeme, bur rather the essence that defines reality, Life. From the new Commandment flows nature itself, and primarily the existence of the one whom it is addressing in the very process by which it engenders it—its freedom as well, without which there is no ethic at all. But what commands has also conveyed to the person it commands what is commanded of him: to live.

What does the task of living mean to someone who is already living? Into the breach opened by this unheard-of question plunge all the fundamental intuitions of Christianity. The first is the definition of a person as Son of God. It is clear that what man has to do, what he must do—but also what he can do—depends on the essence that is originally his. If we interpret man as a natural being (as is done nowadays), it follows that the tasks that may be assigned him are rooted in the processes that are constitutive of such a being, notably in his psychological processes, with psychical processes being reduced to the physiological processes of which they are just the "representatives." There is a prior state of affairs and, within this, a programming, such that human action is merely its unfolding. If, despite everything, a norm may be imposed upon this unfolding, it is only the sum of these processes that might define that norm. For the biological individual (which is believed to exist), it is a matter of "living well"—that is to say, of finding an equilibrium resulting from the proper functioning and harmony of the processes of which he is composed. The idea of an ought-to-be [*devoir-être*], of a duty [*devoir*], of a Law in the sense of ethics, seems deprived of any foundation; there is a natural "morality," whose job, by means of some kind of "psychoanalysis," is to reduce this Law to the wish for a harmony resting on the organism's structures, and prefigured within them.

When "man" is understood in his condition of Son generated in the original Ipseity of absolute Life, there is also a prior state of affairs. It is no longer programming but rather pre-destination—the radical and essential pre-destination by virtue of which, through his condition of Son, a person is destined to be *this living person generated in absolute Life's self-generation, living only from it, able to accomplish his own essence only in the essence of this absolute Life.* It is this radical and essential pre-destination that Paul is thinking of when he writes to the Romans: "We know that in all things God works for the good of those who love him, who have been called according to his purpose. For those God foreknew he also predestined to be conformed to the likeness of his Son, that he might be the firstborn among many brothers" (Romans 8:28–29).

Those called are Life's called, called by Life to be its Sons. They were known in advance by Life, because it is by joining itself to itself that Life has joined each of them to itself; it is in its self-revelation to itself that each has been revealed to himself. But this self-revelation of absolute Life is its original Ipseity, whose effectivity is the First Living. Thus each of the sons revealed to himself in Life's self-revelation can be so only in the Ipseity that belongs to this self-revelation of Life's, only in the Arch-Son. In each of the Sons, the Arch-birth of the Arch-Son must be accomplished if he is to be born in turn. If he is able to be born and if he is born, if he is to be joined to himself in the effective and singular phenomenological Ipseity of Life in the First Living, then the latter must already have been born. The First Living was the first experience with itself of any conceivable living and thus of any Son who is asked to repeat the condition, "to be conformed to the likeness of the Son," as the Apostle says. Because life's self-generation is implicated in the Arch-generation of any conceivable living person, the pre-destination was that each transcendental living Self should repeat in itself the condition of Arch-generation, to wit, the Arch-Son himself, "that he might be the firstborn among many brothers."

The radical and essential pre-destination implied in the condition of Son (identical to his Arch-generation) is what constitutes the principle of the Christian ethic, the Commandment. John perceives this Commandment in its original form, in God's phenomenological life and identical with it. He calls it God's love. God's love is the first and only Commandment of the ethic. "The commandments 'Do not commit adultery,' 'Do not murder,' 'Do not steal,' 'Do not covet,' and whatever other commandments there may be, are summed up in this one rule: 'Love your neighbor as yourself'" (Romans 13:9). But why love others, why love yourself? If what is at issue, in them and in me, is the person-in-the-world, there is hardly any reason to do so. The most pessimistic doctrines, for example Schopenhauer's, remain quite distant from Christianity with regard to their judgment of people, who, as Paul says, are "filled with every kind of wickedness, evil, greed, and depravity. They are full of envy, murder, strife, deceit, and malice. They are gossips, slanderers, God-haters, insolent, arrogant, and boastful; they invent ways of doing evil, they disobey their parents, they are senseless, faithless, heartless, ruthless" (Romans 1:29–31). And according to Peter, "Their idea of pleasure is to carouse in broad daylight. They are blots and blemishes, reveling in their pleasures while they feast with you. With eyes full of adultery, they never stop sinning; they seduce the unstable; they are experts in greed—an accursed brood!" (2 Peter 2:12–14).

It is only insofar as the other or myself is considered in his condition of Son that the Commandment becomes comprehensible. But this happens only to the extent that the condition of Son refers to the process of absolute Life's self-generation. This is what the Commandment is. It only commands as a function of what Life is. The Commandment is only a Commandment of love because Life is love. Life is love because it experiences itself infinitely and eternally. Because it is Life, "God is love," as John says (1 John 4:8). It is because God (as absolute Life) is love that he commands Love. He commands it of all the living by giving them life, by generating them in himself as his Sons, *those who, feeling themselves in infinite Life's experience of self and its eternal love, love themselves with an infinite and eternal love, loving themselves inasmuch as they are Sons and feeling themselves to be such*—in the same way that they love others, inasmuch as they are themselves Sons and inasmuch as they feel themselves to be such. If the Commandment only prescribes love because the One who commands is himself love, it is because *far from resulting from the Commandment, love is on the contrary the presupposition of it.*

The immersion of the Commandment in absolute phenomenological Life, which experiences itself in the enjoyment and love of self, is what ultimately overturns the ethical relation according to which the Commandment determines acting and acting determines reality. According to that relation, the Commandment is powerless, as acting and reality lie outside it. It is because Kant assimilated the Commandment of love to an ethical commandment separated from reality that he was able to mount against Christianity what he believed was a radical critique and to substitute for it his morality of duty; but this was a vain pretense; since one cannot command someone to love when that person does not love, how could one command him to do his duty by respecting a law that prescribes it? Why would respect for the rational law come more easily to someone's soul than love? Kant does not perceive that in Christianity the Commandment of love is not an ethical law, nor is it addressed to a person who has to be persuaded (one knows not how) to love. In the Commandment of love, Christianity is addressed to a Son, to someone who, given to himself in life's self-giving and thus in the infinite love that absolute Life bears within itself, bears this love within himself as what engenders him at each moment. Only because it is joined to itself in life's *pathētik* embrace, edified in the love in which Life eternally loves itself, embracing itself and loving itself within this love, having become an ego in it and taking its power from it—for this sole and unique reason is the ego, constituted by this Commandment of love and drawing its condition of Son from it, able eventually to obey it.

John recognizes at the ground of the ethic the immanence of the Commandment in the process of self-generation and absolute life's love of self, in which each living person is engendered in his condition of Son: "And this is love, that we walk in obedience to his commands. As you have heard from the beginning, his command is that you walk in love" (2 John 6). Similarly, in the First Letter: "This is love for God: to obey his commandments" (1 John 5:3). If to keep the Commandment, to live in the Commandment, is to live in love, then one who does not observe the Commandment, who does not keep it, cannot remain in a state of love: "If anyone has material possessions and sees his brother in need but has no pity on him, how can the love of God be in him?" (1 John 3:17). Someone who, born of love in the sense that has been explained and holding from birth the condition of Son, still comes to lose this love, this person has also lost his condition of Son, and inasmuch as he is alive only in this condition, he is already held in death: "Anyone who does not love remains in death" (1 John 3:14). That the Commandment of love is absolute Life's love of self (which generates within itself each living person in his condition of Son), and consequently that the loss of love is the loss of this condition, are affirmed by John equally explicitly: "This is how we know who the children of God are and who the children of the devil are: anyone who does not do what is right is not a child of God; nor is anyone who does not love his brother" (1 John 3:10).

The connection between the fundamental concepts of John's ethic emerges here. First there is the essential link between the Commandment and practice. Because the Commandment is identical with the process of the generation of livings in his condition of Son and thus with the creation of life in him, in his living praxis, Commandment and praxis, Commandment and acting go together—the acting of the living proceeding from the acting of absolute Life within him, from its unceasing work. Commandment and action are originally consubstantial with generation. It is only after the fact, in the nonpractice of the Commandment, when the person no longer holds himself in a state of love and finds himself expelled from the condition that was originally his, that Commandment and practice diverge in a kind of catastrophe—from which the Old Law's ethic arises. Then, emptied of its substance, the Commandment requires a practice with which it no longer coincides; one no longer sees where it comes from or how it derives its power.

The second connection demonstrated by John combines the concepts of praxis and truth. Because acting belongs to life and is only possible within it, its phenomenological status is that of life, its self-revelation like *pathētik* self-affection. It is this *pathētik* self-affection that constitutes the very possibility of any power and any conceivable action, which is only in a position to be exercised if it is in possession of itself in and through this *pathētik* self-affection. But life's *pathētik* self-affection, its infinite love of self, defines the original essence both of Truth and of Life. That acting belongs to Truth and Life's original essence springs from this key verse: "*We know that we have come to know him if we observe his commands*" (1 John 2:3) We do not observe commands as scholars observe a molecule in the microscope. We do not observe them like scribes and Pharisees analyzing and commenting upon the Law. We observe them by putting them into practice. *In the practice of the Commandment of love, absolute Life gives the Son to himself by being given to the self who acts, in such a way that in this practice it is God himself who is revealed, who loves himself with his infinite love.* "The man who says, 'I know him,' but does not observe his commandments is a liar, and the truth is not in him. But if anyone observes his word, *God's love is truly made complete in him. This is how we know we are in him.* Whoever claims to dwell in Him, *must live as Jesus did*" (1 John 2:4–6, my emphasis).

The belonging of acting to truth and to the *pathētik* flesh of its love, its capacity while being exercised to effectuate this truth and this love, is the foundation of the Christian ethic and its power to reintroduce each into his condition of Son. The correlation in the Commandment of love between acting and truth is explicit; this is what makes acting the site of the emergence and recognition of the Truth: "Dear children, let us not love with words or tongue but *with actions and in truth*. This then is how we know that we belong to the truth" (1 John 3:18, my emphasis). This is why action's power of revelation is constantly affirmed and revelation leads back to action, which is thus nothing but the process of this revelation being accomplished. This self-revelation, and thus the possibility of recognition of what is implied in the condition of Son, is offered everywhere in the Commandment of love as its realization: "This is how we know who the children of God are"; "This is how we know what love is"; "And this is how we know that he lives in us" (1 John 3:10, 16, 24). Also, what always permits this recognition is no less clearly indicated: it is the acting of the Commandment of Life. "He who does justice . . . who loves his brother, who lays down his life, who keeps his commandments" (ibid).

The "observation" of the Commandment, the actualization of the process of generation that has led each to his condition as Son and thus to the reinsertion of that person into his original condition—such is the ethical behavior in which love arises: "Whoever has my commands and practices them, he is the one who loves me" (John 14:21). The one who loves me in fact means: in the action of this someone, the self-revelation of the essential Ipseity in which he is engendered is the pure enjoyment of this Ipseity, the love of Christ. And the Gospel continues: "He who loves me will be loved by my Father," which means that because the self-enjoyment of the Arch-Son is just the self-enjoyment of absolute Life embracing itself and thus loving itself eternally, the one who loves Christ carries all that within him: the self-enjoyment of Christ like the Father's self-enjoyment, such that it is present in each Son inasmuch as he feels himself in the Son's self-enjoyment, in which the Father's self-enjoyment is accomplished— Life's infinite love of self. Ultimately, therefore, this is the essence and final goal of the generation of each person within absolute Life: that Life may embrace itself in him as soon as he is alive. "And I too will love him and show myself to him" (ibid.)—to him who in his self-enjoyment is nothing other than Christ's self-enjoyment as the Father's self-enjoyment.

The Christian ethic is the culmination of the decisive phenomenological and ontological implications that compose the kernel of Christianity. Thus it leads in exemplary fashion to its Truth—to the mode of revelation of absolute Life, which is the essence of this Life and God himself, as it appears in the extraordinary question from Judas (not Iscariot), which arises, seemingly unexpectedly, right in the middle of the chapter we have been discussing: *"But, Lord, why do you intend to show yourself to us and not to the world?"* (John 14:22, my emphasis). The answer contains the decisive implications we have tried to make explicit, and does so with stupefying density: "If anyone loves me, he will put my teaching into practice. My Father will love him, and we will come to him and make our home with him."

11

The Paradoxes of Christianity

The Christian ethic introduces us to a certain number of paradoxes. Because this ethic is rooted in the founding intuitions of Christianity, these paradoxes come from Christianity itself. Some of them, however, are purely superficial, and we will allude briefly to them. Others seems to rock its foundations. So the question is whether they really undermine Christianity or rather allow its solidity to be tested.

A first paradox arises regarding what we call the critique of works. This critique contests the possibility for a person to be saved on account of his own works, that is to say, on account of the acts of which he is the author. But how can such a criticism be made of an ethic that explicitly grants acting, specifically an action that is the doing of an individual, the power to reestablish him in his original condition of Son and, in this way, save him? Moreover, it is in the repeated assertion of the necessity of obeying the Commandment of love, in its fulfillment, that John situates salvation. It is not only in the work of love that love proves itself, but it is in work that love is nurtured and from work that love takes its reality. Since salvation consists in the realization of love, it comes from work. No less explicit is the formation of this thesis in James's Epistle: "Was not our ancestor Abraham considered righteous for what he did when he offered his son Isaac on the altar?" (James 2:21). The reference to effective action here takes on substance, since it is the very hand of Abraham about to strike his son that is held back by the angel, as we see in so many famous paintings.

It is the very act, the real and monstrous act of cutting the throat of his own son, that encapsulates salvation. Of course, to accomplish such an act, Abraham needed to have absolute faith in his God, but it is the act and it alone that makes faith effective. Before the act properly speaking, the faith appeared to be undermined by a sort of doubt, which held back the act. It is by going on to the act, by throwing oneself frantically into it, that faith attests that it is faith, an absolute faith that is only possible thus. This is why James says in his Epistle: "His faith was made complete by what he did"; and again, "You see that a person is justified by what he does and not by faith alone"; and more categorically, "Show me your faith without deeds, and I will show you my faith by what I do" (James 2:22, 24, 18).

As we know, it is in the name of Faith that Paul denies works the power to confer salvation, or (as he says) righteousness, "the righteousness that comes from God and is by faith" (Philippians 3:9). As for Faith, it is itself the effect of grace, so that salvation ultimately comes through grace. But then, "If by grace, then it is no longer by works, if it were, grace would no longer be grace" (Romans 11:6). The question of whether man can save himself, that is to say, through his works, or whether he owes his salvation solely to grace from God (hence arbitrary), is a question that will occupy theologians as well as believers for centuries, who will ask whether, if salvation comes only from a grace freely granted by God, it is still worth the effort to go to so much trouble.

Let us be content here to observe that the question of whether man can assure his salvation by his own works is alien to Christianity and ought not to have been posed in this way. This appears to be true if one refers once more to one of its founding intuitions, namely, that man in the sense that we understand it nowadays, the democratic man, for example, the autonomous man capable of acting by himself, does not exist in the New Testament. What exists is someone who, through his transcendental birth in absolute Life, is a Son and is only possible as such. From absolute Life the Son takes not only his condition as living but also the possibility of acting, in the way we have stated: insofar as, given to himself in absolute Life's self-givenness, he finds himself now in possession of himself and all of his powers, now able to put them into play and thus free to do so. But if it is the possibility of acting that is given to man—through grace, if you want to put it that way—then how could a single one of his acts escape this condition, arise from an initiative for which man is truly the foundation? What Paul criticizes in the pretense that works save through themselves is this belief that they are the doing of man and result from his autonomous activity. In the Epistle to the Romans, shortly after the assertion that salvation does not come "by works" but rather "by faith," comes the unequivocal declaration: "You do not support the root, but the root supports you" (Romans 11:18).

Therefore what is at issue are "human" works coming from man's own power and thus explicable by it. The other objection to such works is that they are works of the Law—which means that man has produced them by taking the Law as model. In addition to the powerlessness of man incapable of producing by himself the saving work comes the powerlessness of the Law to accomplish itself through that work, such that the two forms of powerlessness are superimposed and definitively undermine the efficacy of "works." As for the Faith that Paul abruptly contrasts with them, it must also be understood in the light of the founding intuitions of Christianity, not as a form of thought but as a determination of Life. As we have observed, Faith is not produced in the field of knowledge, as a sort of knowledge of inferior degree, whose object is presumed without being truly seen, and perhaps without ever being visible—a knowledge that is not only inferior, then, but illusory. Faith is not a signifying consciousness that is still empty, incapable of producing its content by itself. Faith is not of the realm of consciousness, but rather of feeling. It comes from the fact that nobody ever gave himself life, but rather that life gives itself, and gives itself to the living, as what submerges him—from the fact that in life he is totally living, as long as life gives him to himself. Faith is the living's certitude of living, a certitude that can come to him ultimately only from absolute Life's own certitude of living absolutely, from its self-revelation, without reservation, in the invincible force of its Second Coming. Having entered into him in its own certitude that life is for living, Faith is within the life of each transcendental me as the feeling it has of absolute Life. From this comes its irrepressible power, not that of the transcendental ego placed in itself and in its I Can in absolute Life's self-givenness, but the power of this self-givenness, its invincible and eternal embrace. This is why Faith never takes its force from a temporal act and never mingles with it. It is the Revelation to man of his condition of Son, the grasping of man in Life's self-grasping.

Only human works, then, may be opposed to Faith, not the Commandment of love to which Faith leads. If it is just absolute Life's experience inside any person, then Faith is also that of absolute acting, acting revealing itself to be that of a Son (no longer that of a man). This feeling of self, this love of self of absolute Life's, as a person feeling within Faith his condition of Son and acting according to this feeling, is referred to by Paul in Galatians as "faith acting through love" (5:6). In the end, Paul means the same thing as John does. At the core of each conceivable action, of the ego's I Can, there is this other acting, that of absolute Life, which reveals itself to itself by joining the ego to itself, the Arch-Revelation of Arch-generation, the all-seeing Eye to which each act, even the most modest, owes being linked with itself and being able to act—the all-seeing Eye that precedes it and accompanies it as its most interior and most inevitable possibility. This unbreakable connection between the Arch-Revelation of absolute Life in any living ego and the simplest act by the latter appears in the stunning statement in Apocalypse: "I am he who searches hearts and minds, and I will repay each of you according to your deeds" (2:23).

As soon as we examine one of Christianity's paradoxes, we are brought back to its founding intuitions. Rather, then, than enumerating these paradoxes, then locating them and offering a solution for each, it is better to proceed in the opposite direction: to gather these intuitions together so as to recognize in them the origin of all the paradoxes that are their inevitable result and thus so many "proofs"—not factual proofs but in some fashion apodictic ones, receiving their validity from the Source itself, from absolute Life and the eternal process in which it generates all livings.

Four founding intuitions that form the essential kernel of Christianity also make all of its paradoxes intelligible. These are:

1. The duplicity of appearing.
2. The antinomic structure of life itself, a structure that we have not yet discussed but which will appear later.
3. The difference between Life and livings, that which separates the (absolute) self-affection of the former from the (relative) self-affection of the latter.
4. The decisive significance of praxis and Ipseity in life's essence.

First, then, the duplicity of appearing means that in Christianity everything is double. First of all, appearing or the mode of appearing, is double: on the one hand, there is the way Life appears, grasping itself immediately in its own pathos without ever putting itself at a distance; on the other hand, there is the way the world appears, as the "outside"—the horizon of exteriority against whose background everything shown to us in the light of this "world" (both things and ideas) becomes visible. So on one side is *pathētik* and in-ecstatic Life, and on the other, the ecstatic truth of the world, the apparition of this milieu of exteriority in which everything is shown to us as exterior. *Because the way of appearing is double,* what appears, *even if it is the same, nevertheless appears in two different ways, in a dual aspect.* Thus our singular body appears to us in two different ways: on the one hand as this living body whose life is my own life, inside of which I am placed, with which I coincide at the same time as I coincide with each of its powers—to see, take, move, and so on—such that they are mine and the "I Can" puts them into operation. On the other hand, it appears as a body-object that the "I Can" sees, touches, feels—the same as any other object. But what is true of my body is true of each of my behaviors: lived by me from inside in the identity of my own life, and at the same time appearing to me from the outside, as to others, in the form of a behavior similar to any other objective process.

Everything is double, but if what is double—what is offered to us in a double aspect—is in itself one and the same reality, then one of its aspects must be merely an appearance, an image, a copy of reality, but not that reality itself—precisely, its double. Two eventualities are then offered: that this double, this exterior appearance, corresponds to reality, or that it does not correspond to it. In the second case, appearance is a trap; it is the appearing of an acting that is not produced from where acting draws its possibility, in the invisible life of the person. For example, there unfolds an external conduct that is reputed to be that of fasting, with all the characteristic aspects of fasting, and yet the one who behaves in this way, of whom we say that he is fasting and who presents all the aspects and marks of fasting, is not really fasting. Similarly, someone adopts the posture of a believer and makes all the right gestures, but does not in fact believe. In instituting the permanent possibility of the trap and the lie, the duplicity of appearance unfolds a universe whose principle is hypocrisy. Hypocrisy does not establish itself in the form of an already realized state of affairs, as if all the detectable behaviors in such a universe were hypocritical. In this case, no hypocrisy would be possible. It is precisely in the guise of an always open possibility that the duality of appearing makes hypocrisy reign in a metaphysical system constituted and defined by this duality. Precisely because the metaphysical system of Christianity rests on appearing's duplicity and is therefore a system based on potential hypocrisy, Christ railed against it endlessly and with unexpected virulence. Because there is the permanent possibility of hypocrisy in such a universe, "values," advocated by John more than anyone else, are the values of truth, which is the Truth of Life and exists only in Life—where duplicity has become impossible: before the all-seeing Eye of God himself.

But what also reigns, at the same time as the possibility of hypocrisy and the duplicity of appearing and through them, is paradox. Christian paradox is not the opposite of common opinion, even if it is contrasted with opinion. Paradox holds together two truths that exclude each other, such that, although each is possible if considered in isolation, the fact of asserting them at the same time about the same reality seems inadmissible. Someone may well believe or not believe, he may fast or not fast, but for this person and not another to believe and at the same time not believe—that he fasts and at the same time that he is not fasting—this is not possible. Unless appearing itself is in fact double, such that in this double way of appearing, the same thing or the same reality—to believe, not believe, fast, not fast, be someone and not another—also finds itself doubled, puts on a double appearance, that of belief and unbelief, fasting and the absence of fasting. Belief and unbelief, fasting and the absence of fasting, are possible at the same time within the same individual because they are appearances, each having the actuality of its appearance and being incontestable as such. This copresence at the same time, in the same individual, of two opposite and contradictory yet apparent determinations, both equally shown, is what we have called hypocrisy. Hypocrisy is the prototype of the paradox whose nature we are trying to elucidate—paradox, like hypocrisy, therefore, takes its principle from the duplicity of appearing.

However, in the duplicity of appearing of the same reality, there is something else we have seen: that this reality is real only once, there where it embraces itself in the flesh and in the irreducibility of its pathos—whereas its exterior apparition in the world's "outside-oneself" is precisely just a simple appearance. It is permissible to conceive that nothing in life's effectivity corresponds to this appearance: no real faith lies inside the exterior conduct of faith—since this faith is only real in life, as the experience that each living has within him of absolute Life. This is why Christianity can turn worldly values upside down, not as the result of a resentment of these values, which would lead it to denigrate and hate what it does not possess, but because these "values" are only an appearance in the world: the appearance of fasting, of faith, of love, of the strength that belongs to love—in short, the appearance of what only becomes effective within life. The duplicity of appearing opens a space of interplay between reality and its counterfeit. One mode of appearing, that of Life, makes the former (reality) possible; another one, that of the world, its counterfeit. So Christianity does not turn values upside down; on the contrary, it assigns them their unquestioned place. In granting values to Life, it withdraws them from the world. By the same token, it distinguishes two fundamental values, or rather, fundamental value and the place of all values, on one side and, on the other, counter-value and the foundation of all counter-values. Truth and Life versus Lies and the world. This is why Christ says: "You are from below; I am from above. You are of this world; I am not of this world" (John 8:23). He says "I," meaning Life and Truth, and "the world," meaning the counterfeit, life, hypocrisy. "I, the Truth, Life [*Moi, la Vérité, la Vie*]": Life's self-revelation, which is Truth, is accomplished in the Ipseity of the First Living, in this Me that is Christ.

If the duplicity of appearing has conferred a dual appearance on everything, such that one of them alone contains reality, while the other is in fact only a double, flimsy and empty, then a criterion is required if one wants to be able to decide which is appearance and which is reality, and to make this a legitimate decision. Each appearance, overall, has for itself the effectiveness of its apparition, and so it is a phenomenological given like any other. Here Christianity does overturn values, the values of truth, everywhere substituting the truth of Life for that of the world. This is where its revolutionary character lies. If anything goes without saying in the eyes of Western thought and its rationality, it is indeed that the criterion of any conceivable truth resides in perception, whether sensory or intelligible. Consequently, the criterion of any rationality consists in the fact of taking this perception as the foundation of any assertion that pretends to be rational insofar as it leans on perceptible information and firmly sticks to it. This is the criterion of any rational knowledge, as well as that of common sense, which Christianity abruptly turns upside down. For Christianity, the truth no longer consists of showing itself in the world's light, but on the contrary, one might say, by avoiding this. The same is the case with life: never showing itself in a world and not taking its manifestation from it, it is no less revealed in its *pathētik*, unimpeachable flesh. This radical overturning of the criterion of any truth is a paradox because it completely upsets ways of thinking about humanity, whether of today or of ancient times. Beyond these ways of thinking, ways of doing and the practical conduct of societies, as well as individuals, are also overturned.

In effect, from this paradox flows a multitude of consequences, which are themselves paradoxes; here we confine ourselves to mentioning or recalling some of them. The first is the action of grace addressed by Christ to his Father to be made known not to those who have knowledge but to those who do not: "Anyone who will not receive the kingdom of God like a little child will never enter it" (Mark 10:15). It is a paradox that he grants knowledge of the Essential to those who know nothing—but only an apparent paradox, if this Essential is a Life that is foreign to knowledge but consubstantial with all those it generates as its Sons. Still more of a paradox is situating the criterion of truth not in its universality but, on the contrary, in an absolute singularity, in a Me, as prestigious as it may be: "I am the truth!" [C'est Moi la vérité!]; "I will give you words and wisdom" (Luke 21:15). This is also just an apparent paradox if it is true that the first and last possibility of any truth is its self-revelation in the essential Ipseity of a First Living. But still a paradox, if the overthrow of knowledge, of its criterion of evidence, of its character of universality, all necessarily correspond with the overthrow of all laws, both theoretical and practical— and thus of the wisdom that relies on them and on observing them. "Has not God made foolish the wisdom of the world?" (1 Corinthians 1:20). This is just as apparently paradoxical if, along with life, laws reign other than those that govern the course of things and by which people seek to regulate their actions. Other laws: those of life, precisely.

These are the laws of life that ought to be taken into account if we would now understand a new series of paradoxes, which no longer rest on the duplicity of appearance but take their principle from Life itself and its own Truth. The issue now is Life's self-revelation in its pathos. It is this mode of original revelation of life that constitutes the principle of the weightiest paradox. *Because this mode of revelation is offered in itself as an antinomy, it determines the antinomic structure of life itself,* independently and beyond any opposition to the world and its truth. So the antinomic structure of life is a universal structure; it involves any possible life whatever, and thereby, everything that draws from life its own possibility: any conceivable living. The clear apperception of life's antinomic structure constitutes what we will call the second founding intuition of Christianity.

The mode of revelation proper to life consists in the pure fact of experiencing oneself. We now know that there are two ways of experiencing oneself: the way of absolute Life, which is God's, and the way of each living, of the living I myself am. To experience oneself in the latter way is to be radically passive with respect to one's own life, to submit to it at each moment in a submitting that is stronger than any freedom. It is to suffer what one experiences and thus what one is, to bear it, to bear oneself, to suffer oneself, such that this "suffer oneself," this "bear oneself," is the sole mode of access that leads each person to himself. This mode of access is life. It is truly the phenomenological structure of life to which "suffer oneself" refers. Because "suffer oneself" is the structure of life, by the same token it finds itself to be the structure of the living—the living who is given to himself only in life's self-givenness, a self-givenness that is merely this "suffer oneself." This self-givenness of life, in which the living is given to himself, this "suffer oneself" that constitutes the phenomenological structure of life and thus of any person, has a phenomenological substance that we have recognized as pathos, a pure and transcendental affectivity, the concrete affective flesh in which (everywhere and always) life affects itself inasmuch as it is life. What we now perceive, then, is that *this pathos is by no means indeterminate*, but always takes the concrete form of a specific tonality, that of the suffering included in the "suffer oneself" and constituting its essence. The transcendental affectivity that belongs to life's essence as the original mode by which it is phenomenalized is a particular (yet fundamental) affective tonality, the tonality of suffering that determines from the very start, in its entirety, any possible life and hence any person.

In experiencing oneself in the "suffer oneself" of life, each person relates to himself in such a way that he bears himself, finding himself charged with self without having wanted it but also without ever being discharged of this charge that he is for himself. Charged with self forever, he cannot break the tie that attaches him to himself in the "suffering" of the "suffering oneself." This tie is his ipseity, the ipseity of his Self. Ipseity is not identity, the simple identity with self of a "me" defined by this formal and empty structure, the formal and empty structure of A = A. So empty is this identity that it is lost from the first step, broken into difference—the difference of A from itself, a difference to which this identity is identical. The true ipseity is an affective tonality that is fundamental and irresistible, a pure phenomenological tonality in which, suffering and bearing oneself, the Self is thrown into itself, in and through this suffering, to suffer and to bear this Self that it is. This charge is heavy. Heavier still is not being able to discharge it: so heavy that, under this burden that cannot be removed, suffering changes into a pain that is unbearable, yet consubstantial with the person's life and with his ipseity. From the suffering of this Self charged with self in the suffering of his ipseity there arises anxiety, the anxiety of the Self to be a Self—this Self that he is without being able to avoid or escape this condition, the fact that he is a Self, and, even more, this particular Self that he is now and will be forever. Taken to its extreme, this anxiety is called despair. Anxiety and despair do not happen to "me" as a function of the vicissitudes of a personal history, but are born in "me," in the phenomenological structure of the Ipseity that makes "me" a Self, and in the affective tonality of the "suffer oneself" in which the essence of this Ipseity consists.

In the "suffer oneself" of its Ipseity and in the suffering that comes to it from the inexorable character of this suffering, the "me" feels itself and has the experience of self; therefore it is put in possession of itself and of each of the modalities of its life: it enjoys itself, it is enjoyment, it is Joy. The stronger the suffering in which, thrown into self, given up to self, overcome by this burden that it is for itself and which it cannot get rid of, the "me" experiences itself in the suffering of this "suffer oneself," then the stronger is this testing, the more violent the grasp in which it grasps itself and is carried away with itself and enjoys itself—and the stronger is the joy.

Thus is disclosed to us the antinomic structure of life as the antinomy of the fundamental affective phenomenological tonalities in which life is revealed to itself by feeling itself in the flesh of its own pathos—in such a way that this pathos does not contribute to a hazardous succession of external events but is split (because of the structure of the mode of revelation proper to life) into two different and contrasting affective tonalities. But we have to understand this opposition between two phenomenological tonalities that are coconstitutive of life's self-revelation. This is precisely not an opposition in the usual sense, an opposition between opposite terms. Instead, Suffering and Joy are linked by an essential affinity, which refers back to a primitive unity: the absolutely primitive original unity of Suffering and Rejoicing. Suffering appears to be the path that leads to enjoying, and thus its condition. It is only in experiencing oneself in the "suffer oneself" that the life of the living Self comes into itself, such that suffering is veritably a path and a way. It is the test that life must pass so that, in and through that test, it attains itself and comes into itself in that coming that is the essence of any life, the process of its self-revelation.

But to suffer is not a way or a path in the sense in which we usually understand it; it defines no place in which one would have to be so as to leave it to enter into another place and stay there in turn, in that place where joy reigns. On the contrary, "to suffer" dwells inside "to rejoice" as *that which leads to joy inasmuch as it dwells within it,* as its internal and permanent condition. It is only in its "suffer oneself," insofar as that occurs, that life attains itself in the self-enjoyment of its own rapture. It is only at the limit of this suffering, when it is carried to a paroxysm in extreme suffering, that joy finds itself borne to its extreme point and elevated to its paroxysm, to the extreme point of beatitude and joy. This is the antinomic structure of life, its division into the dichotomy of affectivity, between the opposed tonalities of suffering and happiness, such that the former can only lead to the latter, inasmuch as suffering takes place and does not stop taking place within happiness, as what gives it to itself, as its internal and insurmountable condition.

Blessed are those who suffer. The hallucinatory proposition pronounced before the centuries, before the earth and the sky existed, was stated by Christ himself: "Heaven and earth will pass away, but my words will never pass away" (Luke 21:33). The co-belonging of suffering to joy as its interior and unsurpassable condition of possibility—this is the second founding intuition of Christianity, one that has not come up before now. This second founding intuition is thus tied to a new series of paradoxes, those that are enunciated in the Beatitudes. While the paradoxes analyzed until now have rested on the duplicity of appearing, on the double truth of Life and the world, the paradoxes of the Beatitudes relate in an essential way to life and its internal structure. Most of them express the original co-belonging of suffering to enjoyment. This co-belonging defines the Arch-structure of suffering, which wills that it be in the accomplishment of suffering and in its own becoming that having joy comes along and is accomplished, and only in this way.

This series of paradoxes consequently takes a single form: beatitude is affirmed as the lot of those who are plunged into suffering. Neither suffering nor the beatitude to which it leads, and still less the relation that unites them, is a simple fact. Suffering and beatitude—and the implication of the former within the latter and so the latter within the former—are essences, processes of becoming ruled by the a priori structures of the phenomenalization of phenomenality, as the latter happens in the living of life. Hence, in any effective living, for it to be so, to suffer and have joy are joint and contemporaneous modes of its *pathētik* self-affection. This is the reason why there are no particular conditions that motivate suffering, which instead derives from its phenomenological structure—the suffering that allows life to be carried away with itself in self-enjoyment. Similarly, blessed are the poor, the afflicted, the hungry, the persecuted, those who suffer calumny, those who suffer for justice. The Beatitudes are not added to their suffering, after the fact, by a kind of synthetic adjunct, like a sort of recompense or promise, a recompense or promise held in abeyance elsewhere than within the suffering itself—in another world that supposedly follows it. The Beatitudes do not follow upon suffering except insofar as suffering is the path that leads to them, a path outside of which no access to Beatitude is possible. This is because suffering belongs to living, whose Beatitude is just its achievement. It is this internal link between suffering and Beatitude that makes the latter arise inevitably wherever the former has reigned. The future that in Matthew (5:3–12), as well as in Luke (6:23), links the Beatitudes to various forms of suffering and persecution takes the form of the apodictic: far from signifying the exteriority and contingency of the link that unites the fundamental tonalities of living in the Archstructure of pathos, it presents its inexorable character.

A difficulty remains. We understand that the antinomic structure of life is the basis of a paradox, to the extent that ultimately paradox appears as the simple formulation of this structure and thus as its immediate confirmation. But does the antinomic structure of life—of the mode of phenomenalization by which its own phenomenality is phenomenalized—not contradict this phenomenality? Life is a self-revelation. It reveals itself, not only in the sense that it is what carries out revelation but, as we have seen, in another sense, in that what it reveals is itself. This determination of life's self-revelation is found again in each of its modalities, which make pain be pain, hope be hope, hate be hate, precisely as each modality indubitably feels itself. Each sensation is what it is because it feels itself in its immediate suffering, and thus what it feels is itself, "what it is" purely and simply without any possible discussion. We know that upon this decisive trait of each of life's modalities (which he improperly calls *cogitationes*), Descartes will base the certainty of the *cogito*. But if pain is that insurmountably and incontestably possible pain, if the sensation is invincibly this sensation, then suffering, too, is this suffering such as it experiences itself in the self-revelation of its own pathos: it is this suffering phenomenological flesh and nothing else. How can we then say that it is joy, this joy whose affectivity, whose tonality, differs so obviously from that of suffering—how can we say that the summit of its "to suffer" is the summit of this joy?

Another difficulty arises from examining the Beatitudes. While Matthew gives eight, Luke cites four—which he follows with four maledictions. But the first two maledictions are strange; their following on immediately from the Beatitudes causes an unease, a sort of contradiction that might recall the one we just mentioned regarding suffering, which was that at the same time as it is suffering in its phenomenological flesh and thus in its self-identity, it must also be something else—joy. The first malediction says "But woe to you who are rich, for you are your own consolation" (Luke 6:24). The object of this malediction is really the identity with self and thus the certitude of each modality of life, the fact that each of them, immediately experiencing itself, is what it is—and nothing else. Thus the experience of wealth, the joy it procures, what is said to be its "comfort"—this joy as it feels itself, then, is what is cursed. Cursed is the fact that one of life's modalities may be what it is: joy a joy, satisfaction a satisfaction. This identity with self of any modality of life's immediate feeling of itself is demolished by the second malediction. This satisfaction, this joy, this happy sentiment that life has of being itself and so enjoying itself—this is what is broken, torn apart, dislocated, destroyed, blown up, abolished. "Woe to you who are well fed now, for you will go hungry" (Luke 6:25). The plenitude of life and the feeling of satisfaction it brings—this must yield to a great tearing apart, to the Desire that no object can fulfill. Here the understanding of the paradoxes of the Beatitudes relates to the third founding intuition of Christianity—not the simple duplicity of appearing, not the antinomic structure of life, but the difference that separates Life from the living person and the former's self-affection from the latter's.

The first difficulty is that suffering might be its contrary, joy. If I truly suffer and if what characterizes any suffering is its identity with itself or, to express it phenomenologically, this specific affective tonality, irreducible to any other and which experiences itself as it is—as this suffering, and this one as opposed to that one—how can we sustain the idea that amid this suffering precisely, confusing me with its impressionable and suffering flesh and identifying me with that suffering, that I am yet happy? But the whole problematic of Christianity, its conception of man as a transcendental me generated in absolute Life and thus as Son, has now and forever demolished that objection. This is because this suffering is only joined to itself in the manner in which the living Self is joined to itself— not by itself, but in the self-givenness of absolute Life and in it alone. When a suffering experiences itself, *there is still within this ordeal something other*: it is not that suffering that experiences, and what it experiences is never limited to itself alone, either. What experiences when suffering . . . itself is absolute Life, and what is when this ordeal of self takes place is not only its own content, the specific tonality of this particular suffering. Inevitably and at the same time, the absolute Life that gives suffering in itself is given to itself in the Ipseity of this suffering, in its self-givenness. Suffering's self-givenness outstrips each suffering, and it only gives suffering to itself inasmuch as it first gave the Self to itself. And suffering has only given the Self to itself inasmuch as it was first given to itself by giving the Self to itself. The Self is living only in life—it would never experience itself if it did not first experience life, if life did not first experience itself in the Self, as the Self experiences itself; if life did not experience itself in the Self and the Self did not experience itself in life each time that it experiences something, so as to be able to have done so; if absolute Life did not feel itself in the Self and if the Self did not feel itself in Life in each suffering that it experiences.

Such is the transcendence present in any immanent modality of life, for example in any suffering; there is not some exteriority in which this suffering would find the means to avoid the self and flee itself. It is within suffering, on the contrary—since, in its radical immanence, it is crushed against itself and overwhelmed by itself, as it were, by the oppressive part of its content and by this burden it is for itself—that the work of absolute Life's self-giving that gives it to itself takes place. Suffering is within Life, as that which is of another order than it, that does not come from it, and to which alone it owes its coming into itself, to which this particular suffering first owes the experiencing of itself and of living. Thus, suffering is always more and other than itself. In it is always revealed—as what reveals it to itself, yet more hidden and more contestable than its own—another life, the "to suffer" and "to rejoice" of absolute Life, whose suffering is never just a modality.

But because suffering never reveals itself without there being revealed in it at the same time what suffering reveals to itself, therefore in fact it is never alone but always surprised, surpassed, submerged, by this antinomic structure of life that inhabits any life and thus any of life's modalities. *It is not suffering itself but the "to suffer" included in it as what delivers it to itself that leads to the "rejoicing" implied in any "to suffer" and made possible by it.* And the sharper the suffering, the more it gives to feeling that "to suffer" enveloped in it as what gives that suffering to feeling and throws it into itself as an unbearable burden, then the more this "to suffer" given to feeling in the excess of this suffering will give to feeling the "rejoicing" it achieves —and the more surely the suffering at the summit of itself will produce beatitude. *It is the phenomenological structure of absolute Life that the Beatitudes enunciate.* The Beatitudes describe to man his condition of Son—a Son finding in the essence from which he is born his phenomenological predestination, that of reproducing in himself the destiny of absolute Life, its perpetual coming forth, in the "to suffer" and through it, in the joy of self and in the exhilaration of this rapture. It is because suffering bears within it this "to suffer" and gives it to feeling more strongly than any other tonality of life that all those whom it strikes will also bear within themselves what is given at the summit of this "to suffer"—absolute Life's joy of self and its exhilaration.

What the Beatitudes celebrate and what they bless is the ultimate metaphysical situation, which wills that within each form of life, even the most unhappy, there is accomplished the essence of absolute Life, its self-givenness according to the structure of the "to suffer" in which it comes into itself in its *pathētik* embrace. But from this same relation between each particular form of life and absolute Life arises the malediction; this is what supplies its motif. "Woe to you who are well fed now." In the plenitude of its living, does not life exercise its highest purpose? How could this plenitude become the stake in a contest, let alone the object of a curse? But it is precisely not absolute Life (whose "to suffer" leads to self-joy) that is cursed—any more than the unhappy life that always feels this "to suffer" in how it is immersed in its suffering without having wished it. What is cursed is what experiences itself—and thus the pleasure of experiencing oneself and of experiencing pleasure, and to be living—as its own good, as what comes from it and thus comes back to it, as something it has somehow produced. *This illusion is the transcendental illusion of the ego.*

As we have seen, the ego attributes to itself all the dispositions and capacities that it discovers within it. Because, given to itself in absolute Life's self-givenness, it finds itself to be in possession of itself and thus of this living Self and can then dispose of all the powers that belong to its body or its mind, so that it takes itself, we were saying, as the source of these powers. That it may put them into operation seems to come to the ego from its own power, and moreover this is what defines its power, what it can do, this "I Can," as it refers to itself. But the ego considers that everything it experiences, and notably the pleasure of experiencing itself and living, in the same way comes from itself, having its source within. This illusion reaches its extreme point in the case of autoeroticism, in which the person reads into his most evident experience the notion that he is producing his own pleasure. When, in the ordinary eroticism of heterosexuality, this pleasure comes from the other as much as from oneself, it is in any case a person and the body of a man or woman that is the origin of all that he experiences and notably the pleasure that he gives himself or by the intermediary of the other, who is like him.

The transcendental illusion of the ego, we see increasingly clearly, consists of a person's forgetting of the condition of Son. This forgetting, present in all the attitudes that the person actively determines, is the real object of the curse, which is not wealth, but wealth lived by people as their own property. It is the absolutely general way the Self's constant experience of self is lived by it as something coming from itself—it is this way of living, of experiencing oneself, the feeling of having an autonomous life—this is what is cursed. "Well fed" means fulfilled, filled with possessions. But in reality, it is the self that attributes to itself the merit of finding itself in this situation in which it is showered with everything, because it first granted itself the merit of finding itself in that situation that is its own, as if it had gotten there all alone, into the transcendental condition of being this living Self—as if, generated in absolute Life's self-generation and in it alone, it had not first been a Son.

For someone feeling himself as the source of all his powers and all his sentiments, especially his pleasures, someone who lives in the permanent illusion of being a self-sufficient ego having only from itself its condition as ego as well as all that thereby becomes possible for it (acting, feeling, enjoying)—to that person what is lacking is no less than what constantly gives this ego to itself and is not it: absolute Life's self-givenness, in which this ego is given to itself and everything else is simultaneously given to it (its powers and pleasures). *This terrifying lack in each ego of what gives it to itself*—what it is missing even when it feels itself as lacking for nothing, as sufficing to itself, and especially in the pleasure it has of being itself and believing itself the source of this pleasure—this is what determines the great Rift. This lack and absolute void is the Hunger that nothing can satisfy, the Hunger and Thirst for Life, which the ego has stopped feeling in itself at the same time as its condition as Son, when, in pleasure, it takes itself for the source of this pleasure and identifies with it as its own property. "Woe to those who are well fed now, for you will go hungry" (Luke 6:25).

What is one hungry for, in this Hunger that comes to all those who are well fed, as the misfortune that none of them will escape? What is lacking to each person who sees himself as the site and source of his pleasures and powers, even the power that gave him to himself, and doing so, gave him, in experiencing himself, the possibility of experiencing the power that gave him to himself to enjoy himself and to enjoy the power that gave him the joy of self? It is absolute Life, for which all those who are "well fed" will hunger if each is satisfied with himself as the source of this satisfaction. That they are hungry for absolute Life—whether this absolute Life is the single Food that can satisfy the Hunger, especially the hunger of those who are well fed, or else the sole Water able to quench the Thirst of all those struck by the curse because they live their satisfaction and pleasure as their own doing—is stated in the uncompromising words of the one who speaks about Life as about himself and of himself as of Life: the Arch-Son, in whom Life generates and reveals itself. "I have food to eat that you know nothing about" (John 4:32); "Everyone who drinks this water will be thirsty again, but whoever drinks the water I give him will never thirst. Indeed, the water I give him will become in him a spring of water welling up to eternal life" (John 4:13–14). This Food, finally, is the self-accomplishment of absolute Life, as is also stated: "My Food is to do the will of him who sent me and to finish his work" (John 4:34).

The difference between absolute Life, which gives itself to itself in the hyper-strength of its self-generation, and the life of the ego, given to it without having willed it, always already given to itself without ever having wanted this power to give itself to him and thus to engender itself—this difference is a *pathētik* difference. The hyper-power of one is an exhilaration, the nonpower of the other, a feeling of impotence. Therefore, when the ego is affected by a content that it did not itself produce, this content seems burdensome. And so any life issuing from a birth and thus not cast by itself into birth is heavy to bear. This is the principle of the "unhappiness of being born"—the Arch-fact due to which each person carries the burden of this Self that he or she is without having willed it, without ever being able to decide if he wanted to come into life, into this life that is precisely his own, nor into this Self that is his. Never having been able to will or not to will coming into life or into this ego of his is not at first negative, as we have had occasion to observe. It is only after the fact, once its transcendental birth is accomplished, that a living Self or an ego can ask whether or not it wanted to come into this Self that it is. Its question always comes too late. *The sentiment of forever being burdened with self without having wanted to* is the sentiment it experiences as an unhappiness at being born, in the anguish that arises from this unhappiness. But this sentiment of being forever burdened with self without having wanted to *is precisely not given by the ego to itself, nor does the ego determine its conditions, nor does it even bear this burden*: only absolute Life's self-givenness gives it to the ego, what carries and bears it is only what makes it bearable to itself, the "to suffer" of absolute Life, in which that Life comes into itself in the exhilaration of its original Ipseity. "Come to me all you who are weary and burdened, and I will give you rest. Take my yoke upon you and learn from me, for I am gentle and humble in heart, and you will find rest for your souls. For my yoke is easy and my burden is light" (Matthew 11:28–30).

Why is this burden (that the ego is for itself) so heavy to bear, while that of absolute Life—which also has the experience of itself—is so light? Because it is absolute Life that throws itself into self in the absolute joy of itself and the infinite love of self, in the absolute living in which nothing is borne if not its unlimited joy and love. This absolute joy and love is experienced by the Arch-Son in the essential Ipseity in which absolute Life experiences itself. This is why—since the experience it has of self is that of absolute Life (the "to suffer" that is only "to have joy")—its burden is so light. The idea that the Arch-Son does the will of his Father and is nothing other than that will—"I always do what pleases him" (John 8:29)—that the self-affecting accomplished in its Ipseity is that of absolute Life and thus of the love with which God loves himself, and finally that, in this way, he keeps his commandments, the commandments of love—these are ideas that clarify the enigma of John's First Epistle: "This is love for God: to obey his commands. And his commands are not burdensome. . . . " (1 John 5:2–3).

This transformation of the heaviest burden into something lighter, this magic transubstantiation, too, of the greatest suffering into the exhilaration of unlimited love—all this only takes place in one in whom—in the image of Christ—absolute Life's self-affecting has been substituted for the simple person's self-affection, given to himself without having wanted to, yet in and through this absolute Life's self-affection. All this happens in him only if—living his condition of Son and being nothing else, feeling himself in the experience of infinite life and living from this experience—he is born a second time, regenerated in a second life. Because this second birth announces itself pathetically, with the brusque mutation of the heaviest burden into the lightness of absolute living and its love, it is incontestable. Its explanation through words, though, opens a new series of paradoxes, which unveil Christianity's third founding intuition, the one that now concerns us and leads to this paradox.

The difference between absolute Life's self-affecting, which is brought into itself, and that of the ego, given to itself without having any hand in this givenness, places us in another situation of aporia. On the one hand, the ego that has not brought itself into self appears functionally deprived of this power to do so (the power of living)—if the power of life is precisely to bring itself into self and thus to experience itself and live in the "to suffer" and "to rejoice" of this living. As regards this power to live, to affect oneself, to feel oneself, and thus to be a living self and a living me—the ego is totally impotent. But on the other hand, this ego, essentially deprived of the power to be brought into itself so as to feel itself, to be joined to itself and to be a Self, still feels itself as joined to itself, it is this Self joined to itself, this Living Self, from which this me and this "ego" that inhabits it draw their possibility. Its impotence is lived and carried to its summit, as in the suffering in which, experiencing its own life and bearing it as an unbearable burden, it equally feels it has nothing to do with the fact of experiencing and bearing, of experiencing itself and suffering itself and enjoying itself. This power is stronger than any other, the invincible and inalienable power of life, which suddenly occupies the whole place of its impotence that has become the unlimited power of life. This ego at the summit of its impotence is submerged by the hyper-strength of life. "*Cum impotens tunc potens sum,*" "For when I am weak, then I am strong" (2 Corinthians 12:10). Paul's amazing statement suddenly clarifies the condition of Son: if the ego that is nothing is despite everything an ego and a living ego, it is because in it God is everything. To be nothing and yet to be a living ego is to bear in oneself absolute Life's self-affection, which joins it to itself and outside of which it would not exist. Such is the paradoxical condition of the Son that Paul formulates: it is at the summit of my impotence, of my powerlessness to be for myself the ego that I am, that I experience—as what joins me to myself in the Ipseity of my "me," as myself—the unlimited strength of life.

The contrast between absolute Life's self-affection (in which this life engenders itself) and the relative self-affection, let us call it, in which the ego experiences itself given to itself but not by itself, leads to a radical questioning of the latter. Ultimately there is only one self-affection, that of absolute Life, because the self-affection in which the ego is given to itself is only absolute Life's self-affection, which gives the ego to itself by giving life to itself, a self-affection without which no person or ego would ever live. Such is the paradoxical condition of the ego: that of being wholly itself, having its own phenomenological substance (to wit, its own life as it experiences it), yet being nothing by itself, and taking this phenomenological substance (its self-affecting) from a phenomenological substance that is absolutely other than it, from a power other than its own, of which it is absolutely deprived, the power of absolute Life to be thrown into life and living.

It is this paradoxical condition of the ego—that of Son in truth—that is expressed in the great Christian paradoxes, especially the greatest of all: the one that proposes that the ego, existing not at all by itself, never exists as its own phenomenological substance, either, as an autonomous reality. Hence someone who wants to establish himself upon that reality and base his existence upon a life that is supposed to be his own—that person will just as quickly lose his life, any conceivable life that he believes to be his own but which only affects itself in absolute Life's self-affecting—which is God's life. The words of the greatest paradox resound three times: "Whoever finds his life will lose it, and whoever loses his life for me will find it" (Matthew 10:39); "For whoever wants to save his life will lose it, but whoever loses his life for me will save it" (Luke 9:24); "The man who loves his life will lose it, while the man who hates his life in this world will keep it for eternal life" (John 12:25). Paul states it a fourth time: "In our hearts we felt the sentence of death. But this happened that we might not rely on ourselves but on God, who raises the dead" (2 Corinthians 1:9).

From the fact that the ego, taking its living phenomenological substance from life's phenomenological substance, is nothing in itself (that is to say, "nothing" according to the non-Greek concepts of Christianity, meaning not nothingness but death), there results a number of consequences that have determined the Christian ethic. They are linked to the transcendental illusion of the ego, and here it will suffice to recall them briefly. If the ego is nothing in itself, it follows that any ego wanting to pose as the foundation of its action and base that action upon itself will find that action cut short. This action is not just pretending to develop from the ego and the power it attributes to itself, but also takes this power as its purpose, concerning itself with things and other people only in relation to itself, its advantages, and its prestige. The more the ego leans on itself with a view to elevating itself, the more the ground disappears under its feet. But the more the ego forgets itself and confides itself to life, the more it will be open to the unlimited strength of that life and the more strength will surge up in it, making it invincible. "For everyone who exalts himself will be humbled, and he who humbles himself will be exalted" (Luke 18:9–14). And later: "No one who has left home or wife or brothers or parents or children for the sake of the kingdom of God will fail to receive many times as much in this age and, in the age to come, eternal life" (Luke 18:29; also Matthew 19:29). The one who is placed in the first rank will be placed last, and the one who is placed last will find himself first, and so on.

The same invincible logic, truly a decisive phenomenological condition, that of Son, unites Christianity's paradoxes, precepts, and commandments. This condition reflects another, of which it is the "image": the Condition of the One who, co-engendered in the process of absolute Life's self-generation and thus consubstantial with it and eternal like it, is no less felt in him, in his Arch-humility, his staggering coming-into-himself as the coming into self of absolute Life: "Not as I will, but as you will" (Matthew 26:39).

That self-affecting—in which the ego is given to itself and thus as a living Self is nothing other than absolute Life's self-affecting giving the Self to itself by being given to it—carries on a phenomenological level extraordinary consequences. In the life that is extraordinarily its own (life before regeneration and before rebirth), in which it is given to itself without having wanted this, in the previous subjection of its freedom and independent of it, the ego, as we have seen, bears itself and bears its life as a burden from which it cannot be released—for example, by separating or distancing itself from its life. It is only within the space of thought, in the exteriority of a "world," that such distancing would be possible. (This is another proof, if one were necessary, that the Truth of Life is totally foreign to the world's truth and has nothing to do with it.) This property of the ego's life of bearing itself without being able to escape itself is also that of each of its modalities, which, as life's modalities, have the same phenomenological structure as life. Let us return a moment to this property of each of the modalities of our life to be what it is. Thus, let us say, a suffering bears itself without being able to be separated from itself or avoid what is oppressive in its being. Because it is riveted to itself without being able to break this link that links it to itself, "it is what it is"—which means: it experiences itself as it experiences itself. In this way of experiencing itself as it experiences itself resides its truth—the fact that each of life's modalities, reduced to what it experiences when it experiences itself, is absolutely certain. Thus the ego goes about its life from certitude to certitude—even though it does not think about it and *because* it does not think about it. Its life is the succession of its sentiments, each buried in its unthought-of certitude, inasmuch as, in its invisible subjectivity, each of them is felt as it feels.

And nevertheless Paul says—and this declaration comes before modern thinking, before followers or opponents of Descartes, philosophers of "consciousness" or of the unconscious, and precedes them by many more billion light-years than separate us from the Big Bang—Paul says: "Do not cling to your own sentiment" (Romans 12:2). And again: "I care very little if I am judged by you or by any human court; indeed, I do not even judge myself. *My conscience is clear, but that does not make me innocent.* It is the Lord who judges me" (1 Corinthians 4:3–4). More violently, Christ says to Peter, who reproached him for foretelling his Passion: "Get behind me, Satan! You do not have in mind the things of God, but the things of men" (Mark 8:33).

In effect, if all the sentiments that an ego feels and that compose its life are felt as they feel themselves in their immediate self-giving, then the latter is not their doing, nor the ego's. Nor is it this ego's self-givenness to itself in the Self of its Ipseity. Nor does the latter take from itself what joins it to itself. The self-givenness of these sentiments, of this ego, of this Self, and of this Ipseity that is their basis, is that of absolute Life giving itself to itself in the original Ipseity of the Arch-Son. Thus the truth of sentiments is not their doing, but God's. That this Truth of sentiments is not their own but God's is explained by the radical gap between these sentiments and God himself. How could the basest and vilest sentiments—those that habitually occupy people's lives, the sentiments of cupidity, jealousy, resentment, vengeance, but also boredom or disgust—how could these sentiments (given to themselves as so many indubitable *cogitationes* that are what they are, in their splendor or most often in their misery) nevertheless not owe their truth to themselves but to life's truth? It is not to themselves that they owe their givenness to themselves, any more than to the ego to which they belong, any more than this ego owes to itself its givenness to itself. Rather, they take this self-givenness from absolute Life and from it alone, which is the absolute self-affection apart from which nothing is given to itself nor given in any fashion—apart from which there is neither living nor world.

But because each sentiment is only given to itself in the givenness to self of absolute Life, then the absolute Truth of Life inhabits each sentiment: by being revealed to itself, it reveals it to itself and illuminates it so that it reaches its smallest corners, it hits it as the core of this light that is not seen and that sees everything. In that core, in each sentiment, the most fleeting or the most revolting, resides the Judge, the implacable Judge, the all-seeing Eye, the God "who sees what is done in secret." "The Judge is standing at the door" (James 5:9); "God, who tests our hearts" (1 Thessalonians 2:4); "The face of the Lord is against those who do evil" (1 Peter 3:12); "God, who does not lie" (Titus 1:2); "Your Father, who sees what is done in secret" (Matthew 6:6); "For the word of God is living and active. Sharper than any double-edged sword, it penetrates even to dividing soul and spirit, joints and marrow: it judges the thoughts and attitudes of the heart. Nothing in all creation is hidden from God's sight. Everything is uncovered and laid bare before the eyes of him to whom we must give account" (Hebrews 4:12–13).

To this series of paradoxes explicitly formulated by the Gospels and related to Christianity's founding intuitions, for which they are offered as so many decisive illustrations, may be added another that is not formulated in the texts but results from the interlacing in them of two theses that are apparently contradictory. On the one hand, the Christian ethic rests on a repeated denunciation of simple words—"It is not the one who says Lord! Lord . . . "—to which are contrasted acts, sole depository of life's reality, in which the relation of the living to that life and thus to God takes place. On the other hand, the role devolved onto the Word, whether oral or written, is immense. Within tradition, this role has never been contested—on the contrary. That the Word is not only important but essential and decisive is not only maintained by a tradition that considers Scripture as the foundation of faith, but also, in these Scriptures themselves, the role of the Word (Scripture itself) is exalted. Paul's verse cited above will suffice to show this: "For the word of God is living and active. Sharper than any double-edged sword . . . " (Hebrews 4:12) But it is Christ himself who puts the word into its own place, that of Life. And since Life is eternal, so too is its Word, according to the verse already cited from Luke: "Heaven and earth will pass away but my words will never pass away" (Luke 21:33). The word—whose critique of the Law has shown that it lets reality escape and is therefore stricken with powerlessness and alien to life—how could that word be called living and identify itself with life, be consubstantial with its eternity? This is the final paradox we must elucidate.

The Word of God, Scripture

The question of the Word immediately arose at our first encounter with Christianity inasmuch as it presents itself in the form of a text. From the start, the text of the New Testament gives itself as different from any other by virtue of its divine provenance, which is manifest in the fact that the telling of events relative to Christ's existence is constantly broken up by quotation marks that introduce another speech, not that of the person relating these events, Matthew or Mark, Luke or John, but that of Christ himself, that is to say, God. "Looking at his disciples, he said, 'Blessed are you who are poor, for yours is the kingdom of God'" (Luke 6:20). If the Word of God reaches us like a double-edged sword, this is not only because of the stupefying character of what it says, but precisely because it is He who is speaking.

And that was the first difficulty. It is Christ who speaks but his words come to us only in the account given of them by Matthew, Mark, John, and Luke in the text of Scripture. Reinserted into this account, caught in the text, the word of the Scripture has become similar to the words spoken by men; it is a collection of unreal significations incapable in themselves of presenting a reality other than their own—notably the reality of He who speaks through them, the reality of Christ and of God. Thus a first vicious circle is drawn, of the powerlessness of the word, and hence the powerlessness of the Law and of the ethical Commandment, which is merely its consequence or example. The powerlessness of the ethic means the Law's inability to produce the action it prescribes. It is this powerlessness that has provoked the decisive displacement effected by the Christian ethic, from word to deed, to deeds foreign to language and outside it but immersed in life, whose action coincides with the very movement of this life.

A singular parallel is then drawn between the question of ethics and, more generally, that of Scripture. The powerlessness of the word is exposed in both of them. However, the ethical dictum is aware of its weakness and instinctively calls on the deed, to which it confides the ontological task of its realization. But Scripture is more than an ethic and not limited to a set of precepts, as important as they may be. What most essentially characterizes Scripture, and what the legitimization of the precepts depends upon, as we have seen, is the claim of divine origin. But upon what authority does the Scriptural word call to establish its divine character? What resources does it possess to overcome the inherent ontological deficiency of the realm of signification, of language? On the ethical plane, the substitution of the New Law for the Old Law raised this difficulty. The New Law, the Commandment of love as John conceives it, in laying down the principle of deeds instead of an edifying but inoperative precept, is an effective power, not the simple power of the ego but the hyper-power of absolute Life with the formidable weight of its *pathētik* determinations—suffering, joy, love. It has swept away the traditional ethic, its formal legalism, its powerless moralism, and all the effects of this powerlessness: its quibbles, casuistry, hypocrisy. But in the case of Scripture, on what foundation could the word establish the truth of what it says, if it is incapable of doing so by itself?

Here another of Christianity's decisive intuitions presents itself—or rather, the same one as before but in another form—and so we already possess it. This intuition (too often overlooked and yet explicit) is that there exists *another word than that spoken by people.* This other word speaks otherwise than do human words. What it says is other than what human speech says. Because it speaks otherwise, is says something else. Because it speaks otherwise, the way it should be understood differs, too, from the way one understands people's words. This other word, which speaks otherwise than human speech and says something else and is heard in another way, is the Word of God.

The habitual declaration (at least by believers) that Scripture is the Word of God is a highly equivocal affirmation, which we understand to mean that because it is addressed to people, Scripture for this reason uses the words people use. This speech is human speech in its form and way of speaking. But what it says—in this language comprehensible to people—has content that is not human but sacred. Inspired by God, it transmits to people what God has to say to them, to reveal to them. The content of Scripture is divine revelation, but this revelation is made to people in the language that is their own. Now, how is a human language capable of receiving and transmitting divine revelation? Or, inversely, how can divine revelation take the form of human language, and why would it be forced to do so? Divine revelation, in other words, would not be revelation as divine but as it expresses itself in human speech, taking its form, in order to be understood by people. But how could this revelation, made accessible to people in human speech, revealing itself to them in the form of their own speech, prove its divine character? How, beyond its human nature, is such speech in a position to attest that it comes from God? God must have requested his capability to reveal himself—to reveal himself to people in any case—from a power of revelation other than the one that constitutes his own essence.

What we need here to escape this set of paradoxes is a radical elucidation of the essence of the word, which will establish that there are two kinds of word. First, there is the human word, composed of individual words that carry significations. Considered in their immediate written presentation, Scripture is a word of this kind, a set of texts obeying the general laws of language, which people use and which allows them, as we believe, to communicate with each other and to make themselves understood. The other Word, with which we are now dealing, differs in nature from any human speech. It understands neither words nor meanings, neither signifier nor signified, it has no referent, it does not come from an actual speaker, nor is it addressed to some interlocutor, *to anyone at all who might have existed before it—before it spoke*. It is this other Word that allows us to understand Scriptural speech and, in addition, to understand that this speech is of divine origin. This other Word allows us to understand the content of the Scriptural word, as well as the divine origin of this word, which is the sole Word of God. Therefore, we must examine the nature of these two kinds of word: that of Scripture, similar to any human word, and this other Word, older and functionally different, which allows us to hear the Scriptural word, its content and its origin.

The human word relies on language, which is composed of words that relate to things and are like signs of them. In this respect, the word acts as an instrument or medium, by conferring a name on something that is already there, to grasp it, to manipulate it symbolically. But, however it is conceptualized, this instrumental function of the word relies on a phenomenological basis that is dual. On the one hand, the word that designates the thing — whether an oral or visual sign—must show itself, even if in the course of ordinary language we do not pay attention to the word itself but only to the thing it designates. On the other hand, there is the thing that must also appear, and all the more ostensibly, since it is what the word is targeting. Thus the word cannot say the thing unless it gives it to be seen. In truth, what the word gives to be seen is not only that of which it speaks but also what it says about it, the set of properties or predicates that it attributes to it.

If we reflect on the kind of apparition implied in any language, on its phenomenological basis, we clearly see that this apparition is nothing but what we have called throughout this book the truth of the world. It is in a world that the thing designated by the word appears; similarly, it is in a world that in the same way all the predicates (real, imaginary, or ideal) conferred on it are shown; it is in the world, finally, that the word (visual or aural, but also the ideal portion words always include) is shown to us, as fugitive or marginal as this apparition may be. Because it finds its phenomenological basis in the world, because each of its constituents—words, significations, targeted things, and the predicates attributed to these things —is also shown in the world, the speech of people belongs to this world in the radical sense that speech finds there its irresistible phenomenological foundation. So we will call it the world's speech. Human speech says by showing in the world. Its manner of saying is a make-seen, that make-seen that is only possible within the horizon of visibility of the "outside." What is said in the world's speech therefore presents a certain number of traits resulting directly from this speech's way of showing:

1. It gives itself by showing itself outside in a world, in the manner of an image.

2. It gives itself as unreal. Let us consider the first verse of Trakl's poem entitled "A Winter Evening":[1]

> Window with falling snow is arrayed,
> Long tolls the vesper bell,
> The house is provided well,
> The table is for many laid.

The things referred to—the snow, the bell, the evening—named by the poet and called into presence by their names, are shown to our minds. Yet they do not take a place among the objects surrounding us, in the room where we are. They are present, but in a sort of absence. They are present in that, evoked by the poet's words, they appear, and absent in that, even though appearing, they are not here. This is the enigma of the poet's word: it makes the thing appear and thus gives it Being, but such that, although said by this word, the thing does not really exist. The word gives it Being by withdrawing Being from it; it gives the thing but as not Being.

3. It is not only the poet's speech that gives in such a way that it withdraws Being from what it gives, by its very fashion of giving. Any human speech does the same, offering what it names only in a pseudo-presence, such that the thing named, as long as it only exists in and through this nomination, does not really exist. I may confine myself to saying: "A dog is man's best friend," but there is still not, by virtue of this statement, any real dog or man. This is the powerlessness of human speech, its radical powerlessness to place into actual existence everything it speaks about, everything it says. The powerlessness of the traditional ethic—the precepts of the Old Law—to produce the deeds it prescribes is just one particular case of this powerlessness. Speech's powerlessness to bring to existence what it names is not due to chance, to some exterior and contingent obstacle. It is the very way it speaks that de-realizes in principle everything of which it speaks. It is its way of showing in the world's exteriority that, placing everything outside itself, therefore strips it of its reality, leaving behind only empty appearance.

4. If, by stripping everything of its reality by throwing it outside itself in the world's exteriority, the world's speech gives only an empty appearance to be seen, reduced to an exterior "aspect," then how could such speech put us in touch with Life—the Life foreign to the world, which is never shown in that world, which has no "aspect" and no "outside"? Life that never separates from itself but that embraces itself in the immediacy of its *pathētik* flesh? Life that holds in itself all reality but also excludes from itself all unreality? Life touches itself in every point of its Being, and where it touches itself, there where it is life in its living, there is neither past nor future nor present in the sense of the world's present, nothing imaginary, no signification, no "thought content," nothing that is not the plenitude of living, in the "to suffer" and "to rejoice" of its *pathētik* self-

affection. All the decisive intuitions of Christianity, those of a phenomenology of life, form a unit. They defy the world's speech to communicate to us a parcel of life's reality, if only in the form of an empty signification. We should add that neither this speech nor the world itself are at the origin of this signification, which would never appear in the field of our experience if the thing of which it is the signification had been given to us elsewhere, in another Word. This is the final intuition of Christianity, of a phenomenology of life.

The other Word, the Word of God, is Life. Life is a word because, like any word, it is phenomenological through and through: it shows, it makes manifest. In this the Word of God shares with the world's speech the common trait of producing a manifestation, an appearing—in such a way that in this appearing something can be shown, can be said. But here, also, the word of God differs radically from that of the world, to the point that to understand the former one has to lose sight, as it were, of what we ordinarily understand as a word: the one spoken by people, the one that says by making visible in the world what it says. If the divine Word is also phenomenological in essence, if it is revelation, the crucial question it poses relates to a radical phenomenology: *How does the divine Word reveal,* what sort of appearing does it deliver? Or even: How does the divine Word speak and what does it say? Now, the Word of God reveals, speaks as Life. The Word of God is the Word of Life, the Logos of Life, recognized by John. Life speaks and reveals because in its essence it is the original revelation, the self-revelation, which reveals itself, being nothing other than the fact of revealing itself.

How does life reveal? In the "to suffer" and "to rejoice" of its living, in the phenomenality of its pathos. What does it reveal in its *pathētik* phenomenality? Itself. We have established this previously. Life reveals in such a way that what is revealed is itself and nothing else. It affects itself such that the content of its affection is itself and nothing else. Unlike the world's word, which turns away from itself and speaks of something other than itself—of something else that in this speech finds itself thrown outside itself, thrown away, deported, stripped of its own reality, emptied of its substance, reduced to an image, to an exterior appearance, to a content without content, both empty and opaque—Life's speech reveals Life and gives Life. Life's Word is life's self-giving, its self-revelation in the enjoyment of itself. The Logos of Life, the Word of Life, the Word of God is precisely absolute phenomenological Life grasped in the hyper-powerful process of its self-generation as self-revelation.

Power is generally attributed to speech. Power reaches its height when it receives an ontological signification. Then it has the power to create, that is to say properly, to institute within Being. Thus the act of naming things has the property of making them exist. This ontological capacity of speech to confer Being on what it names is ordinarily reserved for God. That is where his all-powerfulness lies, an all-powerfulness that is his word—a word that has only to be spoken for the whole order of everything that is to arise immediately from nothingness at the simple sound of his voice and then to submit to the details of his organization. In this domain, moreover, it is not long before God has emulators or rivals. On the model of God, the modern artist boasts of being a creator, creator of a work that is supposedly richer, more surprising, and assuredly more novel than the nature created by God. In this way, the artist supposedly wins out over God by his inventive genius and his sophistication. In the case of the writer, the power of words to raise unknown worlds is still more evident.

The analogy between divine creation and the creative act of the modern artist is one of the commonplaces of criticism in our era. We can now perceive its naïve but hidden presupposition. The word that serves as prototype for the idea of aesthetic or divine creation is the world's word—the word that names objects by making them visible within the horizon of the "outside." What characterizes such speech is its incapacity in principle to lead to the effective existence of that of which it speaks. Hence the specifically magical character it assumes when one wants to make it play this role. This is what magic is: to pronounce words, if possible intelligible, to which is attributed the power to establish a reality that the words, as empty significations, are incapable of producing.

By what paradox has the world's word, incapable of producing anything real, been taken as the prototype and principle of creation? Because, for want of creating what it is speaking of, it at least has the property of giving it to be seen, if it already exists—or of producing an appearance of it if it does not exist, as in the case of the poem. What is decisive for our argument is the fact that the world's speech is taken as the archetype of any speech, whether the word of God or that of people. The word that names birds, fish, the colors of their wings or scales, fire, trees, water, clothing, shoes, food, excrement, and so on is supposedly the one that is going to let us understand the interior essence of divine Life, since it is the original Word, Life's Logos. This external designation of things is supposed to explain to us how the Word of Life speaks to each of the living and makes itself understood by each of them—what is signified for them by hearing the Word of God and, if the latter is offered as a call, what the nature of this call may be, and what kind of response it expects. And finally, if one says that Scripture is the Word of God, a Scripture composed of words and meanings like any human speech, then it is in the light of this, the ordinary speech of people, that we are supposed to understand the Word of God!

However, with the intuition of a Word of Life, these naive presuppositions and exterior paradoxes are exploded by Christianity. At the same time, the whole set of relations organized around the word, the relation of the word to what it says, to the one who hears it, as well as the nature of hearing, are turned upside down. Above all, the very work of the word, its operation, changes totally. The Word of Life does not sustain any reference to the things of this world any more than to the world itself. It is used neither to create them—a task that the human word only really manages in magic— nor even to unveil them; the world and things of the world are, quite simply, foreign to its field of action. Moreover, the Word of Life does not "act" in the sense usually given this word, which we have denounced—in the sense of a creation of objects, of their pro-duction, especially of an objectification. The operation of the Word of Life is not an "action" of this kind but a generation, in which what is generated remains internal to the power that generates it because the power that generates remains internal to what it generates. So the Word of Life is not only a generation but a self-generation. It is life's self-generation as its self-revelation. It is this power to reveal itself in generating itself that is expressed in the notion of Word; it designates the phenomenological power of absolute Life. Absolute Life is a word because it generates itself such as to reveal itself in this self-generation—even more profoundly because it generates itself by revealing itself. For this reason, by generating itself, absolute Life engenders within it a Logos, precisely that of Life, which is consubstantial with it. Life speaks at the beginning, inside this Logos that is its self-generation *as self-revelation*—as Word.

Because Life generates itself by revealing itself in the Word of Life, this Word of Life does not speak only in life's self-generation, where it is consubstantial with the Father, where it is its own Logos. Everywhere that Life's self-generation (and thus its self-revelation, and thus its Logos) is implicated, there too speaks the Word of Life. The Word of life does not speak only at the beginning: it speaks in all livings. What the Word of Life says within any living is his Living. In this way it generates them by giving life to them, that is to say, by allowing them to reveal themselves in its own self-revelation—in the self-revelation consubstantial with its self-generation. Thus each living lives only from the Word of Life, inasmuch as he lives. What the Word of Life says to him is his own life. And because this Word of Life is love—absolute Life's self-revelation in the enjoyment and love of self— what it tells him is his own love. Thus is defined with an unprecedented rigor the constellation of relations that are organized around the Word, such that, grasped on the basis of the Word of Life and no longer on the basis of the world's word, these relations are effectively overturned.

In the world's word, the relation of this word to what it says is the world itself; it is exteriority. This is why everything of which this word speaks is exterior to it: it is the tree that is green, the square that has four corners, and so on. Because it is exterior to the word, what it says is different from it. The word that says that the tree is green is itself not the tree, it is not green. Precisely because the word that makes visible is exteriority, then the difference of everything it says and makes visible is exterior to that word, different from it. The fact that what the word makes visible is the world, difference, and exteriority produces a decisive consequence, which we have already encountered several times because it is rooted in the very nature of phenomenality. This consequence is terrible: the functional indifference of this word toward everything it says. Whether it concerns a tree, whether this tree has leaves or not, whether a geometric figure has so many sides, whether it concerns a broken tool, a goat, an equation, a hydroplane, a reality or an image, a prescription or a concept—it doesn't matter much. The most decisive trait of this indifference of the world's word, implied in the difference in which it shows everything, is the following: never do what is said in the world's word, nor its genre, nor its properties ever result from the nature of this word, to wit, the mode of appearing in which it makes visible everything it does. Never does the nature of what is unveiled depend on the nature of the unveiling, since it is that of the world. This is why, unable to penetrate what it says and never understanding it in its internal possibility, understanding nothing, the world's word confines itself to a simple statement, stated and repeated: "This is . . . ," "There is. . . . "

Any word is heard or is at least susceptible to being heard. We hear words and pay attention to them or not, but we do so only to the extent that we a priori possess the capacity to understand them. This capacity to hear the word precedes any particular listening and makes it possible. In the world's word, the capacity to hear this word rests on the fact that we are open to the world. There is a possible hearing only of what is outside us, given to be heard by us in this "outsideness" that is the world. In the same way as speaking means making seen in a world, so hearing signifies perceiving, receiving what (from thus being shown to us in the world) might in fact be perceived and received by us. It matters little whether we are dealing with a visual, aural, or ideal phenomenon. Thus to speak and to hear have the same phenomenological foundation, apparition in a world. The same Gap is constitutive of primal Hearing, of which speaking or listening are modes. The fact that Hearing—the possibility of hearing in general, of speaking or listening—resides in this Gap from the world results in a fundamental uncertainty about everything that is said and heard in this way. This is because, separated by this Gap from everything that is said and heard as something outside, different from him, the one who listens is thereby reduced to conjectures and interpretations about his subject.

This is even more evident in the nevertheless privileged situation in which it is supposedly the same person who speaks and who listens, who listens to his own words. This situation is that of moral conscience where, in effect, a person supposedly hears a voice that speaks to him about himself but also comes from him, from his depths, as if he were speaking to himself by some trick of the voice of the moral conscience, exhorting him to moral action. This Depth of a person from whence speaks the voice of moral conscience has been interpreted differently by various philosophies. What matters is that *the word of moral conscience is interpreted in the light of the traditional concept of the world, as the world's word.* This word speaks by making heard what it says in an "outside" where it resonates. What it says resonates in this outside; it becomes accessible, audible, and one can either pay attention or ignore it. In any case, what is said is an external content, whether sensible or intelligible. To the extent that it is shown as external content, what is said can be heard. To speak and to hear presuppose the world and its openness. The person who speaks and hears must be open to this world.

One of the most famous descriptions of moral conscience is the paradigm of the situation we are describing. According to Heidegger, man is

Dasein, open to the world. In moral conscience *Dasein* itself addresses an appeal to itself. Because this call, even though coming from *Dasein*, comes to him in the world's openness, it comes to him from outside, from "afar."[2] This call from afar requires a whole problematic. Separated from the word that launched it as it is separated from the person who should hear it, the appeal is mysterious. This is why it gives rise to many misunderstandings, among which is the whole range of philosophies of moral conscience or moral philosophies—except Heidegger's. Still, when he wants to be more precise about the content of this call from moral conscience, he too simply proposes his own philosophy as a response. The content of the call of moral conscience that *Dasein* addresses to itself without knowing it is somehow to know it, to understand it, and thus to be understood in its truth: as *Dasein* thrown and surrendered to the world to die there. Such is the obscurity of the call and the gratuitousness of the response that, between the Word and its hearing, a primal Gap has slipped in that separates them forever. So in effect it comes down to interpreting them as one can and wants. In any case, phenomenology has given way to hermeneutics and commentaries, or rather, to endless hypotheses.

The constellation of relations organized around the word also includes the fact that the word is addressed to someone who is able to hear or listen to it. It goes without saying that every word is addressed to someone. But as soon as this relation between the world and the one who hears it ceases to be considered a trivial fact, we are in the presence of a fundamental problem, one of the most difficult of all those confronted by philosophy. For the word to encounter someone who is capable of hearing it supposes an essential affinity between the nature of this word and the nature of the person who is destined to hear it. But this affinity is much more than a simple affinity. It must involve a basic compatibility, which within Christianity is no longer mysterious. Rather it is tossed into our faces as what constitutes our very essence. The original compatibility between the Word and the person who must carry inside the possibility of hearing it is the relation of Life to the person. Such a relation consists foremost in the fact that Life has engendered the living. Engendering itself in its essential Ipseity and engendering in the latter the living as a Self and as the transcendental me, the Word of Life has thus engendered he whose responsibility is to hear it. That one who will hear the Word does not preexist it. Here, unlike with human dialogue, there is no interlocutor waiting for a word to be addressed to him.

Nobody is there before the Word, before it speaks. But the Word engenders the one to whom it is destined. The call does not find but extirpates from nothingness the person it calls in its formidable appeal, which is the call to live—an ontological appeal inasmuch as being draws its essence within Life and only from Life.

Moreover, engendering the one to whom it is addressed and doing so by making him a living, the Word of Life has conferred on him in his very generation (somehow even before he lives, in the very process by which he came to life, in his transcendental birth) the possibility of hearing it—the Word he heard in the first spasm of his own life, when he experienced himself for the first time, the life whose embrace of self, whose Word, has joined him to himself in the very surge of its Self and for ever after. Thus the possibility of hearing the Word of life is itself for each person and for each living Self contemporaneous with his birth and consubstantial with his condition of Son. I hear forever the sound of my birth, which is the sound of Life, the unbreakable silence in which the Word of Life does not stop speaking my own life to me, in which my own life, if I hear that word speaking within it, does not stop speaking the Word of God to me.

Since the possibility of hearing the Word of Life is consubstantial with my condition of Son, certain consequences follow. This consubstantiality implies in the first place an essential co-belonging between me (the living transcendental me) and this Word of Life. I belong to the Word of Life in that I am engendered in its self-engendering, self-affected in what then occurs as my own life, in its self-affection, self-revealed to me in its own self-revelation—in its Word. Therefore there is an abyss separating the Word of Life from the world's word. Whereas the world's word, different from everything it says and makes visible in the world's exteriority, by the same token manifests its total indifference toward everything it makes manifest in this way, the Word of Life does not cease to embrace in itself the person it is addressing; it is consubstantial with what it reveals, with the person who is revealed to himself within the Word's self-revelation. At no moment does it let that person go outside it, but rather holds him within, in its radical immanence, as this living Self that he is; the word does not stop speaking to him while he is speaking to himself. Its speech is not made up of words lost in the world and stripped of power. Its word is its embrace, the *pathētik* embrace in which, holding itself, it holds the person to whom it speaks by giving him life—by giving him to be embraced within this embrace in which absolute Life embraces itself. The embrace in which absolute Life embraces itself is its love, the infinite love with which it loves itself. Its word is that of love, in the end the only one that the anguished people of our day, lost in the world's ennui, still want to hear. But what does this word say to them? Just itself, just their own life, too—the unspeakable happiness of experiencing oneself and of Living.

Because the possibility of hearing the Word of Life is consubstantial with the condition of Son, another consequence follows. If we understand the possibility that is given to any living Self of hearing the Word of Life as an appeal that this word addresses to him, then the schema we usually use to interpret this call (and as a corollary, its relation to a likely response) proves totally inadequate. This is because, once again, the word is grasped as the world's word, with respect to both the word that addresses the call and the word that is supposed to respond to it. The word that speaks in the world and the call it addresses are worldly things, visible or audible. And the word whose role is to reply must first hear this call, receive it as something it can receive only by opening up to the world—in this Hearing that is openness to the world as such. It is a mediation of the exteriority of the world that links the call and the response.

In this way, call and response are different, exterior to each other, separated from each other in this Difference that is the world. Separated from the call, the response must turn toward it to hear it in the world where it resounds. It can equally well not do so: turn away from it, not hear it, or just not respond to it. The response is contingent in relation to the call. This contingency, the possibility for the response to respond or not respond, is what we call its freedom. But, as we have seen, the structure of the world's word, which speaks by speaking in the world and by hearing what resonates in the world, has separated call and response now and forever.

In the Word of Life, by contrast, the difference between Word and Hearing, the call and the response, has disappeared. Because the Hearing in which I hear the Word of life is my own condition of Son, my own life engendered in absolute Life's self-engendering, this Hearing has no freedom at all with respect to what it hears. It is not the Hearing of a call to which the person has license to respond or not. To be able to respond to the call, to hear it in an appropriate listening, but equally to turn away from it—it is always too late for all that. Life, thrown into itself, has always already thrown us into ourselves, into this Self that is similar to none other, that at no moment ever chose to be this Self that he is, not even to be something like a Self at all. No person has the opportunity to ignore the arch-coming of the Revelation, which has given him Life. Whether he remembers or forgets it arises only from his own thought and in no way affects his condition as a living. Life has only one word that never goes back on what it says, and nobody evades it. This Parousia without memory and without failure of the Word of Life is our birth.

The radical significance of the opposition between the world's word and the Word of Life is ultimately measured within Christianity by a decisive criterion: action. In the light of this criterion, the world's word is characterized by its radical powerlessness to produce the action corresponding to what it says—or, more radically, to produce any action whatsoever. This powerlessness marks any ethic of Law; it is what motivates the shift from the Old to the New Law. If the Old Law must be not abolished but completed, it is for the very simple but decisive reason that it cannot be completed by itself. Its intrinsic content (its prescriptions or interdictions) is not primarily at issue, but rather the fact that, deprived in itself of the force necessary to produce action corresponding to prescription, the enunciation of a rule remains a representation in the mind that leaves unchanged the believer's way of living and acting. But this is all that matters, because living and acting define reality. Because the Word of Life carries in it a primal Acting, the eternal process in which life never stops engendering itself—because, more precisely, as self-revelation of this Acting, it is hyper-Acting that leads acting itself into effectivity—then, far from being opposed to reality, as is the world's word, the Word of Life is tied to it. This tie is so tight that not only does the Word of Life contain reality but it produces it in some fashion, to the extent that any reality, that of Acting itself, presupposes a first revelation, the Arch-Revelation of Life and its Word.

We must now reexamine a previously encountered difficulty. This concerns Scripture considered as the foundation of Christian revelation. Isn't this revelation said in the Word that we have stopped calling that of the world? Isn't Scripture composed of words bearing meanings? If the world's word is characterized by its powerlessness, doesn't this affect Scripture as a whole? It is not only the Old Law, but also the New Law (since it, too, is formulated in the language spoken by people) that proves incapable of spanning the abyss separating language and reality. Does Christ not speak to people in their own language? Isn't it in this language (which is their own) that

the Truth he has brought them is revealed? Doesn't the fact that this revelation is uttered in the world's word, that it takes the form of propositions and sentences imprisoned in their world of unreality, render inoperative the Christian revelation itself, Scripture as a whole?

Here it suffices to recall that text, here Scriptural text, has never been the object of our study. This is because any text aims at an object, or (as they say), has a referent. So it is not the text that gives us access to the object to which it refers. Because the object shows itself to us, the text can refer to it, and more generally, the word can speak of it. In the case of the world's word, it is the world's light that allows the word to speak of anything shown in this light. What is shown in the light of the world is by no means limited to material things. When I say that in a circle all the radii are equal, that $2 + 3 = 5$, that science permits progress, that aesthetic value differs from moral value, that if I think therefore I am, then a horizon of visibility is unfolded so that, in the clear space opened by this horizon, everything that has just been said is shown. Not only is the content envisaged in each of these propositions shown in this "outside" dug out of a "world," but the propositions themselves that aim at these various "contents" only appear on that horizon.

We have contrasted the world's word—whose phenomenological essence we have just recalled as the way in which it speaks by making visible in a "world"—with the Word of Life, whose power of revelation is identified with the self-revelation of Life itself. Grasping the essential connection that is established between the Word of the world and the Word of Life and, in this way, how it is possible to understand the former thanks to the power of the latter, leads to deeper reflection on Scripture. This connection between the two words, the one spoken by people and the other by God, is indicated to us in Scripture, in fact. It tells us how one can understand it, too—what sort of Hearing may lead us to what it wants to tell us.

Scripture says that we are Sons of God. Saying this, it speaks in the manner of the world's word. It utters propositions that relate to a reality different from the propositions themselves, to a referent situated outside them—to wit, these Sons of God, about whom it affirms that this is what we are, this is our condition. Relative to its worldly word, this referent—the condition of Sons of God—is exterior to them. Scripture does not have the ontological power to bring it into being, to make it exist, any more than does any other human word. It says but cannot prove that we are the

Sons of God. But this referent, which is exterior to it and which it cannot bring into existence, *this is where we are, we the living*—living in Life, generated in absolute Life's self-generation, self-revealed in our transcendental Self in the self-revelation of this absolute Life, in the Word of God. By saying, "You are Sons," the worldly word of Scripture turns away from itself and indicates the site where another word speaks. It achieves the displacement that leads outside its own word to this other site where the Word of Life speaks.

So we cannot avoid coming back to the singular analogy established between the word of Scripture and the Christian ethic—an analogy that relates to the fact that, in the end, the prescriptions of this ethic are inscribed in Scripture and form an integral part of it. In the same way that, in the case of the ethic, the precept that is prisoner of its unreality gives way to Life's Commandment of love, unfolding in each person its *pathētik* essence, so that the word of Scripture refers back to the Word of Life that speaks to each person his own life, making him a living. But it is not the word of Scripture that lets us hear the Word of Life. Rather, it is the latter, by engendering us at each instant, by making us Sons, that reveals within its own truth that truth recognized by the Word of Scripture, to which it testifies. The one who listens to this word of Scripture knows that it speaks true, *since inside him the Word that establishes him in Life listens to itself.*

So do we really need Scripture? Isn't it there to be understood after the fact? Isn't its truth recognized only on the basis of a truth we already carry inside us—and so, in its prior accomplishment, since the beginning of Life in us, could easily do without Scripture? But what does "being recognized after the fact" mean? A philosophic argument that has been accredited since Plato says that the possibility of any knowledge—for example, the possibility of hearing Scripture—is always just a re-cognition [*re-connaissance*] that presupposes the knowledge [*connaissance*] in us of what we are thus (for this reason) merely rediscovering, re-cognizing in things—in this case, in Scripture. This thesis concerns Christian revelation only if it undergoes a modification so essential that one may ask if it is still the same idea. This modification (or perhaps subversion) is as large as the abyss separating Greek thought from Christian intuitions.

If it is prior knowledge in us that makes possible the effective knowledge of everything we can grasp—which is therefore just the reminiscence of this first knowledge—then everything depends on the nature of that knowledge. So it is not sufficient to advance, along the Platonic line of argument, that only atemporal contemplation of Ideas that are the archetypes of things allows us to know them by recognizing them for what they are—as Descartes again asserts in his famous *Meditations*, by making the idea of a person that I carry inside me the condition that allows me to take for people these hats and coats that I see from my window passing along the sidewalk. What most matters is the nature of this primitive knowledge that is in me, the reminiscence of which makes possible any ulterior knowledge in the form of a re-cognition. What is in question, at the same time, is the nature of recognition. Is it of the same order as primitive knowledge? If it is the reminiscence of primitive knowledge, does that mean that it is related intentionally to it in a memory, which is to say, in a thought? Is primitive knowledge itself a thought, a seeing? Are both, or either, unfolded in the world's truth? Finally, what does the "in me" of primitive knowledge mean—of this knowledge that I must in effect possess in some way, so as to be able to know on the basis of it, by relying on it, everything that I will know and will be capable of knowing?

In Christianity, primitive knowledge—notably that which allows us to recognize the truth of Scripture—is the condition of Son. Therefore, it is not me, the ego, who is capable as ego, through my thought or my will, of re-cognizing that Scripture is true. It is not me who decides that this voice is the voice of the angel or of Christ: it is only the Word of Life in me. It is only because I am the Son generated at each moment in the self-generation of Life, self-revealed in the self-revelation that is its Word, that the Word of Life can tell me that I am this Son, and in this way that what Scripture says (to wit, that I am the Son) is true. The nature of primitive knowledge, as Christianity conceives it, is therefore unequivocal: it is life's self-revelation. It is precisely because it is life's self-revelation, in which I am self-revealed, which I carry inside me (like this primitive knowledge), that I can re-cognize everything that I will re-cognize on the basis of it. By the same token, it is the nature of re-cognition that is determined. It is not the mode of manifestation in which I re-cognize the Archetypes of things (and thus these things) for what they are, it is not the primitive Seeing in which I contemplated these Ideas for the first time—-it is not a Seeing, it is not the world's truth. Pathetically, by giving me to myself in the embrace in which it is given to itself, Life has let me experience that I am the Son, and only this *pathētik* experience, since it is accomplished in me, allows me to recognize the truth spoken by Scripture in the word it addresses to people: that I am the Son.

One doubt remains. If by my condition of Son I experience this condition such that it is not possible for it to be otherwise, what good is it to say so in the word of a man, addressed to men, to empirical individuals lost in the world—which I, the transcendental Son of Life, am not? What good, once again, is Scripture? This question has been answered at length. It is man's forgetting of his condition of Son that motivated the promise and coming of a Messiah, all of his words and deeds—in short, the content to which the text of the Old and New Testaments refers. It is precisely, we might say, because man forgot his condition of Son that he needs Scripture to remind him of it. But how can a man hear Scripture, listen to its word, know that what it says is true? Because the Word of Life speaks in him. But how in turn can this Word of Life be heard by man? Does he not constantly forget it, even when it constantly speaks in him, establishes him within life?

Man's forgetting of his condition of Son relates not only to the Concern for the world in which he constantly invests himself. As we have seen, it is the phenomenological essence of Life that makes Life what is most forgotten, the Immemorial to which no thought leads. Because Forgetting defines its phenomenological status, life is ambiguous. Life is what knows itself without knowing it. That it suddenly knows it is neither incidental nor superfluous. The knowledge by which one day life knows what since the beginning it knew without knowing it is not of a different order than the knowledge of life itself: it is a *pathētik* upheaval in which life feels its self-affection as absolute Life's self-affection. This possibility, which is always open to life, to suddenly experience its self-affection as absolute Life's self-affection, is what makes it a Becoming. But then, when and why is this emotional upheaval produced, which opens a person to his own essence? Nobody knows. The emotional opening of the person to his own essence can only be born of the will of life itself, as this rebirth that lets him suddenly experience his eternal birth. The Spirit blows where it wills.

Yet Scripture remains as the always open possibility of the Becoming, in which any conceivable regeneration consists. That the emotion without limits in which the self-affection of each living is experienced as that of absolute Life in him, and thus as his own essence (as this essence of life that is also his own), that such an emotion (as Revelation of his own essence) happens to someone who reads Scripture, and it says to him nothing other than his condition of Son, is by no means astonishing. Thus, from the moment that this condition of Son is precisely his own, *the condition of Faith is always posited*. Only God can make us believe in him, but he inhabits our own flesh.

Christianity and the World

The major objection addressed to Christianity at different times and in many forms is that of turning people away from a world that constitutes both the only real and tangible world and (for this reason) the true domain of those who inhabit it, the "inhabitants of this world"—we people. The "world": this one here—the earth, with its elements, its horizons, its temporality, its laws—everything circumscribing the circle of concrete possibilities that define "human existence" and by the same token set its finitude. It is in this world, relying on it and fashioned by it, that all the projects and actions we are given to undertake take on shape and consistency: the itineraries we must follow, the time required to follow them, the set of arrangements to observe, the sum of the efforts to supply. Of course, these conditions change constantly, and expertise and technology cause them to evolve all the time. But these changes and this evolution happen on the basis of a preexisting state of affairs, upon which one can act only by starting from there. This irresistible prerequisite for all modifications and all possible inventions—possible on the basis of it and only in this way—is the world itself. So this world is the imprescriptible horizon of all human behavior and ambition.

To turn people away from this world that constitutes their true domain, and literally the ground and fulcrum of all their movements and activities, means to hurl them into the imaginary. This is the reproach: the invention of a fantastic (or even phantasmagoric) other world, a place of imaginary satisfaction of all the desires and all the aspirations that a person cannot realize here below—the "beyond" that the here below calls forth as the indispensable complement for all lacks and all frustrations. That an incapacity to obtain, by an effective transformation of reality, and hence by work, satisfaction of the multiple impulses within the human being leads outside reality is something for which we have at least two examples and thus two proofs. The first is provided by the ordinary course of individual existence, in which the dreaming portion measures the size of non-satisfied aspirations, that is to say, efforts from which the individual has shrunk. What desire has not been able to obtain in fact, it at least forms in images. But there are aspirations to which no work of any sort can respond. Here is where "reality" reveals its true nature: that against which one can do nothing, that which defies any kind of acting designed to modify or deny it—for example, the mourning of a cherished person, or death in general. Here the only "work" is to accept reality, specifically the death of the loved one—to accept a world whose finitude is precisely death itself.

In the second example of this process, the incapacity to satisfy desire leads to fabulation of a beyond: Christianity. Here the issue, to be clear, is the prior conception of reality. Reality having been understood as the world, inevitably there is raised against Christianity the criticism, supposedly decisive, of "fleeing" reality. That this flight should end in the construction of a false "other world" is merely one possible consequence. One could also conceive others. The very idea of "flight" does not come first. What is found at the origin of this whole process is the misunderstanding of reality in itself, the refusal or incapacity to recognize its true essence—the world as it gives itself to us and thus as it is. Thus, this misunderstanding does not lead first or necessarily outside the world but is manifest inside the world itself through a series of contradictions. The most significant is the attempt to erect a new reality, a new Kingdom, by misunderstanding the conditions of reality. Such an attempt can only result in the disappearance of all actuality, in a pure "void"—in this empty place, alien to reality, that is Christianity's Heaven.

It is remarkable that such a criticism was especially addressed to Christianity in the Romantic Age, when the figure of Christ held for so many thinkers a very special fascination. The young Hegel was more given to criticism than to fascination. What he reproaches Christ for is constantly contrasting the invisible and the visible, such that reality is shattered and so, as prisoners of this contrast, individuals can lead only broken lives. On the one hand, Christ tries to found himself exclusively on the first of these terms, on the pure and infinite love of God, by rejecting all that is not him, all that has the mark of the world. Hence he has to renounce many things, individuals' relations with the society in which they live, their relation to political organization (to the Jewish state), and also to the various associations they maintain among themselves in social activity, and all external manifestations of life. "A great number of active relations and living relationships were lost."[1] The destiny of Christianity is foremost that of any historical form that wants to develop by misunderstanding or rejecting an essential part of reality; by constantly encountering this, it can only (in this permanent conflict) take the path of decline and disappearance. The tragic destiny of someone who takes his affirmation of himself only from his opposition to the world, meaning to reality—from what is now only the "Opposite of the World"— is the destiny of Christ. The young Hegel thought this and described it as follows: "Because what he saw in God were his own collisions with the world, his flight from the world, he had need only of the Being opposed to the world, in which his own opposition to the world would be grounded."

But there is more. Christianity splits reality between "here below" and "the beyond." If someone who is opposed to the world inexorably collides with it and in this lost cause must admit his powerlessness, it is because this bad world is reality, not a part of it but the only effective reality, whereas what is contrasted with it, in the name of which he thinks he can condemn it, is only an empty Heaven. What Christ teaches is purity of the heart, an internal and unlimited love. But what is a love that is not "realized" and does not act? To be realized, to act, is to confront the world, not by maintaining an external and formal opposition to it, but *by transforming it*. To transform the world, to make a real modification occur, is to recognize its laws, to use them, and to produce because of them a change that always presents itself in the form of an objective determination, as this particular effective reality that always results from an action that is also particular and that everyone can see, which is there for each and every one of us. The young Hegel contrasted the "unaccomplished" life with the "accomplished" one, in which the accomplishment consists of this multiplicity of concrete activities that compose the infinitely rich and varied weft of the world of people. Outside this richness and this objective variety, there is only an empty subjectivity. But objectivity for Christ was "the greatest enemy."[2] This is why the refusal of objective determination is supposed to involve Christianity in an "amorphism" deprived of content. By turning away from the world on Christ's example, the disciple not only loses the concrete richness of life, but what is offered to him in exchange for this "renunciation" is literally nothing except this absolutely empty representation of an imaginary Heaven.

Is it necessary to stress the reverberations of such a criticism? The whole Hegelian system reproduces it constantly in various forms, of which the most famous is perhaps that of the "beautiful soul." Incapable of getting out of itself, of confronting the world and really acting, the beautiful soul can only rely on this interior purity and "in this transparent purity, evaporate like a wisp of smoke in the air."[3] Such criticism is not only found among a number of Hegel's contemporaries but will inspire one of the most striking positions within Marxism. It is no longer an issue of dreaming of some interior perfection that relies on itself, nor even of sketching a harmonious system of actions in which this perfection would be possible. Nothing can be done within a person, no change capable of affecting his real being that does not presuppose as its precondition a real change in the world—a world whose true essence is not primarily natural but social. There is a frequently cited statement by the young Marx: "Philosophers have only interpreted the world in a different way; what matters is to transform it."[4]

Thanks to Marxism, the critique whose origins we have just recalled broke out of the narrow circle of philosophy to become one of the commonplaces of modern ideology. As regards the problem we are concerned with here, it bears the following traits: a rejection of any "beyond," which is definitively assimilated to an illusory imaginary; attention and interest devoted exclusively to this world, knowledge of which is all that matters. This interest is not just theoretical but also practical. If metaphysical illusions must be removed and knowledge become scientific and turn toward the objective universe, it is precisely because it is no longer a matter of assuring one's salvation in "Heaven," but of transforming this world. Scientific and ethical ideals shift at the same time. Mentalities merely express this shift. If in the twentieth century, in a country like France, a great number of Christians have lost their faith, it is because this faith was a faith in the "beyond." What ought to have taken its place quite naturally was the effective transformation of this world and adherence to forces that were engaged in this direction. The ethical ideals of Christianity—love of others, solidarity, generosity, justice, and so on—could well have been conserved, and in fact they were; it was simply a matter of realizing them. What Christianity was finally reproached for was not its morality but its moralism. The problem was not its ideals but that by projecting them into an empty heaven it reduced them to pious wishes instead of bringing them into daily life, through struggle and contradictions in the difficult history of humankind. Entire generations have repeated this catechism. But the critique is not confined to our era. Because it is rooted in the heart of things, it revives ancient themes: "One should cultivate one's own garden," "Do not aspire to immortality, O my soul, but live to the limits of one's power," and so on.

When brought into rapport with the founding intuitions of Christianity, what are such criticisms worth? On what "evidence" could they be justified? To return to the young Hegel, it is totally erroneous to pretend that Christianity has split reality into two realms, of the visible and the invisible, and thereby plunged human existence into the rift. Such assertions, with the "critical" consequences that we have reviewed, testify only to an absolute incomprehension of the "spirit of Christianity" and of the decisive thesis that underlies it. This thesis is that there exists only one reality, that of Life. It is precisely because life is invisible that reality is invisible—not just a particular domain of it, a particular form of life, but any possible life, any conceivable reality. It is invisible not only in the sense of that imaginary and empty place that is called Heaven, but invisible in the sense of that which experiences itself—like hunger, cold, suffering, pleasure, anguish, boredom, pain, drunkenness—invincibly, outside the world, independently of any seeing. And which, experiencing itself in its invincible embrace, is incontestable. It is living and thus "real" even when there is nothing else, *even when there is no other world* (according to Descartes's equally invincible argument). So there is no opposition between the visible and the invisible, between two forms of reality. Within Christianity nothing is opposed to reality, and there is nothing other than life.

The second criticism moves beyond the limits of incomprehension into the absurd. Christianity is reproached for an attitude that Christ himself constantly and vehemently denounced. Did the Good Samaritan abandon himself to the vaporous dreams of his beautiful soul when he bent over the traveler covered with blood to help and care for him, when he carried him to the inn, when he came back to settle the bill and check that he was getting well? Do the seven works of corporal mercy lead us outside this world? Who, then, in barbaric times, in the Middle Ages, for example, built the first hospitals? Who drained swamps and spread agricultural and livestock-breeding techniques? Who provided teaching in all domains? Were the seven works of spiritual mercy any less constraining? Who taught a person to let another pass in front of him? Doesn't the *whole Christian ethic* effect a displacement from the order of words and pious declarations to the order of action? Isn't what is decisive about such a displacement the presupposition of the unreality of the world and of pure thought, their assimilation to the empty and almost imaginary place of unaccomplished impulses, of intentions not followed by effects—whereas reality is unequivocally entrusted to action and to it alone? Before taxing Christianity with moralism and reproaching it for turning people away from action and reality, *it would be better to inquire into the conditions that have allowed such a reproach to see the light of day and to target a doctrine that recognizes as true and truthful only the real, and as real only action.*

These conditions are nothing other than the whole set of presuppositions that comprise the truth of the world. That they extend their hold over almost the totality of the development of Western thought, to the point of determining it almost entirely, by no means suffices to establish their validity, especially since a suspicion cannot help but arise that they might be a simple formulation of a prejudice of common sense. What is more immediately evident than this: reality is what we see? Action does not escape this rule. The modification it produces is itself something that one can see; it is a "transformation of the world." The circle implied in this series of "evidences" is apparent, though, when we ask: What is evidence, what phenomenon does it involve? What shows itself to us is evident—what one can see, with the body's eyes or the spirit's. What shows itself to us, what one can see, is what is seen or can become visible, within the horizon of the world's visibility, within its truth. Thus the world's truth is the presupposition—hidden or conscious—of all the theses that identify reality, especially that of action, with this truth, with the world itself. From a philosophical point of view, it is the extraordinary originality of Christianity to perceive this circle and to radically challenge it.

To challenge it with regard to action, specifically. It is not sufficient to investigate action and denounce fine sentiments and empty declarations, a denunciation to which anyone could easily rally. *What is in question are the conditions for effective and real action and thus the conditions of reality itself.*

The conditions for effective action are not the circumstances in which such an action is capable of occurring. For example, when we say, "The child should be tall enough to be able to reach the door handle, otherwise he could not open it," or else, "The working classes had not reached a sufficient level of maturity to acquire a clear vision of the forces at work and to organize themselves accordingly," such conditions are still merely exterior, contingent, and variable conditions for action—they are historical. They define a situation that is more or less complex but particular, in which one can guess whether such and such an action, itself particular, would have a chance of succeeding. They by no means work back to the ultimate and essential possibility of what makes, in each of these cases, something like an "action" possible—that the child *will be able to extend his arm* to the handle, or that people *take up* weapons and *run* to the barricades. Far from elucidating the internal possibility of acting, worldly theories of action simply presuppose it, without even perceiving it as a problem.

It is precisely this interior and ultimate possibility that Christianity seizes upon. *It seizes it at the profound level where it is identical with the possibility of the ego itself.* Because it is a transcendental ego, this fundamental I Can whose genesis we have described, a person is capable of acting—absolutely not as an empirical individual, as a person belonging to the world. This is why one's action is no longer a worldly action, an objective process, but the action of this transcendental ego, of this I Can that alone can act. Christianity has taken to its limit the analysis of this interior and ultimate possibility of acting. The genesis of the fundamental I Can that I am, which alone can act, is the transcendental birth of the ego. Analysis of the ego's birth has shown that each of the powers that compose the being of this ego—to take, walk, and run, but also to think, imagine, and so on—is only possible if given to itself, and thus put in its own possession and hence made ready to be exercised. But this givenness to self of each of our powers as the indispensable precondition of its exercise resides in the givenness to self of the ego, in which resides the givenness to self of absolute Life, which takes place nowhere else. Thus the simplest act, presupposing in itself Life's self-givenness, nothing other than its self-revelation, each humble act carries within it this self-revelation of absolute Life, the all-seeing Eye of God, we called it—such that it takes place "before God."

Here the theses that situate action in the world appear superficial. Not only are they incapable of taking account of the metaphysical and religious aspect (we might call it "Dostoyevskian") of human acts, of the "Judgment" that seems to be invincibly attached to each of them. On the philosophical plane, they are powerless to distinguish human action from a simple objective displacement, a natural process. This is because they are content with a simple acknowledgement of the latter, and so are not in a position to work back to this internal possibility of acting without which no action could be produced. In the same way, they cannot take account of the essential fact that all action is tied to an individual who is its agent. Like the possibility of action, the possibility of the "I" of the "I Can," on the basis of which action is always produced as an action individual by its very nature, also escapes them.

Christianity is not only opposed to superficial descriptions that interpret acting as an event in the world. Starting with its own intuitions, it can understand perfectly well why such descriptions are inevitable, produced everywhere and received as faithful expressions of the phenomenon of action. Christianity in fact by no means misunderstands the world's truth, that way of appearing we have described at length, which as an effective mode of appearing is incontestable. But Christianity circumscribes its sphere, refusing to this mode of appearing the power to exhibit reality in itself—especially the reality of acting. Thus, in the world, acting only appears in the form of an external behavior that lets reality escape because reality is held within life. Thus the duplicity of appearing explains why human acting manifests itself in two different forms, of which one contains the reality of this acting, while the other, the external behavior of fasting, for example, is only action's empty shell.

But the pitiless denunciation of ethical appearance refers back to the phenomenological intuitions that define the division between reality and illusion. The splitting of action into true acting and fallacious behavior corresponds to a duality of the body. On the one hand, there is *the body in the world's truth*, which people take as the real body, and in fact as the only real body, the one you can see in the world, the visible body, the body-object ranked alongside all the objects of the universe and sharing its essence, that of having extension: *res extensa*. On the other hand, there is *the body in Life's Truth*, the invisible body, the living body. According to the phenomenological definition of truth as life, identical with reality, it is the invisible body that is real, while the visible body is only its exterior representation.

This new Christian paradox can be established philosophically. The body that is seen presupposes a body that sees it, a power of vision—which can be exercised only if put into possession of self, given to itself in absolute Life's self-givenness. Thus there is a transcendental genesis of the real body in life which, as the transcendental genesis of the I Can and thus of any conceivable power, is no different from the transcendental birth of the ego. With the concentration of all form of power in life and, moreover, with the identification of the generation of this power with the self-generation of absolute Life itself, it is the entirety of reality that finds itself returned to its site of origin, to invisible life itself and to its hyper-power. Far from the invisible designating the empty site of an illusory heaven, it is upon it that is built any conceivable power, and thus any effectivity that contributes to a power. In the invisible any conceivable body and any form of reality literally take on shape. The objections made to Christianity about its flight from reality merely ignore the essence of that reality.

But then, we might say, if reality is concentrated within transcendental life to the point of being identified with it and giving itself to feeling only in its invisible pathos, is it not suddenly this world that is empty? Can the radical overthrow of concepts relating to reality that Christianity effects be turned against itself? We can no longer reproach Christianity for fleeing reality if reality resides in life, if the real body is the living body—not this visible object that naive tradition has always taken as our veritable body. But doesn't the visible as a whole, now stripped of its pretension to exhibit reality, any conceivable reality, find itself thrown into the realm of shadows? What can we do with a world reduced to a fallacious game of appearances? What can we do in this world if it is no longer anything? The reproach addressed in modern times to Christianity by post-Hegelian thought is barely disturbed, and to some extent it remains valid. Christianity is certainly not flight from reality if any reality lies within invisible life; but it is indeed flight from the world if, deprived of reality, the world is given over to appearance. Doesn't Christianity, as well as Christ, succumb more than ever to the young Hegel's criticism, that in any case (whether or not it can be identified with reality) it is "the Opposite to the world"?

We have to say a little more about the latter if we want to understand how, *far from turning us away from the world, instead Christianity is the means of access to what is real in that world—to the unique reality*. We recall our preliminary study of the world's truth, which showed how this Truth is split between appearing in the world and what appears in it. On the one hand, there is appearing in the world, its "outside," this horizon of visibility in which all things of the world are shown to us. Then there is what appears in it: all the things that, being shown in it, constitute the "content" of this world. *It is the content of the world that constitutes its reality.* Such a content is dual: social and natural.[5] It is the social content that is the most important, so let us concentrate on that.

The social refers to all the concrete activities by which people constantly produce the totality of goods necessary for their existence. It suffices to inquire into the nature of these activities in order for the worldly definition of reality to be exposed as vacuous. All these activities, which form the content of society, undoubtedly appear in the world. It is in this world that we can see them and, we think, recognize and describe them. But as long as we confine ourselves to seeing them, we do nothing. If, seated in the bleachers of a stadium, I watch an athlete who is trying to beat a record, I am not running myself. The manifestation of a race in the world's "outside" is totally foreign to the reality of the race. The reality of the race is situated nowhere else than in the living body of the one who runs, in the fundamental I Can of the transcendental ego, which utilizes its powers to the extent that it is in possession of them, each of these powers being given to itself in the self-givenness of this ego, itself given to itself in life's self-givenness. All the activities that constitute the content of society—social praxis —have acting as their essence. It is from this essence that they take their properties, even their possibility. They take their properties and their possibility from Life's essence and from it alone. If this set of human activities constitutes the content of the world, what appears in it, its reality, then we have to say: what appears in the world owes nothing to appearing in the world. The world's content owes nothing to its truth. By turning us away from the world's truth, Christianity does not turn us away from its reality; on the contrary, it indicates to us the place where reality lies and leads us to it. This decisive thesis, for Christianity, for the world, and for ourselves, is what we must now establish. We will do so with two crucial examples, since they question the reality of this world: first, what is called the "economy," which constitutes the substratum of any society; and second, relations with others, without which there is no social world, either.

By "economy" we usually mean two things: on the one hand, a particular domain of reality with its specific phenomena and their laws, and on the other, a certain science that is defined like any science by what it selects and isolates out of the whole to take as its object of study. The particular domain of reality, designated under the title of "economic reality," is that of social labor and the phenomena linked to it: salaries, merchandise, value, money, capital in its various forms, and so on. As for the science that studies this "economic reality" in its various aspects, it is called "political economy" or else (more simply but in an amphibiological way) "economy."

In order to establish the pertinence of the fundamental concepts of Christianity in comparison to the "content" of the world and its reality, we refer to the analysis by Marx, one of the greatest thinkers of all time, the only person to have cast upon society and its economy a transcendental gaze capable of producing the principle of their intelligibility. In line with the duality of the concept of economy, Marx's critique is dual. On the one hand, it is a critique of "political economy," that is to say, of that science that studies economic phenomena and their laws. This critique is radical in that, beyond questioning certain theses of the English school, of Smith and Ricardo notably, it takes aim at political economy in general, the very possibility of a science like economics. This critique of the possibility of an economic science is radical only because it is first a critique of economic reality itself.

What does a critique of economic reality mean? Contrary to the illusion of economists, which Marx called fetishism or economic materialism, it means there is no economic reality, in the sense in which one speaks of reality as something that exists in and of itself and that in some way always has. But labor, the salary paid in exchange for this labor, the consumer goods produced by it, and the money that results from this labor, various exchanges, and industrial, commercial, and financial activity in general—isn't all that quite real, constituting, as is partly evident, the "content" of this world? Here the decisive intuitions of Christianity upset this system of evidence. Behind all these so-called "economic" and "social" activities, what is acting, as we have just recalled, is the transcendental ego, whose every power is given to itself in the givenness to itself of this ego, such that this fundamental I Can is alone capable of walking, lifting, striking—of accomplishing each of the acts implicated in each form of labor. Because it is only given to itself in the self-givenness of life, this I Can is living and exists only as such. Taking its possibility from life, it takes from it all its traits—it is living and thus invisible, subjective, individual, and real. For a number of the essential traits flowing from the essence of action, we cannot find any economic index. Walking, talking, carrying, striking, and even running, singing, and so on—these activities are all modes of acting but have nothing economic about them. Labor, then, inasmuch as it consists of such acts, has nothing economic about it.

This was Marx's fathomless intuition. He reproaches the English school, and all economic science, for having treated labor from the start as an economic reality, without seeing that there is a prior question on which everything depends. To labor considered naively as economic in itself, as it is by both nineteenth-century and contemporary economists, Marx contrasts "real" labor, asserting its original and essential phenomenological determinations: labor is "subjective," "individual," and "living." Thus labor is understood as a mode of acting, and it is unequivocally related to the essence of acting, to life. If labor (and, even more precisely, all human activity) constitutes the content of the world, its reality, then in fact we have to say: the world's reality has nothing to do with its truth, with its way of showing, with the "outside" of a horizon, with any objectivity. The reality that constitutes the world's content is life. Here is the new evidence: far from fleeing the reality of this world, a Christianity that knows only life deals only with this reality.

The proof of the living character of the world's "content" is brought out in Marx's economic analysis as a whole. He proposes a transcendental genesis of the economy, and we should briefly retrace its stunning construction. According to Marx, reality is by no means economic. One can analyze a sugar cube and never find its price. One can analyze any human activity, whether it is recognized as labor or not, and never find there something like a "salary" or money or exchange value. Everything that might be said to be "economic," and so be examined by a science like "political economy," is in itself foreign to the world. "Economic reality" is the product of an invention by the human mind. A world, the people who inhabit it, who produce in it the goods necessary for their existence, who maintain among themselves a network of complex relations—all that could very well have been produced, and still economy (economic reality and the science of that reality) might nevertheless be absent from this world. This again is one of Marx's ideas.

How did an economy in itself foreign to the world's reality arise, then? Why has it developed to the point of extending its domain over the world and determining it altogether? Here the founding theses of Christianity make an unexpected appearance. *Only, in effect, the invisible essence of life explains the appearance in the world of an "economy."* Here is how.

With each form of human activity taking its essence from acting and thus from life, labor finds itself defined by that life. Since life contains reality, labor is itself real. Since it carries within it a basic ipseity, this real labor is individual. Since life is subjective, work is subjective. Since it is living, work is living. These, as we have said, are all the traits recognized by Marx in labor: real, individual, subjective, living.

In the concrete activity by which people produce the goods that are necessary to them, a moment occurs when, due to the growing complexity of this activity, people must exchange the product of their labor. How can you exchange x amount of merchandise a for y amount of merchandise b when these goods are qualitatively and quantitatively different? How can you define the weight of salt that should be given in exchange for some quantity of animal skins? Why, as a function of the sum of work required for the production of the salt and for that of the skins. Therefore, the only possible criterion of exchange is labor. In fact, in the many exchanges constantly occurring, what is exchanged is not merchandise but the labor that has produced them. Since exchange presupposes equality, the exchanged labors should be equal. But as a mode of acting and drawing its essence from this action, each of these labors is real, subjective, individual, living—invisible. None lends itself to any measurement, quantitative or qualitative. This is the aporia: exchange presupposes the measuring of labors but this is impossible.

And here is the solution: the invention of economy. If the exchange of merchandise presupposes measuring the real labor that has produced them, and if this measuring is impossible because the labor is invisible, then it becomes a matter of constructing objective entities to represent these modalities of invisible action and be their equivalents. The invention of economy consists in the construction and definition of objective equivalents that are supposed to represent invisible real labors and permit comparing them and thus calculating and exchanging them. Economy is nothing other than the result of this genesis: the set of objective "representatives" of action, representatives reputed to be their equivalents.

What do these "representatives" consist of but the representation of real labor, positioned before the gaze, in the world's truth, in the form of an objective norm, of what finds its reality in the Truth of Life: living work. And since everything shown in the world's truth is unreal because it is shown there, so the set of objective equivalents to living labor is also unreal, or more precisely ideal, because they are concepts. The genesis of the economic consists therefore in the construction of a set of ideal and unreal objective equivalents of living labor—notably the prime example among them, "labor" in the sense of economics, the economic labor done by economists that Marx called "abstract," "social" work. Economic work is precisely the unreal representation of real and invisible work.

This is not the place to explain the construction of each of the ideal objective equivalents of living and invisible labor, equivalents that are constitutive of economic "reality." Let us confine ourselves to a few essential observations. Objective economic "reality" is ideal and unreal, like each of the equivalents of labor from which it is constituted. Thus the economic universe by which modern thought tends to define the "real" content of society is only a universe of abstractions, each arising from the substitution, for an invisible and unrepresentable modality of living action, of a parameter in which one tries to represent the properties of this action—properties that take their reality only from life. The economic entities are not confined to representing living labor but proceed from them. One of Marx's key ideas was that exchange value, money, capital, and so on are produced by the living subjective form of labor and only by it. The economic universe as a whole constitutes the "content" of this world, which proceeds from life and refers back to it. Of this content, the world's truth offers us an inefficient appearance, whereas the Truth of Life reveals its veritable nature, the action that produces economic objects and determines their history. Far from fleeing economics, Christianity's intuitions lead us back to the principle of its development and make it intelligible.

It is on the plane of concrete relations with others that the reference of the world's "content" to the invisible essence of life presents itself with invincible force. This time it is not a matter of analysis, by a phenomenology of life, of "economic reality," its nature and functioning. The declarations of the New Testament, of Christ himself, enter directly into play in order to produce, in this domain of the experience of other people more than in any other, their revolutionary effect.

Since the other, "others," the "neighbor," is just another me, an *alter ego*, its essence can only be identical to mine. It follows that everything that Christianity has asserted on the subject of this "me" that I am also holds good for this other "me" that is the other's ego. The transcendental birth of the ego pertains to the other just as much as to me. The consequences of this observation, usually considered trivial, are immense, however, and overturn everything that could be said or thought in an implicit way, then or now, about relations with others. If there is a presupposition that goes without saying and on which any approach to this relation inevitably relies, then it runs as follows: the other appears to me in the world; he is a Being situated in this world, and my relation with him, consequently, is a form of this relation to the world and is only possible within it. Or else: the other is an empirical individual, worldly, bearer of a set of characteristics that are themselves empirical and worldly. These characteristics, as we know, are of two sorts, some relating to the content of this world—social or natural characteristics, then—while others relate to its Truth, that is to say, to the concrete modes by which the world is phenomenalized: space, time, causality, and so on. Thus such an individual is born in some place, at some time, of parents belonging to some ethnic group, some social milieu, and he is himself bearer of some sexual determination, some property or some physical or mental deficiency, and so on.

But if, by his transcendental birth in absolute Life, the ego, the other ego as well as mine, is the Son of this Life, the Son of God, such that this condition defines his essence and consequently all his essential determinations, then all his empirical and worldly characteristics are immediately eliminated—especially everything that arises from a natural genealogy. Here an observation presented in the course of our preceding chapters takes on a singular focus. What Christ refused for himself—the very idea of a natural genealogy, the idea that a person is son or daughter of a man and a woman, that he or she has parents "in the flesh"—all that is withdrawn from the person, too. A person, by virtue of being a living person in Life, by being its Son, has no other Father than the One who is "in Heaven." All his or her characteristics, flowing from the divine and invisible essence of life, thus have nothing to do with what arises from the world and the truth proper to it. And hence this is valid for the other just as much as for me. The other is no longer what we see of him in the world and what we believe he is. Here is Paul's radical and stupefying statement to the Galatians: "There is neither Jew nor Greek, slave nor free, male nor female . . . " (3:28).

As for the first four negations, we would accept them upon reflection, despite their very strange character. This strangeness relates to the fact that each of them implies *rejection of the visible*. In fact, this person here is really a Greek, and that one a Jew. This one is a master and that one a servant. Why are such characteristics, despite their evident importance, social or spiritual, even despite this evidence, suddenly stripped of meaning, or at least taken as secondary? One might say it is for ethical reasons. It is because we have an ethical idea of a person whose essential reality cannot be reduced to Greekness or Jewishness, still less to a social condition, whatever it may be, that we refuse in effect to reduce him to this condition. But from where does the idea come that makes us accept despite ourselves this sudden disqualification of worldly evidence? If it is a matter of history, then we have to say it comes from Christianity itself. If it is a matter of philosophy, then the idea of an ethical person irreducible to worldly determinations and unfathomable on their basis can only come from his invisible essence—from his condition of Son generated in absolute Life and taking from that Life his veritable reality.

But the two final negations plunge us into uncertainty by their extraordinary character. To be a man or a woman, these qualities of the "human being"—is this nothing but an external, visible, "natural" determination? Or on the contrary, is it not the innermost reality of such a being, his or her sensibility, affectivity, intelligence, way of relating to others and to himself, that is affected from top to bottom according to whether this "being" is a man or a woman? Paul's extraordinary declaration cannot be attributed to the singularity or the excess of his personal thought. On this essential point as on so many others, it is Christ's teaching, which he was not able to hear, that he is taking up in a rigorous way (contrary to the thesis that the Christianity we know is a sort of fabrication by Paul). When the Sadducees, to contest the resurrection, ask Christ, with regard to the seven brothers who died one after another without children and had, according to the Law, each married the same woman: "Now then, at the resurrection whose wife will she be, since the seven were married to her?" Christ answers, identifying the resurrected with angels, that they "will neither marry nor be given in marriage . . . for they are like the angels. They are Sons of God, since once resurrected" (Luke 20:27–36).

Does the determination of a person as Son of God abolish the determination of virility or femininity? Or else, does this abolition only concern the "Son of God" in the strong sense, someone who has identified himself with absolute Life and who, born a second time, resurrected, has become as eternal as Life? Or else, referring to resurrection and to Heaven, is this abolition of sexual differentiation, like this resurrection and like Heaven, just an article of faith? Or else, can Paul's radical thesis (which echoes the no less radical reply of Christ to the Sadducees—the affirmation that the essential reality of the human being is located outside or beyond sexual differentiation), can this affirmation, instead of arising exclusively from Faith, be proved philosophically, not by a speculative philosophy with always problematical results, but by a phenomenology capable of formulating propositions of an apodictic order? Thus it is a matter of knowing if the essential truth of the human being laid bare in the condition of Son leaves sexual determination outside itself, thus authorizing the apparently extravagant declarations of Paul and of Christ himself.

The phenomenological analysis of the condition of Son that we have pursued through this book allows us to answer this question with certainty. It will be shown, moreover, that this question is of decisive interest for understanding the relations with others that now occupy us. Paul's setting aside, in defining a person, determinations like Greek, Jew, master, slave, and finally, man and woman, is radical only in proportion to the weight (or, if you like, the seriousness) of these determinations. To render his statement less implausible, we preferred, at first, to consider the determinations in question in their empirical aspect and thus as purely worldly. And it is true that the enumerated properties are shown in the world. It is from this visible manifestation that they derive their reality in the eyes of common sense. But this is not the case. Far from being reducible to their worldly appearance, the determinations set aside by Paul do belong to life; it is from life that they draw their reality; it is because they are living that they are real. To be Greek or Jew is not limited to the presentation of objective ethnic characteristics that in fact scarcely exist or do not exist at all. To be Greek or Jew is to find oneself determined on the level of sensibility, affectivity, intelligence, ways of acting—therefore, subjectively, according to vital essential modalities—and all this results from belonging to a culture that cannot define itself except subjectively, by the fundamental *habitus* of transcendental life.

To be master, similarly, whether a master in Paul's time or the boss today of a waiter or a factory worker, is to be fashioned by the concrete modalities of praxis, a praxis that is real, individual, subjective, and itself just a determination of living acting. To be a man or a woman, finally, is quite another thing than to present a certain external aspect or recognizable natural properties, such as an objective body that is sexually differentiated. Here again, what is said to be "natural" or "objective" can only be defined on the basis of a certain number of transcendental subjective experiences, for example, the internal and lived unfolding of feminine "sexuality" and, more generally, the internal unfolding of a body that is originally, in the very possibility of its "acting" and its "feeling," a subjective and living body. Why, then, does Paul think he is able to set aside such determinations at the highest "real" point of what makes for veritable reality and a person's condition?

Because this condition is that of Son. Each of the real determinations that are those of a Son are only so—real and living—if given to themselves in the self-givenness of absolute Life that gives this Son to himself. And this holds good for the nevertheless essential determination that makes each Son of Life, here below, in this world, a man or a woman. In this way, the Christian definition reveals its infinite profundity. If we scrutinize, in its most essential subjective transcendental reality, what makes, within each man and each woman, his virile or her feminine sensibility, with the multiple and differentiated modalities that impregnate his or her whole life, where would we find something in common between them, between these virile and feminine sensibilities, something in common that would allow Paul, speaking of human beings, to proffer his stunning declaration, "neither male nor female"? This essential common truth is nothing other and nothing less than what inhabits each determination of virility and femininity, to wit, *the fact that this determination is given to itself and that this givenness to itself takes place in the same way, is the same, for man as for woman.* It is, for each "human being"—man or woman—the condition of Son: the living person given to himself in the self-giving of absolute Life. It is this self-givenness that is Identical in each: Christ, God. Neither male nor female: Son of God.

Now, what is Identical in each person—the self-giving of absolute phenomenological Life in its original Ipseity—determines in its entirety the Christian theory of the relation to another, which now presents a certain number of traits.

The first is that what we dealing with in the relation to the other is never primarily or solely, despite worldly appearance, a Greek or a Jew, a master or a slave, a man or a woman: it is a Son. This means a transcendental Self generated in the self-generation of absolute Life and in its essential Ipseity—Self taking its ipseity from Life and Life alone. It is only in such a Self and through it that any me and any ego are possible. And there is no Greek and Jew, master and servant, man and woman, unless each of these is an ego and a me. Thus any relation to one of them, to "others," presupposes a relation to the transcendental Self without which none of them would be an "other," another ego. But any relation to a transcendental Self presupposes a relation to the process of self-generation of life in the Ipseity of which this Self has been engendered. Any relation to another presupposes the One whose Son he is, without which, being neither a Self, nor a me, nor an ego, he would not be an "other," another ego.

Thus we return to the decisive intuitions placed in evidence in the parable of the shepherd and the sheep related by John and analyzed at length in Chapter 7. It is impossible to have a relation with any me if we do not also enter into relation with the power that has joined him to himself. It is impossible to enter into relation with any other—Greek, Jew, master, slave, man or woman—if we do not first enter into relation with the One who has given this Self to itself in the original Ipseity in which life is given to self, thus giving itself potentially to any conceivable living. What gives each Self to itself, making it a Self, as we said, is its flesh, its *pathētik* and living flesh. But this flesh that is its own has itself a Flesh that is not its own, the Flesh of the giving to self of absolute phenomenological Life in the Arch-Son—the Flesh of Christ. We said it was impossible to touch any flesh without first touching that Flesh.

From this first trait of the relation with the other come a number of ethical consequences. These "consequences" are nothing other than the very principles of the Christian ethic, because this ethic is merely the formulation of the intuitions constitutive of the Revelation of Life. If the relation that unites each Self to itself, making it this self that it is, is in fact the relation of Life to itself, its self-revelation, meaning God, then it is impossible to love God and at the same time not love each of the Selves that God generates by giving them to themselves in His own self-givenness. "If anyone says, 'I love God,' yet hates his brother, he is a liar" (1 John 4:20). And again: "Whoever loves God must also love his brother." This is because "Everyone who loves the father loves his child as well," and from this comes, beyond any possible challenge, a value of absolute attestation: "This is how we know that we love the children of God: when we love God" (1 John 4:21 and 5:1–2). The text adds: "and practice his commandments" (1 John 5:3). We see clearly that these commands are merely the formulation of the radical phenomenological situation in which Life engenders all livings. Moreover, from the latter's point of view, these commands are the formulation of his transcendental birth in his condition of Son. Thus the two famous commands of the Gospels, the two commands to Love, are placed in the radical intelligibility of their identity, which expresses the condition of Son generated in absolute Life's self-generation: "'Love the Lord your God with all your heart and with all your soul and with all your mind.' This is the first and greatest commandment. And *the second is similar*: 'Love your neighbor as yourself'" (Matthew 22:37–38, my emphasis; see also Mark 12:28).

From the Identical in each of us—the self-giving of absolute phenomenological Life in the essential Ipseity of the First Self and thus of any conceivable Self—results the second trait of Christian theory in relation to others. Within the perspective belonging to modern philosophy, but also within the customary representations of this phenomenon, the relation to the other is thought of on the basis of a first term that is the ego itself, more precisely this ego that I am. This is why this first term appears as the origin or center from which the experience of the other begins. We have to understand how the ego that I am can reach that of another, the alter ego, and thus enter into "relation" with it. It is not possible to explain systematically the reasons why all the theories that take the ego as their point of departure for the relation with others have failed—or the network of paralogic that dooms them. We will content ourselves with a few brief observations.

The first piece of paralogic in the theorizations of the experience of the other understood as the other ego is precisely the presupposition of the ego itself. That there is an ego, the other's as well as mine, goes without saying, to the point that the very possibility of something like an ego, the possibility of a Self and an Ipseity in general, never appears as a problem. Thus any theory of the experience of another is itself undermined by an essential lacuna, which a priori renders unintelligible everything it purports to talk about and even effaces its existence. What is radical about the Christian theory is that it places at the foundation of the relation with the other the most irresistible possibility: the very existence of egos between which this relation unfolds. Not their simple existence, in truth, but their very possibility, the possibility of something like an ego of any kind, mine or that of someone else. And this possibility is that of a transcendental Self taking its ipseity from the Ipseity of absolute Life—this is the Christian definition of a person as "Son of God" and as "Son within the Son."

However, if the ego is only possible when generated in the Ipseity of absolute phenomenological Life and the original Self of this Ipseity, then the very terms of the relation with others and this relation itself are overturned. As long as the ego is taken naively as based on itself and self-sufficient, it can in fact furnish the point of departure for the relation to the other, as well as the terms of this relation: the other himself, the other ego. But as soon as the possibility of the ego appears as a problem, as soon as evidence appears that no ego has ever brought itself into its own condition and that this radical powerlessness pertains to the other ego as well as mine, then the ego's incapacity to form the point of departure or the point of arrival for the relation with others is simultaneously discovered, and thus the usual way this relation is posed collapses. *The relation between egos yields to the relation between Sons.*

The relation between Sons implies the Life in which each Son is given to himself. Thus Christianity circumscribes the very dimension in which the relation with the other can take place: in Life and only in it. This is because the terms between which such a relation must be established are themselves not possible unless within this life. But Life not only underpins each of the terms between which the relation with others is established. It also underpins the relation itself, not only the possibility of each of the Sons but also the possibility for each of them to enter into relation with the others, to be with them. How does life underpin this possibility for each of the Sons to be with another, their being-in-common? *Inasmuch as it is itself this Being-in-common.* What they have in common, in effect, is to be livings, carrying this life in them. *The Being-in-common of the Sons resides in their condition of Son.* For this reason, Being-in-common is as easy and as difficult to understand as the condition of Son. For this reason, too, Being-in-common fluctuates as does this condition. Let us look at these two points.

That the possibility for each person to enter into relation with another resides in his condition of Son in fact displaces quite radically the point of departure of this relation, which no longer lies in a person, even if he is understood as a transcendental ego. Nor does it lie in the transcendental Self that underlies the ego. It is beyond the transcendental Self, in what joins it to itself, that the point of departure lies: life, its process of self-generation as the generation of the First Living in the Ipseity of which any living Self comes into itself, mine as well as yours. Only in this process of life is access to livings possible. Only because each living Self comes into itself in this process of life and takes part in this process is potential access preserved for it, in this process and through it, to any conceivable living Self.

This is one of the crucial intuitions of Christianity, that the relation to the other is only possible in God—precisely in the process of divine Life and according to the modalities in conformity with which this Life is achieved. Hence, the way in which any transcendental Self reaches another is the same as the way in which it reaches itself: by passing under the triumphal Arch, through this Door that is Christ in the parable of the sheep reported by John. It is in the very movement (Life being made Ipseity in the Self of the Arch-Son and generating in itself any conceivable Self and particularly mine) in which I reach myself and am given to myself through my transcendental birth, that I also reach, eventually, the other—since I identify myself with such movement and coincide with it.

Here is the second point. Since the Being-in-common of Sons resides in their condition as Sons, it fluctuates like that condition. How does the condition of Son fluctuate? On the contrary, isn't it an invariable essence that must be imperatively present and preserved in its unchanging structure, lacking which there could be no Son, no person in the Christian sense? But according to Christianity, the concept of Son is dual in that, forgetful of his condition, deprived of his original splendor, de-generate, throwing himself into the world and fascinated by it, the lost son is only concerned with this world and all that shows itself to him in it. In this fallenness, his relation with self is modified from top to bottom: it is no longer his relation to self in Life, the ordeal he had, by experiencing himself, of the self-experience of absolute Life in him. The self-experiencing from which he constantly takes his condition as a living he now attributes to himself. Thus he is enclosed within himself. The experience he has of Life within him has become the experience of his own life, purely and simply. Formerly Son, he has become an ego, this ego that takes itself for the foundation of itself and of everything it does. He has entered into the system of transcendental egoism, a system in which he cares only for himself, such that his relation with himself is no longer his relation to himself within Life—within Christ and in God—but his relation to himself in a care for self through the space of a world. What is obscured in this relation to self of a Self caring for itself in the world is nothing less than his veritable Self, which is only given to itself in absolute Life's self-giving, outside the world, far from any Care. What is also obscured is absolute Life, God himself.

Here lies the decisive consequence regarding the relation to others, *since this relation of the Self to the other is of the same nature as its relation to itself.* Both vary in unison and in the same way. Just as the Self in relation to itself forgets what makes it possible, its givenness to itself in life's original Ipseity, so the Self relates to the other by subtracting what in the other gives him to himself—precisely, his givenness to himself in life's self-givenness. He relates to the other as to an empirical individual shown in the world, in the best case as another ego, similar to his own and self-sufficient in his quality as ego. What is ruled out in both cases is the self-givenness of absolute Life in the Ipseity of the First Living One, or Christ/God. Or, to put it from the standpoint of each of these egos, his condition of Son.

Is it necessary to observe that the normal play of intersubjective relations unfolds inside this system of transcendental egoism? Placing himself at the center of this system, each person is concerned with the other only with a view to himself. The other person matters only in relation to my project, is worth something only with respect to me. But because care is always directed outside oneself, its reign over exteriority is never interrupted. Whether the ego is related to itself or to the other, it is always in a world. Hence, the relation of domination between egos can be reversed, as one sees in eroticism, for example. The ego shown in the world as other than itself can then, must then, say: "I am another." In this exteriority and even when he would like to be reduced to it, giving himself to the other as if it were just that, this thing being offered and good to take, this body to possess, he does not cease to live himself and to understand himself as an ego —but an ego that is only open to the world and given in it. And consequently an ego that forgets its very own essence.

In his second birth, by contrast, delivered from the transcendental illusion of the ego, the Son, who never brought himself into the condition that is his, experiences life as what constantly carries him into this condition and gives him to himself. Thus he finds himself placed first within this Life before being placed in Being itself. Where he finds himself placed first is also where his relation to the other begins. Just as his relation to self now repeats the process of his transcendental birth and expresses phenomenologically his condition of Son, so, too, his relation to the other finds itself turned upside down. It is no longer the ego in him that furnishes the point of departure for the relation, but rather, within the Son that he is, life itself. Similarly, it is no longer to another ego that he relates, but to a Son, to Life. Where the Son is placed first, there too, the other is found first. Where the Son comes from, from there also comes the other. Where he begins, the other begins also. The self-givenness of absolute phenomenological Life, in which each Son is given to himself, is the Being-in-common of Sons, the preunifying essence that precedes and preunites each of them, determining him a priori both as a Son and as sharing in this essence, potentially, along with all conceivable Sons, and in this way as "members of God's household" (Ephesians 2:19), "a people belonging to God" (1 Peter 2:9). Access to the other is only by way of the access of a Son to a Son, in the transcendental birth of both, in the self-givenness of absolute phenomenological Life in its essential Ipseity—only in God and within the Arch-Son: "So in Christ we who are many form one body" (Romans 12:5).

From the fact that the Being-in-common of Sons is their Being-in-God and their belonging to a "chosen race," to a "royal priesthood" (1 Peter 2:9) result the prescriptions of the Christian ethic. We see once again that these prescriptions are not unreal and ideal laws, but modalities in which divine action is accomplished, the generation of Sons in Life's self-generation, what Christ calls "the Father's Will." That one should love the other is a prescription any ethic could accommodate, as uncertain as its foundation might be. An ideology lacking any foundation, as for example democratic socialism in our day, could equally well lay claim to it. But that one should love the other who is your enemy, even if he is depraved, degenerate, hypocritical, or criminal, is in effect only possible if this other person is not what he appears, not even this I Can, the transcendental ego who has committed all these misdeeds. It is only if, as Son, the other carries within him Life and its essential Ipseity that he may, in his depravity, be the object of love, or rather not him—in the sense of a person, the one whom other people call a person—but the power that gave him to himself and constantly gives him to himself even in his depravity. The command is to love the other insofar as he is in Christ and in God, and on this condition alone.

This is why, as soon as this condition fails to appear, the imprescriptible love of others also disappears. The other is now just another person, a person as people are—hypocrites, liars, ambitious, sinful, egotistical, blind, fighting ferociously for their own advantage and prestige, no less combative toward others who oppose their projects and desires. Forgetful of their veritable condition and the other's veritable condition, they behave toward themselves and others as mere people. Then the whole edifying morality that wishes to found itself on the mere person, on the rights of man, discovers its emptiness, its prescriptions are flouted, and the world is given over to horror and sordid exploitation, to massacres and genocides. It is not by chance that in the twentieth century the disappearance of "religious" morality has given rise not to a new morality, a "secular morality," albeit a morality without any definite foundation, but to the downfall of any morality and to the terrifying and yet daily spectacle of that downfall.

By implicating God in the intersubjective relation between "people" understood as his "Sons," Christianity has given that relation an incredible depth, a character that is not only *pathētik* but tragic. It is *pathētik* because the substance of this relation is life, whose substance is pathos, and tragic because when Sons either forget their own condition or rediscover it, this relation correspondingly plays out for them their own perdition or salvation. There is salvation when a Son relates to the other as to another Son— as to someone given to himself in the original Ipseity of absolute Life and in the originating Self of this Ipseity. "He who receives you receives me, and he who receives me receives the one who sent me" (Matthew 10:40).

The schools of thought that have reproached Christianity for its flight from any effectiveness, outside the world, toward an imaginary "beyond," find within the living relations between individuals (relations that, even more than the social praxis of which they are also the weft, form the real content of this world) merely bitter disappointment. What lies at the origin of the conflict with all these superficial schools of thought, which have forever identified reality with what one can see and touch, with what is shown in the world, is the radically new definition of reality as life that Christianity offers. It is a phenomenology of life that gives reality its veritable essence, *pathētik* and invisible. Radically foreign to the world, life nevertheless constitutes its real content. Here below, too, life extends its reign. Its concrete modalities are the atemporal substance of our days. Any visible appearance is paired with an invisible reality. With each mouthful of the visible, as Kafka says, an invisible mouthful is given to us: on earth as in heaven.

Conclusion
Christianity and the Modern World

The relation of Christianity to the modern world can only be understood against the background of a radical divergence in their appreciation of what man's veritable Being might be. To a certain extent, modern thought continues the traditional approach, according to which what man is is linked to the knowledge we can have of him and depends on it and its advances. What is more obvious? From this perspective, the veritable Being of man is not a point of departure for knowledge and thus of everything it can teach and show us. We will know at the end of knowledge's development what our Being truly is, when everything that was only vaguely glimpsed in an overall intuition has become the object of precise and rigorous scholarship, what is today called science.

If the veritable Being of man depends on the knowledge we have of him, then in effect an upheaval in knowledge—its nature, methodologies, and object of study—should lead to a complete change in the conception of what a person is. Such an upheaval in knowledge occurred at the beginning of the seventeenth century, as we mentioned, when Galileo contested the reality of the sensible qualities of the universe in order to oppose them, as constitutive of the reality of the universe, to material objects with measurable dimensions. The sensory knowledge of these illusory sensible qualities would be replaced by geometric knowledge of extended material bodies. With Descartes and the mathematical formulation of this geometric knowledge, modern science—a physical and mathematical approach to the material universe—was founded.

Inasmuch as man himself is subject to the type of knowledge that is considered today the prototype of all rigorous scholarship (and thus of any science), so his nature is likewise clearly defined. A man is composed of material particles, and his veritable reality depends on certain specific structures of organization in these particles, especially chemical and biological structures. Let us recall that when he achieved the proto-founding act of modern science as geometric knowledge of material bodies, Galileo attributed the existence and nature of the sensible qualities of objects to the biological properties of the human organism. Thus man is part of the material universe and can be entirely explained on that basis. Whether one likes it or not, this conception of man determines in various ways thought in our era. Man is a trivial thing. Not only is he just a cog in this immense machine, subject to its blind functioning, but he himself does not escape a radical determination that is not only external but internal: he is not even master in his own house!

Such conceptions are linked to science, to the point of appearing as scientific conceptions themselves, as scientific truths in the sense that they make themselves part of science and have to be asserted as such. This is an illusion we have denounced[1] by tracing an insurmountable line between what science says and what is said by many of those who practice it, who believe they are speaking in its name—between science and scientism. To reduce man to a part of the material universe, similarly subject to the physical and mathematical approach of modern Galilean science, it is necessary to have previously reduced any form of knowledge to such an approach: *to presuppose that there exists no mode of knowing other than Galilean science, that is to say, modern physics.* But science by itself is incapable of establishing such a presupposition—a fact that escapes its notice. What does it really see? In the Galilean field, there are only material bodies with their ideal physical and mathematical determinations. Where in such a field is it shown, where can we read the assertion, that it is the unique constituent of any conceivable reality?

One might think in the presence of this field that it shows itself, and that showing is not in itself precisely any of these material objects nor any of their ideal determinations. This showing is the appearing of the world as opposed to what appears in it, a pure appearing that Galilean science never takes into account, even when it is the irresistible condition of everything it does take into account. But something else appears in this Galilean field that it is not concerned with, either: the sensible qualities of things, which Galileo disregarded but without which he would never have had the slightest idea of these things. Their being placed outside the field that will belong to science does not prevent the fact that that field is constituted, positively and negatively, on the basis of them. And then, once these sensible qualities are placed outside the scientific field, what becomes of them? What is their basis if they are foreign to its materiality, its extensiveness, its forms, and their ideal determination? But, in any case, it is another sphere of reality that they define or to which they refer. Moreover, it is another mode of appearing than that of things, than the world's truth, which they presuppose, since the sensible qualities laid out on the surface of things and which seem to belong to things *could have been dissociated from them*—since they refer in all necessity to a sensibility, to sensations and pure impressions, and ultimately, to their manner of appearing and of giving themselves: in the experience of self of absolute phenomenological Life and its *pathētik* self-givenness and only in it. Thus we are sent back to Christianity's decisive intuitions. We have just recalled that the confrontation between these intuitions and the Galilean postulate, which will determine the modern world and its thought, produces an understanding of the relation of Christianity to this world, as well as of their respective opinions on what makes up the veritable Being of a person.

While the knowledge that has become the modern Galilean science of the material universe reduces a person to a part of that universe, to a complex of molecules and particles and the mathematical determinations from which they are inseparable, as they are just the point of intersection of these parametric networks, what does Christianity have to say about the veritable Being of a person? That he or she is the Son: not the son of a biological life, which according to biology itself does not exist, but that of the only life that *does* exist, the absolute phenomenological life that is nothing other than God's essence. Let us leave that last part aside, though, since science neither knows what God is nor recognizes any properly religious assertion arising from "faith." Let us consider this phenomenological life in itself, from a purely philosophical viewpoint, as we have done throughout this book. Of course, one cannot "consider" this life, since we never see it. With respect to invisible life, philosophy (a mode of thought) is as powerless as science, because life in general escapes thought and any intentional aim, any gaze, any "outside," just as it escapes the physical and mathematical knowledge of the material universe, which is merely a particular form of this gaze. But the life that does not show itself in the world, that eludes its truth, reveals itself to itself in its *pathētik* self-revelation, experiencing itself with an invincible force, such that, even if we were to say that no other world exists—no kind of thought, no knowledge or science—still this experiencing of self by life that is its "living" would nevertheless be produced. It is of this invisible and invincible Life that a person is the Son.

However, a person is radically other if the access to what makes his essential Being, *if his own access to himself*, resides in invisible Life and only there. The access by a person to himself is his own essence, his relation to himself, his Self. How a person can accede to himself, how he can relate to himself in such a way as to be able to be a Self is what is explained by the theory of Son (Son of Life, since that is where Sons are). Inasmuch as life gives itself to itself in the original Ipseity of the First Self and in this alone, each Self is given to itself so as to become this Self that it is, the Self of any me and any conceivable ego. But it is only as this Self, as this me or this ego, that something like a "person" is possible. Therefore one has to say not only what we have just said—that man is otherwise if the access to his essential Being, if his own access to himself, is made within life—but also that he would be otherwise if the access to himself were made in the world, in knowledge, in thought, and especially in modern scientific thought issuing from the Galilean revolution and in the field opened up by this science. In the field opened by Galilean science, there are material bodies, microphysical particles, molecules, amino acid chains, neurons, and so on, but no Self. *In the field opened by modern science, there is no person.* It is not that the upheaval of knowledge that resulted from the emergence of the entirely new scholarship of modern science has similarly upset (or at least modified) our idea of a person, what makes his essential Being; rather, science quite simply suppresses it. On the contrary, the obsolete knowledge of Christianity, a knowledge that is two millennia old, furnishes us not with entirely limited and useless data about humans: today it alone can tell us, in the midst of the general mental confusion, what man is.

That man, who is only possible as a Self, and thus as a me and as an ego, should by the same token be possible only where something like a Self intervenes, is rigorously taken into account by the Christian theory of the

Son. That man is the Son of God, Son of absolute Life, does not mean anything other than this: it is in the very movement by which life gives itself to itself in the process of its eternal self-revelation that also is born the Ipseity in which any conceivable Self is given to itself as this Self that it is. Such a process constitutes the transcendental birth of man in God, as his Son, since man carries a Self in him and he is only possible on this basis. That is why man is only possible as a Son of God, why there is no man—no Self—except engendered in Him and by Him, in this process of Life's self-givenness, which is identically that of His self-revelation—the Revelation of God.

However, if man is only possible insofar as he is a Self, and if this Self is only possible in turn if engendered in the process of the absolute Life of God, the decisive consequence is that *the negation of God is identically the negation of man*. It is this dual negation that the modern world places constantly before us, thereby revealing itself as a fundamentally anti-Christian world and thus radically alien to man.

The negation of God results directly from the fact that, never being shown in the world, Life can only in fact be denied, explicitly or not, as long as the world's truth, extending its reign over everything that is, is posed as the site of any conceivable reality. It is precisely with the rise of the Galilean field and the systematic spread of this field as the sole object of true knowledge that (reality being circumscribed to this field) no other phenomenological site appears in which anything like the Living of life can occur—no place for God.

Once again, it is not science that denies God—any more than biology denies life. How could they? We have attributed to biology itself the words of François Jacob—"Biologists today no longer study life"—because, for once, what is said about science by a scientist does not spring from scientism but is absolutely true. But if you think about it, you must admit that this proposition stating the truth of biology cannot be formulated by biology. To know that biology is no longer concerned with life, you have at least to know what life is, which is precisely what biology does not know. The same is true for science in general: that life is absent in principle from the Galilean field is something about which science knows nothing and has no means of knowing. It does not even have an idea of life, which never appears to its gaze. Because they ignore all this absolute phenomenological life and cannot formulate any proposition about it and still less pronounce a denial of it, biology and science cannot be held responsible in themselves for what is happening before our eyes. They are innocent of God's murder.

Because biology and science in general know nothing about God, they don't know anything about the living transcendental Self drawing its essence from life and without which no person is possible. There is no person who is not a me and a living Self, and no Self who does not experience itself in absolute Life's original experience of itself—in God's Ipseity. No more than it could achieve God's murder can science achieve that of man, the man whose true essence it is basically ignorant about, to the extent that it has eliminated the living of life, and thus any living Self, in the very act by which it was constituted. Thus the idea of scientific reductionism, as specific to science and accomplished by it, appears highly contestable. In order to reduce the living transcendental Self (the Self that experiences itself in life's experience of itself and is a Self only in that experience) to the thematic content of Galilean science (for example, to a system of neurons), it is by no means necessary to know everything about those neurons, as elaborate and developed as this knowledge might be. The precondition of any thought process aimed at reducing the true and essential Being of man to biological structures (for example, to systems of neurons) is the prior knowledge of this transcendental Self without which there is no person—a Self that escapes the gaze of biology, as of science in general. Inasmuch as it obeys the presuppositions and prescriptions pertaining to its foundation, modern science finds itself in principle incapable of proceeding to the reductionism with which it is reproached.

Still, the extraordinary progress of this science in modern times, notably biology in the twentieth century, and the spectacular results it has produced, which continue to slowly modify people's ways of life—thereby posing what is called "society's problems"—have given birth to the universal conviction that today science must define the only true knowledge humanity possesses, and by the same token that its object (this Galilean field composed of molecules and microphysical particles) must be the only reality. Hence, while mathematics and its methodologies are alone held as worthy, what is not offered to their examination and does not appear within the domain of knowledge they circumscribe instead is eliminated, stricken from any pretense to be an object of science and thus to be something real. Of course, the living transcendental Self is not shown and cannot be shown in this Galilean field, *and so the motivation of the thesis—that Galilean knowledge is the only truth and that its domain defines the field of all possible reality—cannot be shown there, either.* It doesn't matter! This is now a conviction, not only of science but of the modern mind, which believes itself to be "scientific" and to speak in the name of science: reality is the material universe. It is this modern mind with scientific pretensions that everywhere enters into conflict with Christianity in order to destroy it. From this conflict results the theoretically anti-Christian or a-Christian world in which we are living.

In fact, from the moment scientific knowledge is taken as the only true knowledge and the Galilean field of the material universe that it apprehends is taken as the sole reality, then what does not appear in such a field—absolute Life, which experiences itself outside the world, the Ipseity of this life that is its "experience of self," any transcendental Self drawing its essence from this Ipseity, and finally any "me" that is possible only as a Self—nothing of that exists. "The death of God," a dramatic leitmotif of modern thought attributed to some audacious philosophical breakthrough and parroted by our contemporaries, is just the declaration of intent of the modern mind and its flat positivism. But because this death of God destroys the interior possibility of man, since no man is possible who is not first a living Self and a "me," it strikes at the very heart of man himself. Therefore, at the moment they are challenged Christianity's crucial theses are verified. Just as these say it is impossible to reach a living without reaching Life, to strike a person without striking the Christ and therefore the God in him, so it is impossible to deny the latter without proceeding by the same token to the negation of the former, to spit upon God without spitting upon man. And this is why the elimination of Christianity under the combined effect of Galilean beliefs and their almost exclusive teaching in all places where this teaching is practiced inexorably leads to the debacle of humanism in all its forms.

The defense of the veritable man, transcendental man, is the task that philosophy has always recognized as its own. In modern philosophy, this defense has taken the form of a transcendental theory of knowledge. What characterizes such a theory is that, unlike science, which is concerned with knowledge of the objects in its specific domain, transcendental theory asks about the possibility of any knowledge in general. Thus Kant has shown that the possibility of knowing any phenomenon whatsoever refers back to a priori forms of intuition (space, time) as well as to categories of understanding, forms without which there would be no phenomenon for us, and consequently no science. Transcendental philosophy leads us from what appears to the appearing of what appears. This pure appearing considered in itself is called by modern philosophy "consciousness," "transcendental consciousness," "consciousness of something," "intentionality," "Being-in-the-world," and so on. These diverse systems of conceptualization assert the relation to an "Outside" and the truth of the world as the unique essence of phenomenality. Within the world's truth, though, as we have repeatedly shown, no Ipseity is created and there is no Self, no me, and so no man, either. The incapacity of modern philosophy to preserve man's true being echoes that of science and raises it to a pitch.

The vanishing of the inner possibility of man, of his "essence," makes him an empty shell, a cavity open to all winds and susceptible to being filled by any content. The different contents proposed by modern thought and presented as so many determinations (and ultimately, definitions) of what makes the essential Being of man are naturally borrowed from the different sorts of knowledge that have risen on the Galilean horizon. On the one hand, there are the properly Galilean kinds of knowledge, the hard sciences like physics, chemistry, biology. On the other, there are the so-called "human" sciences attached to certain specific aspects of human behavior: psychology, sociology, economics, law, history, and so on.

The hard sciences ignore everything about man, starting where man finishes, finishing where man starts. If what makes the essential Being of man is the experiencing of itself by a transcendental Self, then it is deprived in principle of neurons, molecules, particles, and so forth—in the very act by which their nature has been decided a priori. This occurred in the Galilean foundation of modern science, which excluded from the universe everything that was human about it: everything sensible, subjective, living.

The so-called human sciences, fascinated by the Galilean model, borrow its mathematical methodologies and strain to extend them systematically. In so doing they remain outside the sphere of what is proper to man as living Selves. In effect, an abyss opens between life and mathematical ideals, separating reality and irreality forever. This abyss was perceived by Marx's transcendental gaze when he asked about the possibility of measuring the living (and thus real) work that made possible the economic exchange of goods. The random and arbitrary construction of ideal economic objects that are presumed to be the representatives (thus the objective equivalents) of invisible life, the invention of economics, was the response of humanity to a practical and unavoidable question.

This substitution of ideal entities for life, on the model of economics, is what the human sciences unwittingly accomplish. Thus they take their specific objects for the definition of reality, while the transcendental Self to which these "objects" always secretly refer (and without which they have no meaning) disappears beneath the superimposed strata of all kinds of parameters. So now the possibility of this living Self, or the transcendental birth in absolute phenomenological Life, has become gibberish for the human sciences. Their objects become analogous to those of the hard sciences, purely Galilean, and any difference between the two types of science tends to be effaced. Henceforth, their contents, too, tend to be identified with each other. Experimental scientific psychology, for example, is now just biology applied to the complex animal that is man. There is no longer even any question of man in his specificity, as a living transcendental Self and possible only in this guise, as something that experiences himself, who feels, who agonizes, who suffers and enjoys, who acts, who wants and does not want.

What is a man who is no longer a me, a person emptied of his capacity to feel himself and thus to "live"? At bottom, this amounts to asking: *What is a person reduced to his apparition in the world's truth?* The answer is: an automaton, a computer complex, a robot—the external appearance of a man without what makes him a man, the transcendental Self. But still, no transcendental Self brings itself into the condition that is its own. Given to itself and feeling itself in the self-givenness of absolute Life and in it alone, any transcendental Self is Son of this life.

Son of Life or automaton is what John perceived in his apocalyptic vision. The automaton is the Beast—or not truly the Beast, since the Beast contains a hidden reference to what might be something like this living and harmonious subjectivity that inhabits us, this *phenomenological* subjectivity that makes us beings of Light in the very bosom of our Night. The Beast still mimics life. What is proposed and defined as a man empty of what makes a man is therefore not the Beast, nor even the Monster. It was not the monstrous Beast that made Marx shudder when he entered a mechanical workshop of his day and saw in the equipment functioning all by itself a sort of terrifying caricature of human action, of "living work." When the material apparatus functioning all by itself is really cut off from any relation with any human activity and is defined by this exclusion, then it is no longer a Beast but something that is foreign to any feeling, any action, any living, to the capacity to experience itself, but that still behaves as something that acts. What Descartes uneasily calls by the name used at the time, the "automaton," John sees in its nakedness, stripped of what is still the subjective condition of this function, this "automatism": not the Beast but its inert copy, inanimate, "the statue of the Beast" (Revelation 13:14).

But "automaton" or "statue of the Beast" exists only on condition that any transcendental Self is destroyed, annihilated—denied. But how can a transcendental Self be denied unless the conditions that make it possible are themselves denied? These conditions are explained by the transcendental birth of this Self, without which no person is possible. They refer back to the generation of the first Self in the original Ipseity in which Life generates itself; they refer to Christ. Someone who denies not man's existence but his very possibility, who undertakes the process of eliminating it in principle and a priori—an elimination that precedes and involves the effective and radical elimination of man—is the one who denies Christ: the Anti-Christ.

The negation the Anti-Christ undertakes is thus double. On the one hand, he denies that Jesus is the Christ (the affirmation that Jesus is the Christ is what defines Christianity; outside this affirmation Christianity does not exist). To deny that Jesus is the Christ is to say that man has no need of being a living Self and consequently a living Self generated in Life and in Life's original Ipseity. In other words, it is not necessary to experience oneself in order to be something like a man. And because such an assertion is absurd, the negation uttered by the Anti-Christ is the negation of man.

But the Anti-Christ proceeds to a second negation. To deny that Jesus is the Christ is to deny that there was a Christ, and also to deny that there was a First Self generated in Life's self-generation as the precondition of this self-generation. To deny that Jesus is the Christ is not only to deny man, but also to deny this First Self and the Ipseity from which absolute Life was engendered, and to deny Life itself. It is to deny the Father and the Son, inextricably. This is what the following verses from John's First Letter say, densely and precisely: "Who is the liar? It is the man who denies that Jesus is the Christ. Such a man is the antichrist—he denies the Father and the Son. No one who denies the Son has the Father; whoever acknowledges the Son has the Father also" (1 John 2:22–23).

Why is someone who denies that Jesus is the Christ a liar? We must think this through if we want to understand anything about the essence of our world and also the singular relation that ties Christianity to this world. In other words, who is the Anti-Christ today, who is the liar? How and why does the Anti-Christ lie? We have established, on the one hand, that a living transcendental Self only occurs in the coming into self of Life and in the Ipseity in which this coming into self takes place and, on the other hand, that no man is possible who is not a Self, if he does not himself come into the Ipseity of this life. If one denies both of these assertions, what remains of man? We asked: *What remains of man outside the Truth of life, in the world's truth?* An empty appearance, a bell that rings hollow. This is the lie: making us believe that man is reduced to something that feels nothing, and does not feel himself, to what Revelation calls "idols that cannot see or hear or walk" (Revelation 9:20), to waves of particles, chains of acids.

Who is the Anti-Christ today, in our time, in our world? Why, the world itself—or rather, the principle on which this world is being constructed and organized. For here we should note that the negation of the transcendental Self of man is not only speculative or theoretical. On the theoretical plane, it is true, this negation involves immense consequences. As we have seen, the content of any knowledge about man is not only modified but totally changed when this content is interpreted not as a Self, but precisely as a reality in itself foreign to this Self and to transcendental Life, from which it is born. The very honorable assertion that Jesus is a man (albeit an exceptional and extraordinary man whose erecting of a magnificent morality should in any case inspire respect) proceeds to a hidden but no less radical negation of the being of the Self. Here an apparently modest and well-meaning assertion takes a scandalous turn. To say that Jesus is a man, to speak simply of "Jesus," is to deny that he is the Christ and to treat this marvelous man as a liar—since it is true that Jesus always explicitly referred to himself as the Messiah and that the theme of the New Testament, the passionate confrontation with the priests, and moreover, *what Christ says about himself and his own nature,* all rest solely on the tirelessly repeated affirmation—the foundation of the Christian faith—that he is the Christ.

But we have to grasp this question of whether Jesus is just a man— exceptional, extraordinary, and so on—from a still more essential perspective. *Within the truth of Life such a proposition is quite simply absurd.* In the Truth of Life and in the metaphysical light of this truth, man, the living transcendental Self, is only generated in this Life and in the original Self of its essential Ipseity. We have established at length[2] that there is no man except as "Son of God" and "Son within the Son." So then, if the Son does not exist, no man is possible. The Allegation of the Anti-Christ—the assertion that the Christ is just Jesus and that Jesus is just a man, that he is not "Jesus Christ"—is not only the liar's greatest deceit, but also philosophically untenable. Just as it is impossible to conceive a living without presupposing the absolute Life in him, and just as it is impossible to live as this living without experiencing this life within ("absolute" because no living brings this life into himself, but only experiences himself in it), therefore no me and no Self has ever had the power to bring itself into its Ipseity, into this condition of being a Self and a me. It is only within Life and within the Ipseity in which it has become Life that something like Selves and transcendental me's are possible.

But we are not going to return to the consequences, infinite and quite fatal for man, of the Anti-Christ's thesis. I have said that this assertion has not only theoretical value but also determines practice. Upon the Anti-Christ's Allegation (even when this Allegation is completely ignored these days) is founded the organization of the whole modern world. Any form of organization acts and rests upon this. Acting itself implies an I Can without which no power can be exercised, without which no action is possible. This I Can that relies on the ego thus leads back to a me, to a Self, and finally to the Ipseity of absolute Life—to Christ/God. Such were the presuppositions of the Christian theory of acting. On the one hand, acting is only possible in life, there is only living action—for example, living work. On the other hand, acting is not only unfolded in Life but receives any possible motivation from it, from the life that is not only the ego's, but this absolute Life to which any particular life, all living, and any living Self owe their lives. From the foundation of any particular and concrete action upon the absolute Life that gives the self to itself comes the principle of the Christian ethic— partly an ethic of renunciation, the possibility of rediscovering, in the ego's relation to itself, the power that relates it to itself, the acting of absolute Life. But it is also an ethic of regeneration and second birth, which consists in rediscovering in oneself this acting of absolute Life, and henceforward to live this new life, which is eternal life.

What becomes of action under the imprint of the Anti-Christ? To the extent that the negation of the First Self involves that of any conceivable Self, it destroys the very possibility of acting. What would action be if it did not carry within it a living Self, did not experience itself and reveal itself in life's self-revelation? It would be a blind external process, analogous to all those that compose the universe's fabric. So if it is a matter of organizing and transforming that universe, what kind of knowledge would serve as a basis for this transformation, if it can no longer be, as in man's past, the experience life has of itself in the *pathētik* effort of its living action? It will be the knowledge of Galilean science. *The transformation of the material universe relying upon the physical and mathematical knowledge of this universe is modern technology.* So it is seen as a matter of setting up and putting into operation objective material apparatuses borrowed from this universe and its internal processes, apparatuses constructed and developed in the light of Galilean science. Technology (modern, Galilean, not traditional technology relying on the living body and essentially subjective) is the self-transformation of the material universe thanks to the physical and mathematical knowledge of this same universe, such that in the system of this self-transformation, there is no living left: neither "man," nor me, not Self nor Son nor Arch-Son, not God—no life of any sort. And also such that each element or each constituent of this system repeats its overall structure. A technology in principle foreign to life (and based upon its exclusion) is the essence of action in the era of the Anti-Christ, when the very possibility of the living Self has been denied.

The implementation of that kind of technology carries consequences that are visible everywhere today, to the point that you could say that the modern world is its billboard. Such consequences are necessary to the extent that they merely repeat the presupposition of a system that extends its reign to the whole planet, sowing desolation and ruin everywhere. Along with the destruction of the living Self, the presupposition is its elimination of any form of action and its very destruction, inasmuch as there is no action except living action and its replacement by modern technology, that ensemble of objective material processes that are in themselves foreign to any life.

One of the traditional forms of acting consists of the production process for the material goods necessary for human existence, which is therefore present at the base of any society. What is happening today to this process is the tragic illustration, and thus the proof, of the expulsion of the living Self outside human action, and the consequences of this expulsion. It is only too evident that these consequences—the destruction of the living Self and thus of man—are just the repetition or reappearance of the presupposition of a system that is not only that of the economy but of the modern world as a whole. "Exclusion," notably the exclusion of a growing number of workers from the economic and social circuit (or what we have just called the expulsion of the living Self outside human action) is not an unfortunate byproduct of the senseless extension of a purebred capitalism indifferent to people. The extension of this uncontrolled capitalism goes along with its internal destruction under the effects of the hyperdevelopment of modern technology. By constantly diminishing living work, technology exhausts the source of economic wealth, that is to say, capital itself, which it destroys in turn. But nothing of this would have been possible if man, the transcendental Self generated in the Ipseity of absolute Life, had not been previously eliminated from the Western view and from the organization of the world set up by that view.

If the system of technology that sweeps man away from the surface of the earth proceeds from the negation of man's transcendental Self—or ultimately, from the Anti-Christ—and if the Anti-Christ is the liar, and if today one must cry as in John's time "Who is the liar if not the man who denies that Jesus is the Christ?" then in what way can such a system, revealing its ravages day by day, be called "lying"?

When pilots are trained for supersonic warplanes, those in charge of this training encounter almost insurmountable difficulties. How can you entrust an aircraft of the utmost complexity—and cost—to an apprentice pilot who has not mastered it? And who can attain mastery of it except by being in contact with the aircraft by practicing the maneuvers of takeoff, navigation, combat, landing, and so on, by being able to handle multiple commands and decode multiple signals?

We know that warfare, and everything that prepares for it or is linked to it in some way, has been one of the principle causes of technological progress—at least as long as technology was obeying ends other than itself. The solution here was to simulate a space similar to one in which the pilot will be placed, the ensemble of conditions in which his actions will unfold—the instruments, their placement, and the precise gestures required to use them—exactly to duplicate all the information that he will receive and more generally the whole perceptible universe that will define his field of action, the sensations and impressions of all sorts that he will experience—visual, aural, kinesthetic—in short, the simulation on the ground of the concrete "living" that will be the pilot's in flight and in combat. This solution implied the construction of a set of complex and sophisticated apparatuses—computers, robots, and so on—capable of reproducing faithfully for the pilot not only his immediate instrumental and technological environment, but also his relations with it, the experiences and perceptions that he would have if he were flying a real aircraft.

The internal arrangement of the pseudocabin would be just part of a fictional spectacle, similar to the spectacle and impressions that the student pilot would perceive and feel if he were really flying. What he sees outside, too, would be similar to what he would see in a real flight, in a real sky! The same bursts of light, the same trajectories of phantom airplanes on which he opens fire, the same explosions, the same racket, same looping, same losses of equilibrium, same rockets, same targets, hit or missed, same successes, same failures! A complete and prefect reproduction, in its "physical" and emotional components, of simulated combat—of real fictive combat or, if you prefer, of fictive real combat. In the perfect simulation, as in a hallucination, there is no longer any difference between the true and the false, and there cannot be. But when nothing distinguishes true from false, then a new era begins, a dangerous time, not just of episodic lying but of systematic, permanent, efficient, and ontological lying that can no longer be perceived a such. All series of appearances are false, even when, by their immediate sensory pressure, they impose themselves as real. But this time of a lying that is no longer so perceived, and cannot be, is a time of madness. Madness is nothing but the impossibility of distinguishing appearance from reality—in the example here, the impossibility of establishing a division between the series of simulated appearances and the exactly similar ones that compose the system in reality.

Now let us imagine the simulation in the technical and scientific world of a procedure applied not only in the military domain but to social relations, for example to the erotic relations between men and women. And let us hypothesize that men can use a simulator. The man (like the student pilot) is placed in a certain position and the appearance of a woman's body is gradually unfolded in its various aspects, not as on a two-dimensional screen but beneath his fingers such that each movement of his hand or body discovers a new segment of the female body with its own corresponding movement—to each of his caresses corresponds a woman's caress—while within him are wakened the preset sequences of desire and erogenous sensations. For the user of this erotic simulation, a sort of ontological reversal is produced. Science has reduced the living transcendental Self to a dead object of the Galilean field, to networks of neurons that feel nothing, think nothing, say nothing. So now it is necessary to restore to this automaton some human property or appearance. Special computers enter into the action. Beneath his touching, the appearance of the female body quivers, the eyes close, the mouth twists and starts to moan: all the signs of pleasure are there. The statue of the Beast comes to life, its fictive life mingles with that of the simulator's user. As the Apocalypse says, it is a matter of giving "breath to the image of the first beast, so that it could speak . . . " (Revelation 13:15). This is the marvel—virtual reality—that is going to seduce the inhabitants of the earth, the work of false prophets and false messiahs. *They will make extraordinary machines that will do everything men and women do so as to make them believe that they are just machines themselves.*

To those among the Thessalonians who announced the coming of the Day of the Lord as imminent, supposedly on the strength of letters from him, Paul objected, "That day will not come until the rebellion occurs and the man of lawlessness is revealed, the man doomed to destruction. He will oppose and exalt himself over everything that is called God or is worshipped . . . " (2 Thessalonians 2:3–4). "That is called God or is worshipped": Life, the true Life that animates any true living Self and makes it a true Living Person—Life that denounces the hollow idol, the statue of the Beast, everything given the appearance of a man or a woman yet neither one nor the other. Everything that will accompany "the coming of the lawless one . . . all kinds of miracles, deceptive signs and marvels, as well as all the temptations that evil offers to those who are lost because they did not accept the love of the truth" (2 Thessalonians 2:9–10). The Truth: Life. Signs and marvels: the simulation of Life. Evil: everywhere this simulation takes place, as in the erotic simulator, where a man who wants to embrace a woman, to experience his life where this life experiences itself, in its living Self, in fact only embraces the void, pure Absence, radical evil: NOBODY.

In the simulator, but also everywhere such a metaphysical situation is produced: everywhere a man or a woman is only an object, a dead thing, a network of neurons, a bundle of natural processes—where one is put in the presence of a man or a woman but finds oneself in the presence of what, stripped of the transcendental Self that constitutes its essence, is no longer anything, is only death.

"During those days men will seek death, but will not find it; they will long to die, but death will elude them" (Revelation 9:6).

Men debased, humiliated, despised and despising themselves, trained in school to despise themselves, to count for nothing—just particles and molecules; admiring everything lesser than themselves and execrating everything that is greater than themselves. Everything worthy of love and adoration. Men reduced to simulacra, to idols that feel nothing, to automatons. And replaced by them—by computers and robots. Men chased out of their work and their homes, pushed into corners and gutters, huddled on subway benches, sleeping in cardboard boxes.

Men replaced by abstractions, by economic entities, by profits and money. Men treated mathematically, digitally, statistically, counted like animals and counting for much less.

Men turned away from Life's Truth, caught in all the traps and marvels where this life is denied, ridiculed, mimicked, simulated—absent. Men given over to the insensible, become themselves insensible, whose eyes are empty as a fish's. Dazed men, devoted to specters and spectacles that always expose their own invalidity and bankruptcy; devoted to false knowledge, reduced to empty shells, to empty heads—to "brains." Men whose emotions and loves are just glandular secretions. Men who have been liberated by making them think their sexuality is a natural process, the site and place of their infinite Desire. Men whose responsibility and dignity have no definite site anymore. Men who in the general degradation will envy the animals.

Men will want to die—but not *Life*.

It is not just any god today who is still able to save us, but—when the shadow of death is looming over the world—that One who is Living.

REFERENCE MATTER

Notes

INTRODUCTION

1. My emphasis.—Trans.

CHAPTER 1

1. On the term *phainomenon*, see Martin Heidegger, *Being and Time*, trans. John Macquarrie and Edward Robinson (New York: Harper, 1962), pp. 51–55, and my commentary in *Phénomenologie matérielle* (Paris: Presses Universitaires de France, 1990), pp. 112ff.

CHAPTER 2

1. If life is the essence of God, as it is of Christ and of man himself, the concept of life stands at the core of our search. The reader may perhaps be surprised to see the word sometimes spelled with a capital "L," and sometimes with a lowercase one, occasionally in the same sentence. Let us simply say here that, written with a capital, the terms refers to the Life of God; written with a small letter, it refers to our own life. Since life is one and the same, however, these terminological nuances are intended to refer to one condition or the other (divine or human). Taken in an as yet undifferentiated sense, the word is written with a small "l." But, of course, these are no more than general indications. It is only in the context of our analysis that an attempt is made to provide a radical elucidation of what is meant in each case by "life."

CHAPTER 3

1. François Jacob, *The Logic of Life: A History of Heredity*, trans. Betty Spillman (New York: Pantheon, 1973), p. 299. Referring back to the context: "The processes that take place at the microscopic level in the molecules of living beings are completely indistinguishable from those investigated in inert systems by physics and chemistry. . . . In fact, since the appearance of thermodynamics, the operational value of the concept of life has continually dwindled and its power of abstraction declined. Biologists no longer study life today."

2. Edmund Husserl, *Cartesian Meditations: An Introduction to Phenomenology*, trans. Dorian Cairns (The Hague: Nijhoff, 1964), p. 97.

3. Martin Heidegger, *Sein und Zeit*, p. 50; *Being and Time*, op. cit., p. 75.

4. On the inability of Heideggerian thought to account for the problem of life, see Didier Frank, "L'être et le vivant," *Philosophie*, no. 16 (1987).

5. On the decisive influence of Schopenhauer on European aesthetic creation at the end of the nineteenth and into the twentieth century, see the groundbreaking works by Anne Henry, especially *Proust romancier: Le tombeau égyptien* (Paris: Flammarion, 1983), *Schopenhauer et la création littéraire en Europe* (Paris: Méridiens-Klincksieck, 1989), and *Céline écrivain* (Paris: L'Harmattan, 1994).

6. Heidegger, *Being and Time*, p. 75.

CHAPTER 4

1. Saint Anselm of Canterbury, "Proslogion," in *Basic Writings*, trans. S. W. Deane, 2d ed. (La Salle, Ill.: Open Court, 1995), p. 53.

2. See Chapter 9.

CHAPTER 6

1. Meister Eckhart, *The Essential Sermons, Commentaries, Treatises, and Defenses*, Bernard McGunn and Edmund Colledge, O.S.A., eds. (New York: Paulist Press, 1981). Sermon 6, p. 187.

2. Ibid, p. 187.

3. It was in the light of this concept [*auto-affection*] that I explored the concept of life in *L'Essence de la manifestation* (Paris: Presses Universitaires de France, 1963; 2d ed., 1990, esp. pp. 31ff.

4. Impression is not situated in the world or in the objective body except by virtue of an illusion criticized by Descartes: "Often we are even mistaken in judging that we are feeling pain in some part of our body." See *Principles of Philosophy*, 67.

CHAPTER 7

1. *Moi* can mean both "me" and "ego," as will be discussed in this and the following chapters.—Trans.

2. G. W. F. Hegel, *The Phenomenology of Mind*, trans. J. B. Baillie (New York: Humanities Press, 1966), p. 316.

3. Understanding the essence of a person as a transcendental Self who is radically singular and irreducible to any other rules out scientism's discourse on people. Consider, for example, the views of François Jacob: "Perhaps it will also be possible to produce at will, and in as many copies as required, exact duplicates of individuals, a politician, for instance, an artist, a beauty queen or an athlete. There is nothing to prevent the immediate application to human beings of the selection

processes used for race-horses, laboratory mice or milch cows" (*The Logic of Life*, p. 322). The idea of identical individuals would appear ludicrous, if the reference were not to an "individual" in the human sense but to a transcendental Self, which is in its essence unique. That which comes into the condition of experiencing itself discovers, owing to the absolute singularity of any experience of a phenomenologically realized self, that it, too, is absolutely singular. Two biological individuals who were strictly identical would be no less different as transcendental Selves. We see from this crucial example that it is hardly "scientific" to claim to define man from the point of view of biology, chemistry, or physics—that is to say, by ignoring the principle that makes him a man: his ipseity. The individuality that the biological viewpoint confers on the biological individual is merely that of a thing—a "worldly" individuality, totally foreign to the ipseity without which there is neither Self, nor "me," nor man.

4. Franz Kafka, *Amerika*, trans. Will Muir and Edwin Muir (New York: Schocken Books, 1974), p. 272.

5. *The Sickness Unto Death: Kierkegaard's Writings, Vol. 19*, trans. Howard Vincent Hong and Edna H. Hong, pp. 19–20.

CHAPTER 8

1. I might add that the theories that deny the ego's freedom by transposing into its sphere (about which they know nothing) rules or conceptual systems borrowed from the world's phenomena do not just commit a theoretical mistake: this is secretly motivated. It is the abyss opened in front of man by freedom that is being rejected: the abyss of the possibility of sin. In constructing a system of absolute necessity—belied by experience, moreover—Spinoza's bad faith endeavored to offer man a more sure salvation.

2. See above, Chapter 7.

3. *Le Pélerin chérubinique: Description sensible des quatre choses dernières*, Book 1, distich 289.

CHAPTER 9

1. Saint Anselm of Canterbury, *Proslogium, Monologium*, trans. Sidney Norton Deane (La Salle, Ill.: The Open Court, 1903), p. 3.

2. Jean-Luc Marion's problematic aims to dissociate the question of God from that of Being; see *God without Being*, trans. Thomas A. Carlson (Chicago: University of Chicago Press, 1991).

3. Heidegger, Zurich Seminar, quoted and discussed by J.-L. Marion in *God Without Being*; see also Jean Greisch, *Heidegger et la question de dieu* (1980), p. 334.

4. Heidegger, *Questions III* (Paris: Gallimard, 1966), p. 114.

5. Eckhart, *Treatises and Sermons*, p. 258.

CHAPTER 12

1. Quoted and discussed by Martin Heidegger in *On the Way to Language*, trans. Peter D. Hertz (San Francisco: Harper and Row, 1982, c. 1971), pp. 159–98. English translation in *Poetry, Language, Thought* (New York: Harper and Row, 1971), p. 194.

2. Heidegger, *Being and Time*, op. cit., p. 316.

CHAPTER 13

1. G. W. F. Hegel, *The Christian Religion*, trans. Peter C. Hodgson (Missoula, Mont.: Scholar Press, 1979), p. 197.

2. Ibid., pp. 193–97.

3. G. W. F. Hegel, *The Phenomenology of Mind*, trans. J. B. Baillie (New York: Humanities Press, 1977), p. 667.

4. Karl Marx and Freidrich Engels, *The German Ideology* (New York: International Publishers, 1973), p. 123, Thesis XI on Feuerbach.

5. Reflection on the natural content of the world would show that, due to the senses, this content, too, refers back to life.

CONCLUSION

1. See especially Chapter 3.

2. See Chapters 4 and 5.

Cultural Memory | in the Present

Michel Henry, *I Am the Truth: Toward a Philosophy of Christianity*

Gil Anidjar, *"Our Place in Al-Andalus": Kabbalah, Philosophy, Literature in Arab-Jewish Letters*

Hélène Cixous and Jacques Derrida, *Veils*

F. R. Ankersmit, *Historical Representation*

F. R. Ankersmit, *Political Representation*

Elissa Marder, *Dead Time: Temporal Disorders in the Wake of Modernity (Baudelaire and Flaubert)*

Reinhart Koselleck, *The Practice of Conceptual History: Timing History, Spacing Concepts*

Niklas Luhmann, *The Reality of the Mass Media*

Hubert Damisch, *A Childhood Memory by Piero della Francesca*

Hubert Damisch, *A Theory of /Cloud/: Toward a History of Painting*

Jean-Luc Nancy, *The Speculative Remark (One of Hegel's bon mots)*

Jean-François Lyotard, *Soundproof Room: Malraux's Anti-Aesthetics*

Jan Patočka, *Plato and Europe*

Hubert Damisch, *Skyline: The Narcissistic City*

Isabel Hoving, *In Praise of New Travelers: Reading Caribbean Migrant Women Writers*

Richard Rand, ed., *Futures: Of Derrida*

William Rasch, *Niklas Luhmann's Modernity: The Paradox of System Differentiation*

Jacques Derrida and Anne Dufourmantelle, *Of Hospitality*

Jean-François Lyotard, *The Confession of Augustine*

Kaja Silverman, *World Spectators*

Samuel Weber, *Institution and Interpretation: Expanded Edition*

Jeffrey S. Librett, *The Rhetoric of Cultural Dialogue: Jews and Germans in the Epoch of Emancipation*

Ulrich Baer, *Remnants of Song: Trauma and the Experience of Modernity in Charles Baudelaire and Paul Celan*

Samuel C. Wheeler III, *Deconstruction as Analytic Philosophy*

David S. Ferris, *Silent Urns: Romanticism, Hellenism, Modernity*

Rodolphe Gasché, *Of Minimal Things: Studies on the Notion of Relation*

Sarah Winter, *Freud and the Institution of Psychoanalytic Knowledge*

Samuel Weber, *The Legend of Freud: Expanded Edition*

Aris Fioretos, ed., *The Solid Letter: Readings of Friedrich Hölderlin*

J. Hillis Miller / Manuel Asensi, *Black Holes / J. Hillis Miller; or, Boustrophedonic Reading*

Miryam Sas, *Fault Lines: Cultural Memory and Japanese Surrealism*

Peter Schwenger, *Fantasm and Fiction: On Textual Envisioning*

Didier Maleuvre, *Museum Memories: History, Technology, Art*

Jacques Derrida, *Monolingualism of the Other; or, The Prosthesis of Origin*

Andrew Baruch Wachtel, *Making a Nation, Breaking a Nation: Literature and Cultural Politics in Yugoslavia*

Niklas Luhmann, *Love as Passion: The Codification of Intimacy*

Mieke Bal, ed., *The Practice of Cultural Analysis: Exposing Interdisciplinary Interpretation*

Jacques Derrida and Gianni Vattimo, eds., *Religion*

72406055R00178

Made in the USA
Lexington, KY
29 November 2017